Ethnic Profiling

A Modern Framework

Kimora, editor

International Debate Education Association

New York, Brussels & Amsterdam

Published by
The International Debate Education Association
P.O. Box 922
New York, NY 10009

Library of Congress Cataloging-in-Publication Data
Ethnic profiling: a modern framework/Kimora, editor.
    pages cm
   ISBN 978-1-61770-078-1
    1. Racial profiling in law enforcement—United States.   2. Discrimination in criminal justice administration—United States.   3. Discrimination—United States.   4. United States—Ethnic relations.   I. Kimora, 1956–
   HV7936.R3E84 2014
   363.2'308900973—dc23   2013043210

Composition by Brad Walrod/Kenoza Type, Inc.
Printed in the USA

 IDEBATE Press

Contents

Acknowledgments

I would like to thank all of the authors who contributed their works to this volume. In addition, I would like to thank Martin Greenwald and Eleanora von Dehsen for their professionalism and their patience. This book is timely and necessary for all of those who cherish learning and justice. Finally, I thank my beloved Srijan for his ongoing love and support.

Introduction

How many times is an individual likely to be stopped and searched by police or singled out for special surveillance from immigration authorities? How often will a consumer be followed by security personnel in a retail store or a traveler picked for random searches at an airport? The answer to these questions is frequently determined by the color of a person's skin or her ethnic background. This is ethnic profiling. It is a violation of human rights, and it has exacted a tremendous cost on individuals and on communities.

WHAT IS ETHNIC PROFILING?

Ethnic or racial profiling is the practice of using racial, ethnic, national, religious, or gender characteristics, rather than individual behavior and evidence, as a way of singling out people for investigation. It associates a certain ethnic or religious group with an affinity for a particular crime—Arab Muslims as terrorists; Hispanic males as drug dealers.[1] Ethnic profiling is a form of illegitimate stereotyping and discrimination.

Ethnic profiling can be deliberate or unintentional. It can occur when a police officer exhibits racist behavior or acts on the basis of subconscious negative racial stereotypes. But it can also occur when the police use tactics that impact different ethnic groups unequally. For example, police may use stop-and-frisk practices—a policy of stopping residents based on what an officer deems "suspicious" behavior—that while not defined by reference to ethnicity more disproportionately affect a particular ethnic group.[2]

Although ethnic profiling is usually associated with law enforcement agents, the practice is widespread. Customs officials at international airports have targeted black women for searches because they thought them likely drug carriers, and Immigration and Naturalization Service agents have initiated workplace raids based on subjects' appearance or language, not evidence of wrongdoing.[3] After September 11, 2001 (9/11), some airlines and airline pilots refused to let Arab Americans fly because of "suspicious behavior." Even department store personal and security guards have used racial and ethnic profiling to target minorities for scrutiny.

Some reformers insist that the definition of racial profiling must include not only discriminatory *acts*, but also *discriminatory omissions* on the part of law enforcement. They maintain that the failure of the police to provide the same protections to minority communities as they do to whites, is racial profiling.[4] Retailers, too, are racial profiling when they refuse minorities service or give them service inferior to whites.

Not all profiling is ethnic or racial profiling. Police use criminal or suspect profiling as a tool that enables them to utilize their resources efficiently.[5] They analyze evidence and gather other substantive information about the nature and manner of a crime to construct a profile of the offender that might help them in their investigations.[6] Pursuing a suspect whose description includes race or ethnicity in combination with other identifying factors is criminal profiling and is not considered discrimination. Thus, if the police were to pursue short African American men wearing yellow hats because witnesses described the perpetrator of a robbery in these terms, this would be criminal profiling. However, if a police officer stops and frisks all black men on suspicion of carrying drugs because he assumes black men are more likely to be drug dealers than any other group, he is racially profiling. Criminal/suspect profiling has not been controversial, although there are concerns that vague descriptions risk stereotyping and can lead to racial profiling.

The international community views ethnic/racial profiling as a violation of human rights—it denies people equal treatment under the law—and in the United States, both Democratic and Republican administrations have denounced it as unconstitutional, socially corruptive, and counterproductive. Yet, African Americans, Asians, Latinos, South Asians, and Arabs are still profiled as they work, drive, shop, travel, and even walk through their own neighborhoods.[7]

HISTORY

Ethnic and racial profiling has a long history in the United States. Prior to the Civil War, fear of slave rebellions made whites suspicious of all blacks. Consequently Southern blacks were frequently stopped and required to show identification or passes to prove they were either free or had the permission of their owner to travel. Free blacks in the North feared they could be victims of slave catchers who would sell them into slavery in the Deep South. No one knows how many free blacks were illegally captured and sold, but the numbers may have reached into the thousands.[8]

Racial and ethnic profiling was not confined to African Americans, however. In the mid-19th century, Irish immigrants were seen as lazy, stupid, and prone to criminality, and became scapegoats for a variety of contemporary problems. Chinese immigrants were viewed as belonging to an inferior race. Whites assumed that they were unassimilable and that Chinese neighborhoods were dens of gambling, prostitution, and opium smoking. Anti-Chinese sentiment ultimately led to the Chinese Exclusion Act of 1882, which suspended entry of Chinese workers into the United States.

One of the most dramatic episodes of ethnic profiling occurred in the wake of Pearl Harbor. In the aftermath of the December 1941 attack, anti-Japanese American sentiment increased, fueled by unsubstantiated rumors that Japanese Americans were prepared to sabotage the war effort. Growing demand for government action eventually convinced Pres. Franklin D. Roosevelt to issue an executive order in February 1942 compelling Japanese Americans to evacuate the West Coast. None had a hearing or trial before being transported to internment camps; none were ever associated with sabotage. They were interned simply because of who they were. The Supreme Court upheld the legality of the executive order in *Korematsu v. United States* (1944), ruling that national security interests outweighed individual rights. In 1988, Congress apologized and granted compensation to each surviving prisoner.

In the early 1980s law enforcement officials began using profiling in an effort to prevent crime and as part of the so-called War on Drugs. But legitimate profiling quickly turned into ethnic profiling.[9] In 1986, for example, the Drug Enforcement Administration launched Operation Pipeline, a drug interdiction program that introduced a racially biased drug courier profile for use by highway patrols throughout the country. The training program associated with the operation did not explicitly say that police officers should watch for particular racial or ethnic characteristics but all scripted demonstrations of stops involved drivers with Hispanic surnames.[10]

The country became aware of racial profiling in 1996, when ABC aired "Driving While Black," an investigative report in which three young black men drove around New Brunswick, New Jersey, in a Mercedes Benz. Officers pulled the car over for minor infractions and then searched the car and the passengers. The show clearly demonstrated that police conduct was a result of racial profiling. The program fueled a debate that intensified two years later when New Jersey state troopers killed three young minority men during a traffic stop.

In the wake of the shootings, civil libertarians challenged state and local governments to end racial profiling. By 2005 twenty-nine states had passed legislation prohibiting the practice and/or requiring that law enforcement officials collect data on stops and searches. Yet racial and ethnic profiling continues to this day.

Even before the August 2014 police killing of an unarmed black teenager, Michael Brown, that led to unrest in Ferguson, Missouri, the state's attorney general had published evidence that town police had targeted blacks for stops and searches, although the police were more likely to find contraband on whites they searched. Following Brown's death, civil liberties groups charged that Ferguson was engaged in racialized policing, asserting that in the United States there are two kinds of policing: "one to serve and protect the white community and one to criminalize and control the black community."[11]

In October 2014, the ACLU of Massachusetts issued "Brown, Black and Targeted," a study of over 200,000 encounters between Boston police and citizens which showed that Boston police used racially biased policing.[12] Although blacks made up less than a quarter of the Boston population, they composed 63% of Boston police–civilian encounters from 2007 to 2010. And statistical analysis proved that even controlling for crime, Boston police were more likely to initiate encounters in a black neighborhood or with black citizens. Boston police said they were focusing on gang members and those with criminal records in an effort to make high-crime neighborhoods safer, but of more than 200,000 encounters none led to arrests.[13] Surveys revealed similar problems in a variety of American cities, including New York, where in 2012, the number of stops (133,119) of young black men neared the entire city population of young black residents (158,406).[14]

PROFILING AND TERRORISM

Efforts to prevent further attacks following 9/11 intensified profiling based both on ethnicity and religion. Men from predominantly Muslim countries were required to register with federal agents, be photographed, finger-printed, and interviewed.[15] Thousands were involuntarily detained when they went to register, although none were eventually connected to terrorism.[16]

In 2003 the Bush Administration banned racial profiling in federal law enforcement, but made a broad exception for issues of national security.[17] Consequently, many counterterrrorism programs have raised concerns about ethnic profiling. One such program is the Suspicious Activity Report (SAR) Initiative, a joint collaborative effort by the U.S. Department of Homeland Security, the Federal Bureau of Investigation, and state and local law enforcement partners for identifying, reporting, and sharing information on "suspicious" activities. Under the program, launched in 2008, law enforcement officials file reports of suspicious behavior to central Fusion Centers, which store the information for data sharing by law enforcement and counterterrorism officials. Citizens can report anonymously.[18] The definition of suspicious behavior is vague, however. Anyone shooting a video or using binoculars, for example, can be considered a potential terrorist and placed on an SAR.[19] Supporters of the initiative claim they are not profiling but targeting behaviors. Nevertheless, the program has led to ethnic profiling. For example, a Pakistani-American scientist became the subject of an SAR for walking around a train depot while trying to find the entrance to a building,[20] and three men of Middle Eastern descent became the subject of a report for videotaping the Santa Monica pier in a "suspicious" manner.[21]

Federal officials are not alone in using ethnic profiling in the campaign against terrorism. In 2012 the Associated Press revealed that the New York Police Department (NYPD) has been clandestinely spying on Muslims since shortly after the 9/11 attacks in what one critic termed "a deliberate, decade long policy of outright ethnic profiling."[22] Police infiltrated Muslim communities although they had no specific targets or criminal leads. They spied on people in mosques, eavesdropped in cafes, and recorded the names of political organizers, noting where they lived, worked, and even gathered for sports events. Reports show that they also paid informants to bait young Muslims into making inflammatory statements, which were then sent to the NYPD.[23] NYPD officials and then-Mayor Michael Bloomberg defended the program as counterterrorism efforts needed to keep New Yorkers safe. Yet the NYPD concedes that the program resulted in zero leads to terrorists or terrorist activities.

The debate about ethnic profiling as a counterterrorism tool is ongoing, and the public's reaction to profiling in the name of national security is very different from that associated with policing. By the end of the 1990s, the overwhelming majority of Americans (81%) disapproved of racial profiling (defined as stopping motorists solely on the basis of race). In contrast, shortly after 9/11 a majority of Americans (54%) supported subjecting Arabs to more intensive scrutiny at airports.[24] In 2014, a significant number of Americans (42%) still supported the use of profiling against Arab Americans and American Muslims.[25]

THE DEBATE

The use of profiling has generated a heated, widespread debate. Supporters of the practice emphasize that it has dramatically reduced crime, particularly in minority neighborhoods.[26] They condemn profiling solely on the basis of race or ethnicity but point out that looking at common characteristics of those who may commit crimes is good police work. They maintain that if, for example, blacks are being stopped and searched at a disproportionately high rate, it is because they make up 55% of all drug convictions while comprising only 13% of the population.[27] They assert that average citizens stopped by police should view the encounter not as a violation of rights but as part of a procedure designed to protect their safety. Profiling has proved effective. Why stop using a valuable technique? If the police have used unreasonable racial stereotyping, proper training and discipline will solve the problem.

Opponents contend that despite training, officers have continued to rely on cultural stereotypes and act on their perceptions of a person's characteristics rather than evidence.[28] Critics maintain that the fact that more minorities are arrested for crimes is a reflection of aggressive policing and the inherent racism in our culture, not higher rates of criminality among minorities. When police look for minorities, they will arrest minorities. Opponents contend that an uncritical reading of criminal justice statistics that show an over-representation of minorities in arrest records has been used to justify over-policing. As David A. Harris, professor of law at the University of Pittsburgh, points out:

> Officers concentrate their observations and enforcement activity on drivers and pedestrians who are African American or Hispanic because these people are arrested and incarcerated more often. Since officers focus on these particular citizens, they inevitably arrest more of them than they would otherwise. This means that disproportionate numbers of them enter the criminal justice system as defendants, and are incarcerated. This, of course, becomes justification for the next round of intensive observation and arrest.[29]

Thus, this illogical way of administering "justice" leads to a self-fulfilling prophecy.[30]

Opponents acknowledge that aggressive policing has led to a drop in crime, but point out that profiling has eroded the public's confidence in police and alienates those who may be able to help the police in valid investigations, thus making policing in neighborhoods where profiling is practiced even harder.[31] Critics also contend that ethnic profiling is inefficient: putting resources into stopping and frisking large numbers of innocent people diverts law enforcement from investigating individuals who have been linked to crimes by specific and credible evidence.[32]

Finally, opponents suggest that racial profiling is unlikely to be an effective policing strategy in the long run because criminals can simply shift their activities outside the stereotype. For example, if police profile young Hispanic males as drug carriers, criminals may use another demographic group to move drugs.[33]

CONCLUSION

The future of the country lies in its ability to face the challenges of ethnic profiling with intelligence, education, and candor. We need to acknowledge that ethnic profiling exists and that it is tearing our communities apart. We need to recognize that some people see value in profiling, believing it to be a legitimate way to curb crime, while others believe it will always devolve into racism and demand it be stopped.

Our society thrives when we can debate contentious issues such as ethnic profiling. We invite you to read the essays in this book. We also encourage you to debate the issues presented in the articles in your classrooms and in the street. Do not stop learning until your world is perfect. Clearly, we have some learning to do.

ABOUT THE BOOK

The articles in *Ethnic Profiling: A Modern Framework* do not debate the pros and cons of ethnic profiling. As we've seen, most Americans believe that the use of racial or ethnic profiling for routine policing is wrong. Instead the anthology is designed to raise awareness of the issue so that we can envision ways of addressing it more effectively. The anthology brings together a series of articles that look at the root of ethnic profiling and offer evidence that profiling continues in contemporary America. Essays discuss the effect and effectiveness of the practice and suggest how it might be stopped. Finally, the anthology examines how the rise of terrorism has affected Americans' views on ethnic profiling and presents articles that challenge readers to think about difficult questions: Is profiling in the name of national security constitutional? What are the long-term effects on our democracy of such profiling?

The anthology begins with two articles that look at the theoretical and practical aspects of ethnic and racial profiling. In "Critical Racial and Ethnic Studies—Profiling and Reparations," Rodney D. Coates asserts that racial profiling is part of a larger, more ingrained problem of systematic oppression and racialization in Western culture and that as long as racial profiling is treated as a problem and not a symptom, few actual remedies will be forthcoming. Coates contends that racial elites and nonelites agree that racism is bad, that vestiges of racism yet remain, and that laws and their enforcement should be racially neutral. The degree to which groups and individuals assess such neutrality is dependent on which side of the racial divide they find themselves. Using a literature review, he traces the roots, context, and consequences of systems of racialization. How are these systems preserved, maintained, and perpetuated? Is exploitation at the heart of this dynamic process?

Next Delores Jones-Brown, Brett G. Stoudt, Brian Johnston, and Kevin Moran analyze data about the New York City Police Department's controversial stop and frisk practice. In excerpts from "Stop, Question, and Frisk Policing Practices in New York City: A Primer (Revised)," the authors show that the vast majority of people stopped by the police are black or Hispanic and that the reasons police give for stopping individuals are often vague. Their analysis also demonstrates that stop and frisk is ineffective. While stops increased from 2003 to 2011, the "rate of return"—those found with guns, knives, other weapons, or illegal drugs—declined. In 2013, U.S. District Court Judge Shira Scheindlin ruled that the policy violated the Fourteenth Amendment's promise of equal protection. The city appealed the ruling, but the practice has declined tremendously.[34]

The next three articles look at the effect of profiling on a variety of populations and in various situations. Brett G. Stoudt, Michelle Fine, and Madeline Fox ("Growing Up Policed in the Age of Aggressive Policing Policies") examine the effects of New York City's zero-tolerance policing policy on young people. This policy is based on the assumption that close police surveillance and zero tolerance of low-level crimes (for example, loitering or panhandling) will reduce criminal behavior in high-crime neighborhoods. The authors do not address the question of whether police officers intend to discriminate, but their data reveal that many young people grow up viewing themselves as perpetual suspects because of their age, how they look, or where they live. The authors find that aggressive policing policies not only offer challenges to liberty but also have long-term effects on the attitudes of young people. Particularly for people of color, males, and LBGT youth, their contact with the police is largely negative, and many do not feel comfortable or fear seeking help from law enforcement personnel.

Next, "Profiling Mexican American Identity: Issues and Concerns," by Adalberto Aguirre Jr., describes how law enforcement agencies use "Hispanic identity" to profile Mexican Americans as either drug smugglers or undocumented aliens and discusses the harmful effects such racial profiling has on Mexican American social identity. Aguirre concludes that "racial profiling harms Mexican Americans because it marginalizes their presence in American society. More important, racial profiling enhances the precarious position of Mexican Americans in American society by silencing their voice and tainting their social identity with negative expectations that constrain their pursuit of opportunity in American society."[35]

George E. Higgins and Shaun L. Gabbidon ("Perceptions of Consumer Racial Profiling and Negative Emotions: An Exploratory Study") then summarize the results of their research on the effect of consumer racial profiling (CRP) on those profiled. The authors found that while gender played no role, race and income were important determinants in an individual's reaction to perceived CRP. Blacks were more likely than whites to develop negative emotions from the experience as were higher-income individuals. Higher-income blacks were the most negatively affected.

The next two articles address the effectiveness of profiling. In "Disputed Definitions and Fluid Identities: The Limitations of Social Profiling in Relation to Ethnic Youth Gangs," Rob White discusses the limitations of profiling in dealing with ethnically identified youth gangs in Australia. He argues that anti-gang intervention based on broad profiling will most likely compound the very problem it is intended to address. "[T]he intervention itself can serve to consolidate and concretize gang formation and gang identity. This is especially so if accompanied by aggressive forms of policing. . . ."[36]

We often assume that racial profiling is one-directional—the police profile the public. But as "Racial, Ethnic, and Gender Differences in Perceptions of the Police: The Salience of Officer Race Within the Context of Racial Profiling," by Joshua C. Cochran and Patricia Y. Warren, argues, the race of an officer is important in the public's evaluation of police encounters, particularly among African Americans. The study reinforces the importance of increasing the number of minority officers to improve citizen–officer relations.

Public opinion polls have shown that most Americans do not support the use of ethnic profiling in routine policing, yet as we know, profiling occurs in a variety of circumstances. The next article explores public opinion regarding consumer racial profiling when dealing with shoplifting suspects. In "Public Opinion on the Use of Consumer Racial Profiling to Identify Shoplifters: An Exploratory Study," Shaun L. Gabbidon and George E. Higgins focus on two questions. First, how does perceived effectiveness, the view that CRP is discriminatory, or that the practice is not ethical, influence whether individuals believe that CRP occurs? Second, how is support for CRP influenced by the ethical nature of the practice, its perceived effectiveness, and the feeling that it is discriminatory? The authors found that the majority of the people surveyed thought that CRP occurs; only a very small minority of the respondents supported the practice and felt it was effective. Those who thought that CRP was not ethical did not support the practice; those who thought it effective defend its use.

In "Controlling Police Officer Behavior in the Field: Using What We Know to Regulate Police-Initiated Stops and Prevent Racially Biased Policing," Michael D. White examines the question of how police departments can prevent their officers from engaging in racially biased behavior when stopping citizens. He recommends careful recruiting, training that is tailored to the community and stresses the means and not just the ends of policing, administrative rules that are clear and routinely enforced, and accountability that begins in the chief's office and flows down through the organization to the officers on the street.

The anthology ends with three articles that address the debate about the use of profiling in countering terrorism. First, "The Dynamics of Public Opinion on Ethnic Profiling After 9/11: Results from a Survey Experiment," by Deborah J. Schildkraut, looks at whether Americans, who do not support ethnic profiling in general policing, will support profiling for purposes of national security. Schildkraut found that "support for profiling Arabs and Arab Americans is higher than support for profiling black motorists, that people are more supportive of profiling immigrants than they are of profiling U.S. citizens of Arab descent, and that how people define what it means to be American is a powerful predictor of such support, in some cases overshadowing 'the usual suspects,' including race, partisanship, education, and fearing another terrorist attack."[37] A nativist, right-wing ideology that identifies "American" with white European Christian is the most powerful predictor of support.

Next, in "Racial Profiling and Terrorism," Stephen J. Ellmann addresses the question of whether racial and ethnic profiling is an effective constitutional response to terrorism. Ellmann believes that profiling, while ordinarily unacceptable, may be valuable in protecting the United States from terrorism, but that it comes at a great cost both to those profiled and to society in general. He argues that profiling can be constitutional depending on the circumstances and the programs in which it is used. In determining constitutionality, he concludes that we must assess "the peril faced, the alternatives for facing it, and the impact of profiling in those circumstances, both for good and ill." Ellmann warns, however, that while some profiling may be constitutional, "[w]e have stepped out on to a slippery slope; we must now do all we can not to slide down it."[38]

Finally, in "Profiling in the Age of Total Information Awareness," Nancy Murray questions the long-term effect of the government's counterterrorism surveillance programs. She asserts that under the guise of national security, the federal government is creating an enormous multi-agency bureaucratic system not only to fight terrorism but also to further "predicative policing." Secretive U.S. domestic surveillance programs gather detailed information about individuals to anticipate crimes before they are committed. She warns that these programs are linked to a return of ethnic and racial profiling because they focus on Muslims, immigrants, and particularly black prisoners who have converted to Islam.

The articles in this anthology raise a number of important questions. As you read through the anthology, think about the following:

- Is ethnic profiling ever justified?

- The experience of those groups profiled is very different from the majority white population. What effect does the experience have on those profiled? What is the long-term effect on society in general?

- How can we prevent legitimate profiling from devolving into ethnic profiling?

- Should we permit profiling in the name of national security?

NOTES

1. "Ethnic Profiling: What It Is and Why It Must End," Open Society Foundations, http://www .opensocietyfoundations.org/explainers/ethnic-profiling-what-it-and-why-it-must-end.

2. "Ethnic Profiling," Open Society Justice Initiative, October 2009, http://www.refworld.org/ pdfid/4cc559a02.pdf.

3. "Racial Profiling: Definition," ACLU, https://www.aclu.org/racial-justice/racial-profiling-definition.

4. Ibid.

5. Open Society Justice Initiative.

6. "Racial Profiling: Definition."

7. "The Persistence of Racial and Ethnic Profiling in the United States," ACLU, https://www.aclu .org/human-rights_racial-justice/persistence-racial-and-ethnic-profiling-united-states.

8. Carol Wilson, *Freedom at Risk: The Kidnapping of Free Blacks in America, 1780–1865* (University Press of Kentucky, 1994).

9. David A. Harris, "Driving While Black: Racial Profiling On Our Nation's Highways," An American Civil Liberties Union Special Report, June 1999, ACLU, https://www.aclu.org/ racial-justice/driving-while-black-racial-profiling-our-nations-highways.

10. David A. Harris, "U.S. Experiences with Racial and Ethnic Profiling: History, Current Issues, and the Future," *Critical Criminology* 14 (2006): 216.

11. "The ACLU Response to Ferguson," ACLU, https://www.aclu.org/aclu-response-ferguson.

12. American Civil Liberties Union of Massachusetts, *Brown, Black and Targeted*, ACLU, 2014, http://www.aclum.org/stopandfrisk.

13. Nusrat Choudhury, "Boston Police Have a Racially Biased Policing Problem, and a Golden Opportunity to Reform," ACLU, October 8, 2014, https://www.aclu.org/blog/racial-justice-criminal-law-reform/boston-police-have-racially-biased-policing-problem-and; Missouri Attorney General, "Racial Profiling Data 2013: Ferguson," http://ago.mo.gov/VehicleStops/2013/ reports/161.pdf.

14. New York Civil Liberties Union, "Stop-and Frisk Campaign: The Issue," http://www.nyclu.org/ issues/racial-justice/stop-and-frisk-practices; New York Civil Liberties Union, *Beyond Deliberate Indifference: A NYPD for All New Yorkers* (New York: NYCLU, 2013), http://www.nyclu.org/files/ publications/nypd_report_final_0.pdf.

15. Anastasia Hendrix, "Muslim Registration under Attack: Men from 23 Countries Must Report to U.S. Government for 2nd Year," SFGate, November 20, 2003, http://www.sfgate.com/politics/ article/Muslim-registration-under-attack-Men-from-23-2510840.php.

16. "Troubling Post-9/11 Government Operations Targeting Muslims," Privacy SOS, https:// privacysos.org/subsequentops.

17. Department of Justice, "Fact Sheet: Racial Profiling," June 17, 2003, http://www.justice.gov/archive/opa/pr/2003/June/racial_profiling_fact_sheet.pdf.

18. Homeland Security, "Report Suspicious Activity," http://www.dhs.gov/how-do-i/report-suspicious-activity.

19. Larry Aubry, "LAPD Spying Wrong and Must Stop," *Los Angeles Sentinel*, May 1, 2014, http://www.lasentinel.net/index.php?option=com_content&view=article&id=12973:lapd-spying-wrong-and-must-stop&catid=85&Itemid=175.

20. "Racist Incitement Outside Government Bolsters Racist Policies Within It, and Vise [sic] Versa," PRIVACYSOS, July 14, 2014, https://privacysos.org/node/1460.

21. Thomas Cincotta, *Platform for Prejudice: How the Nationwide Suspicious Activity Reporting Initiative Invites Racial Profiling, Erodes Civil Liberties, and Undermines Security* (Somerville, MA: Public Research Associates, 2010): 45, http://www.publiceye.org/liberty/matrix/reports/sar_initiative/sar-full-report.pdf.

22. Connor Friedersdorf, "The Horrifying Effects of NYPD Ethnic Profiling on Innocent Muslim Americans," *Atlantic*, March 28, 2013, http://www.theatlantic.com/politics/archive/2013/03/the-horrifying-effects-of-nypd-ethnic-profiling-on-innocent-muslim-americans/274434/.

23. Adam Goldman and Matt Apuzzo, "Informant: NYPD Paid Me to 'Bait' Muslims," AP, October 23, 2012, http://www.ap.org/Content/AP-In-The-News/2012/Informant-NYPD-paid-me-to-bait-Muslims.

24. Robert A. Levy, "Ethnic Profiling: A Rational and Moral Framework," Cato Institute, October 2, 2001, http://www.cato.org/publications/commentary/ethnic-profiling-rational-moral-framework.

25. Arab American Institute, "American Attitudes Toward Arabs and Muslims: 2014," http://www.aaiusa.org/reports/american-attitudes-toward-arabs-and-muslims-2014.

26. "Racial Profiling," The Free Dictionary. http://legal-dictionary.thefreedictionary.com/Ethnic+profiling.

27. Ibid.

28. National Institute of Justice, Office of Justice Programs, "Racial Profiling," January 10, 2013, http://www.nij.gov/topics/law-enforcement/legitimacy/pages/racial-profiling.aspx.

29. David A. Harris, "U.S. Experiences with Racial and Ethnic Profiling," 219.

30. Jo Goodey, "Ethnic Profiling, Criminal (In)Justice and Minority Populations," *Critical Criminology* 14 (2006): 207.

31. "The Case Against Racial Profiling," The Leadership Conference, http://www.civilrights.org/publications/reports/racial-profiling2011/the-case-against-racial.html.

32. Ibid.

33. National Institute of Justice.

34. Mike Bostock and Ford Fessenden, "'Stop-and-Frisk' Is All but Gone From New York," *New York Times*, September 19, 2014, http://www.nytimes.com/interactive/2014/09/19/nyregion/stop-and-frisk-is-all-but-gone-from-new-york.html.

35. Adalberto Aguirre Jr., "Profiling Mexican American Identity: Issues and Concerns," *American Behavioral Scientist* 47 (2004): 937.

36. Rob White, "Disputed Definitions and Fluid Identities: The Limitations of Social Profiling in Relation to Ethnic Youth Gangs," *Youth Justice* 8 (2008): 149.

37. Deborah J. Schildkraut, "The Dynamics of Public Opinion on Ethnic Profiling After 9/11: Results from a Survey Experiment," *American Behavioral Scientist* 53, no. 1 (September, 2009), 61.

38. Stephen J. Ellmann, "Racial Profiling and Terrorism," *New York Law School Law Review* 46 (2003): 730.

Critical Racial and Ethnic Studies— Profiling and Reparations

*by Rodney D. Coates**

Critical racial and ethnic studies attempt to understand the process by which systems of racialization are preserved, maintained, and perpetuated. The *critical* designation implies that such studies recognize the multiple dimensions in which systems of oppression operate. These multiple dimensions, of which race and ethnicity are but two, operate interactively and systemically to produce and reproduce structures of exploitation. The social and cultural institutions provide the situational context in which these dimensions interact. Therefore (either implicitly or explicitly), courts and police, schools and churches, friendship and family networks, and various media outlets all serve to preserve, perpetuate, and/ or modify racial attitudes and group formation and systems of racial oppression and exploitation. Finally, as economic, political, and cultural systems of production change, we note similar changes in the various oppressive and exploitative systems. What I am suggesting is a dynamic as opposed to a static process.

This dynamic process is, as indicated earlier, multifaceted, multidimensional, and situationally, historically, economically, and geopolitically specific. Consequently, whereas we focus on singular dimensions of oppression, it is understood that they are embedded in pluralist systems of exploitation. Such pluralist systems of exploitation, with global ramifications, increase the difficulty for those seeking solutions, remedies, and positive change. Current critical attempts to understand these systems of exploitation have centered on issues relating to racial profiling, reparations, and pedagogy. These central issues provide the basis for this special issue of the *American Behavioral Scientist*.

I am constantly amazed at how consistently race is celebrated in U.S. culture. What is so amazing is that many of these celebrations are rarely viewed as being complementary by various racialized segments of our society. The commercialization of racial and ethnic nonelites often serves to reinforce negative stereotypes. For example, during this past Black History Month celebration, one noted the following features on commercial television: *Pootie Tang, Booty Call, Kingdom Come,* and *12 Angry Men*. Pathological representations of Black males are the central feature of all of these programs. As we go from television to the press, the observation is that these same individuals are more likely to be vilified and victimized, they are more likely to be projected as being the problems or the source of the problems, and they are least likely to be projected in a positive light. I am here reminded of a recent set of commercials advertising Viagra—it is noted that two different sets of commercials were produced. One set, featuring a White male in a loving caress with his partner, centers attention to his newfound ability to perform his marital duties. Alternatively, the other, featuring a partner-less Black male, centers attention on his ability to continue to pursue multiple sexual conquests. After her Jezebel role in *Monster's Ball* in 2001, Halle Barry received an Academy Award. Such movies basically reaffirm a cultural devaluation and sexualization of Black women. Internet stores sell videos with titles such as *Black Chicks in Heat, Black Bitches, Hoochie Mamas, Video Sto' Ho, Black and Nasty, South Central Hookers,* and *Git Yo' Ass On Da Bus!* In the privacy of their homes or hotel rooms, Americans can watch Black actresses—Purple Passion, Jamaica, Toy, Chocolate Tye, Juicy, Jazz, Spontaneeus Xtasy, and others—"validate" the belief that Black women are whores (Pilgrim, 2002). Although not often recognized as such, these are clearly evidence of the racial profiling of racial and ethnic nonelites.

Racial profiling, the systematic singling out of racial and ethnic nonelites for differentially negative sanctions, is alive and well throughout America. Whereas most recent research and concern has been in terms of police and crime, a long history of racial profiling has and continues to be well documented. Current efforts led by the ACLU have resulted in multiple lawsuits being initiated, a series of laws being passed, and a number of policies being changed. Unfortunately, as long as racial profiling is treated as a problem and not a symptom, few actual remedies will be forthcoming. To treat racial profiling as the problem, much like treating only the cough that comes with smoking, is to only treat the symptoms. Racial profiling is part of a larger, more ingrained problem in Western culture.

In the raging debate over racial profiling it should be understood that most Americans, both racial elites and nonelites, agree that racism is bad, that vestiges of racism yet remain, and that laws and their enforcement should be racially neutral. The degree to which groups and individuals assess such neutrality is dependent on which side of the racial divide they find themselves. Much like the O. J. Simpson trial, many racial elites view the criminal justice system as basically fair, whereas many racial nonelites view the same system as being basically unfair. Most racial nonelites know with certainty that police, the courts, and the laws unfairly target, systematically restrict, and regularly harm members of their groups. Alternatively, most racial elites know with certainty that their only protection from an increasingly hostile and criminal underclass is the police, the courts, and the laws. Although several factors may account for these differences, the force of the news media cannot be ignored. Evidence seems to support the vilification of racial nonelites. Specifically, Blacks and Hispanics are more likely to be presented as criminals than as victims or more positively (Chiricos & Eschholz, 2002). These types of perceptual biases have dire and negative consequences when racial nonelites confront the legal system (Berger, 2002).

It should be observed that these types of observations are not limited to the United States; in fact, it seems to be universally associated with racial and ethnic discrimination. For example, research conducted in South Africa by Horwitz (1997) and Binnell (1997) documented how racial elites inflate their own superiority by deflating that of racial nonelites. Consequently, whereas they perceive themselves as being superior, they describe racial nonelites as greedy, lazy, sexually aggressive, deviant, disrespectful, irresponsible, dependent, greedy, and backward (Burger, 2002). Furthermore, as seen in Russia, when racial elites also dominate the police, these types of attitudes can result in selective enforcement, extremism, and ethnic intolerance (Punanov & Spirin, 2002).

Globally since 9/11, there has been a rise in fear of immigrants and anti-immigrant hostilities. Xenophobic fears have surfaced in Denmark, the Netherlands, Belgium, England, France, and Italy to name but a few. In this volume, a critical examination into the basis of such xenophobic fears is provided by Philip Kim in his article "Conditional Morality After 9/11? Attitudes of Religious Individuals Toward Racial Profiling." Here Kim discusses how American fears after the attack served to fuel a process whereby Arabs and Muslims were racially discriminated against. What makes Kim's observations so critically important is that he explains how religious affiliation serves to undergird these discriminatory practices. Specifically, his research demonstrates how Protestant, Catholic, and Jewish Americans were more likely to support racial profiling of Arab and Muslims then those who were nonreligious.

Wilson, Dunham, and Alpert, in their article "Prejudice in Profiling: Assessing an Overlooked Aspect," similarly demonstrate the role of prejudice in how police target specific racial nonelites. They show that such prejudice is rooted in the social, cultural, and institutional structure in which and to which police respond. Within this structure, Blacks and other racial nonelites are deemed as more likely than not to be criminally oriented. As a consequence, they are more likely to find their actions scrutinized and their claims of innocence and motives to be more suspect. Under these conditions, rather then being penalized, police may actually be rewarded for racially profiling.

The issue for Aranda and Rebollo-Gill in "Ethnoracism: Profiling the 'Sandwiched' Minorities" is that profiling cannot be understood unless we also take into consideration the global interaction between economic imperialism, culture, history, politics, and racial identity formations. Latinos, targeted because of their cultural identification, also suffer from a form of profiling that the authors call *ethnoracism*. Thus, although some would argue that for Latinos, what some call a sort of colorblindness is actually a mask that conceals a unique form of racism in what they call *ethnoracism*. Ethnoracism is a more subtle form of racism that relies on language, accent, culture, and national origin. Aranda and Rebollo-Gill argue that "discrimination against the other based on ethnic markers, and in their absence, one's own cultural identification, is not just a social-psychological phenomenon. It is rooted in global, systemic ethnoracism" (p. 926).

Likewise, Aquirre documents that Mexican Americans are more likely to be profiled as drug smugglers or illegal aliens. In Aquirre's article, "Profiling Mexican American Identity: Issues and Concerns," research is presented that argues the practice that victimizes racial nonelites essentially aims to legitimize White hegemonic structures that promote values of White superiority. The damage that this victimization does is that it serves to silence and subordinate Mexican social identity in public life. Racial profiling presumes Mexican guilt, questions their legitimacy, and relegates them to a marginalized place in American society. Thus, the Mexican American is more likely to be publicly silent, politically apathetic, and socially invisible.

Moving from the macro to the micro, the next set of authors begins by observing that unless we understand the context that gives rise to racial profiling, we will never understand the content of such profiling. Thus, Parker and colleagues, in "A Contextual Study of Racial Profiling: Assessing the Theoretical Rationale for the Study of Racial Profiling at the Local Level," demonstrate the utility of investigating racial profiling within the spatial context of local areas. Their article explores both the theoretical and methodological challenges faced by those seeking to conduct such research. They conclude the link between community structure, values, and police behavior with racial profiling has yet to be established. Hence their call for further research in that the understanding of links is critically important if local agents are to develop necessary remedies and solutions to the problems associated with racial profiling.

How racial nonelites respond to racial profiling may be the difference between life and death. In cities across the nation, increased levels of incarceration, fear, and even death have resulted as these nonelites have found their opportunities for freedom and security impaired. Bennett, Merritt, Edwards, and Sollers, in "Perceived Racism and Affective Responses to Ambiguous Interpersonal Interactions Among African American Men," explore how ambiguous racial situations may have dire consequences for racial nonelites. Their study suggests that ambiguous stimuli may be more problematic for cognitive and affective processing (and potentially physiological disposition) than overt racism among African

American men. Thus, repeated episodes of racial intimidation, profiling, and discrimination may produce increased levels of stress, hypertension, and other related health conditions.

The basic idea of justice is that if damage has been done then remedies must be provided. In the newly developed American jurisprudence model, we assert that justice must be both racially sensitive and racially blind. Herein we find a paradox, for the historical legacy of the United States has been one of racial sensitivity that has consistently decided in favor of racial elites at the expense of racial nonelites. The reason why our legal structure should be racially sensitive has to do with our racial legacy of insensitivity (i.e., slavery, segregation, Jim Crow, *Plessey v. Ferguson*, Chinese Exclusionary Acts, the Internment of Japanese, Trail of Tears, current and past immigration policies, differential sentencing, etc., etc., etc.). It is strange that the very same racial elites who benefited, sanctioned, and applauded such racially stimulated legal actions now lead the call for a racially blind system. One must however question their authenticity as they now cry, bemoan, and condemn those who seek remedies for past and present damages.

Williams and Collins essentially argue that the history of discrimination, racism, and segregation has produced lasting health consequences for today's African Americans. In "Reparations: A Viable Strategy to Address the Enigma of African Health," they contend that Black-White differences in health are directly related to the lack of access to competent and reliable health care. Such access, limited by segregation and discrimination, has been significantly denied to African Americans. Specifically, they assert that

> these differences in social and economic conditions are largely respon-
> sible for racial differences in health status. Reparations are a potentially
> effective strategy to rebuild the infrastructure of disadvantaged, seg-
> regated communities. Such investment would enhance the economic
> circumstances of African American families and communities and also
> improve their health. (p. 977)

Whereas Williams and Collins see reparations from a single national lens and focus, Hewitt looks at it as a transnational and hence global strategy for remedy.

Hewitt begins by observing the increasing inability and unwillingness of America and other Western nations to effectively deal with the problems they created for survival, effective living, and future hope among racial nonelites. Her article argues that the only solution to this failure is total and complete repara-tions. The world that we live in, the Western sphere of influence, owes its very presence, power, and affluence to the exploitation of African energies, lives, and resources. In "One Capital Indivisible Under God: The IMF and Reparations for Slavery in a Time of Globalized Wealth," Hewitt systematically lays out the damage, the debt, and the cost of such exploitation. Specifically, she demonstrates that such terms as *the underclass, sedimentation of race*, and the misnomer *Afro-pessimism* all essentially blame the victim (i.e., Black people) and not the system for the inexorably, intergenerationally imposed impoverishment of Africans throughout the world. The exploitation and oppression of the African, transglobal in nature, must seek a transglobal remedy. Such a remedy is found in the International Monetary Fund (IMF), which Hewitt asserts is the very embodiment of Western hegemonic systems of racial control. She concludes that through the IMF, special drawing rights from enslaver and colonial nations to African people would be an efficient method of making restitution.

REFERENCES

Berger, V. (2002). A legacy of racism. *National Law Journal, 24*(55). Retrieved August 3, 2003, from http://www.law.com/jsp/article.jsp?id=1032128694425

Binnell, B. (1997). *A discourse analysis of the racial talk and identity construction of a group of working class Afrikaans speakers.* Unpublished doctoral dissertation, University of the Witwatersrand, Johannesburg.

Burger, D. A. (2002). Race, crime and social exclusion; a qualitative study of White women's fear of crime in Johannesburg. *Urban Forum, 13*(3), 53–80.

Chiricos, T., & Eschholz, S. (2002). The racial and ethnic typification of crime and the criminal typification of race and ethnicity in local television news. *Journal of Research in Crime & Delinquency, 39,* 400–421.

Horwitz, K. (1997). *White South African kinship and identity.* Unpublished doctoral dissertation, University of the Witwatersrand, Johannesburg.

Pilgrim, D. (2002). *The Jezebel stereotype.* Retrieved August 3, 2003, from http://www.ferris.edu/news/jimcrow/menu.htm

Punanov, G., & Spirin, Y. (2002). Police didn't notice anything wrong. *Current Digest of the Post Soviet Press, 54*(22), 13.

*Rodney D. Coates** is a professor of sociology and gerontology and director of Black World Studies at Miami University. His specialties include critical race and ethnic relations, political sociology, the sociology of education, and stratification.

Stop, Question, and Frisk Policing Practices in New York City: A Primer (Revised)

*by Delores Jones-Brown, Brett G. Stoudt, Brian Johnston, and Kevin Moran**

[...]

VII. WHAT HAPPENS DURING STOPS AND STOP OUTCOMES

Many people stopped by police officers in New York City are questioned and then permitted to move on, but many are also "frisked," and a portion of those stopped experience the use of force beyond the frisk itself. While the number of documented stops declined by 22% from year-end 2011 to year-end 2012, what happened during stops for each year was quite similar.

During roughly half of all stops in 2011 (not shown) and 2012, officers reported frisking the suspect (55.7% and 55.8% respectively). Officers are legally authorized to pat down the outer clothing of a suspect in order to determine if the person is carrying a weapon. In both years, a very small percentage of total stops resulted in the discovery of a weapon of any kind (gun, knife or other). In 2011, when stops were approaching 700,000 the percent of stops that recovered a weapon was 1.0 or 7,849. In 2012, when the number of stops fell closer to 500,000, the percentage of stops that resulted in the discovery of a weapon was 1.13 (6,027). For both years, a slightly higher percentage of stops (1.7%) resulted in the discovery of some other kind of contraband, excluding weapons (see Figure 6). Contraband is any item that is against the law to possess, including illegal drugs. For both years, guns were the least likely item to be discovered during stops (0.14% in 2012 and 0.12% in 2011, when stops were at their highest).

In a little less than a quarter of stops in 2011 (21.6%), officers used some form of force beyond the pat down. During 2012 the percentage of stops involving force beyond the frisk fell to 17.3 (see Figure 6). According to information captured in completed UF-250 forms, the categories of force include: putting suspects on the ground or against a wall; drawing a weapon and/or pointing a weapon at the person stopped; and using manual force, a baton, handcuffs, or pepper spray during the stop. In both years, searches, which require a greater amount of evidence than do frisks, were relatively low at 8.3% in 2012 and 8.5% in 2011.

Figure 6. What Happens During Stops, 2012

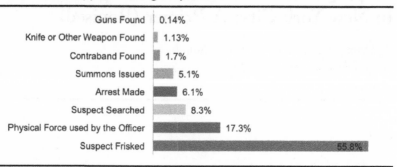

Guns Found	0.14%
Knife or Other Weapon Found	1.13%
Contraband Found	1.7%
Summons Issued	5.1%
Arrest Made	6.1%
Suspect Searched	8.3%
Physical Force used by the Officer	17.3%
Suspect Frisked	55.8%

Data Source: NYPD Stop, Question and Frisk Report Database, 2012 (http://www.nyc.gov/html/nypd/html/analysis_and_planning/stop_question_and_frisk_report.shtml).

Out of 532,911 total stops in 2012, 6.1% resulted in an arrest being made and 5.1% resulted in a summons being issued. Of the 685,724 stops in 2011, 6% resulted in an arrest, and 5.9% resulted in the issuance of a summons. Thus, for 2012, 11.2% of stop and frisk activity concluded with an arrest or summons. In 2011, the figure was 11.7%.[1] The low percentage of stops that resulted in an arrest or summons during 2011 is similar to outcomes in the previous eight years (2003–2010), when the proportion of stops that resulted in an arrest or a summons ranged from a high of 13.7% (2010) to a low of 9.7% (2006).

The New York Civil Liberties Union (NYCLU) refers to stops that do not result in an arrest or summons as "innocent stops".[2] From 2003–2012, nearly nine out of ten individuals stopped in New York City have been innocent. Figure[s] 7[a & b]

Figure 7a. "Innocent" Stops, 2003–2012

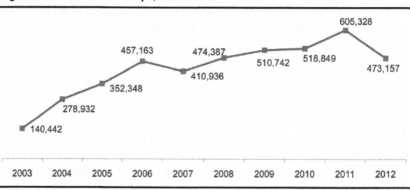

Data Source: NYPD Stop, Question and Frisk Report Database, 2003–2012 (http://www.nyc.gov/html/nypd/html/analysis_and_planning/stop_question_and_frisk_report.shtml).

Figure 7b. Total Stops Compared to "Innocent" Stops, 2003–2012

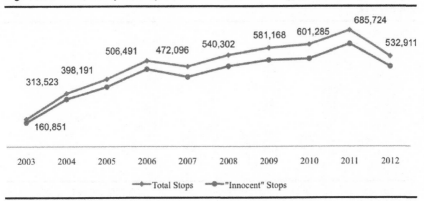

Data Source: NYPD Stop, Question and Frisk Report Database, 2003–2012 (http://www.nyc.gov/html/nypd/html/analysis_and_planning/stop_question_and_frisk_report.shtml).

show the growing number of so-called innocent stops. When compared with the total number of stops annually (see Figure 7b), it is clear that the overwhelming majority of stops engage individuals for whom suspicion of criminality was not confirmed. Data about the percentage of stop and frisk arrests and summonses that are subsequently dismissed for legal insufficiency could not be accessed, but between 6.7% and 30% of UF-250 forms are completed in ways that call the legality of stops into question.[3]

Since 2008, the NYPD made 1,074,145 total arrests. Of those arrests, 16.9% (181,407) were from documented stop and frisk encounters. Thus, over the last five years, more than 80% of the total arrests made by NYPD officers were the results of activities other than stop and frisk. (See Figure 8).

VIII. INCREASED STOPS, MODEST RETURNS

One rationale offered for the liberal use of stop, question, and frisk procedures is that they work to substantially reduce the number of weapons being carried on the streets of New York. In 1994 when William Bratton was Police Commissioner, the New York City Police Department issued Police Strategy No. 1, "Getting Guns off the Streets of New York," which established the Department's plan to eradicate gun violence by stepping up efforts to find and seize illegal firearms.[4] Strategy No. 1 is closely linked with Police Strategy No. 5, "Reclaiming the Public Spaces of New York," which presents the Department's plan to combat "low-level street disorder" to "undercut the ground on which more serious crimes seem possible and even permissible."[5]

Figure 8. Total NYPD Arrests Compared to Total Stop & Frisk Arrests, 2008–2012

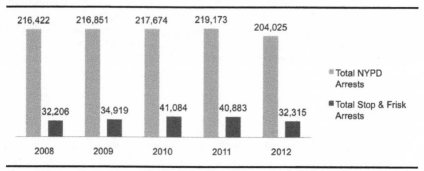

Data Sources: NYPD Stop, Question and Frisk Report Database, 2003–2012 (http://www.nyc.gov/html/nypd/html/analysis_and_planning/stop_question_and_frisk_report.shtml); NYPD annual *Crime and Enforcement Activity in New York City* reports, 2008–2012 (http://www.nyc.gov/html/nypd/html/analysis_and_planning/crime_and_enforcement_activity.shtml).

While the total number of annual stops climbed to nearly 700,000 in just a few years (up from 160,851 in 2003), the number of stops in which, at least, one illegal gun was discovered remained substantially modest in comparison.[6] As Figure 9 shows, the number of guns recovered over the ten-year period 2003 to 2012 ranges from a low of 633 (2003) to a high of 840 (2008), averaging 738 (see note following Figure 9).

While stops have increased each year, except in 2007, a clear pattern of gun recovery has not emerged. The greatest number of guns was recovered in 2008

Figure 9. Recovery of Guns, 2003–2012

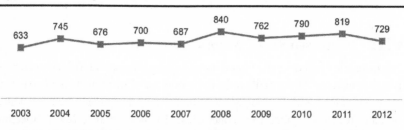

Data Sources: NYPD Stop, Question and Frisk Report Database, 2003–2012 (http://www.nyc.gov/html/nypd/html/analysis_and_planning/stop_question_and_frisk_report.shtml). Note: The number of "guns recovered" was derived by adding whether at least one pistol, rifle, assault weapon and/or machine gun was found during the stop. UF-250 forms do not record the quantity of items found, e.g. 3 pistols and 1 machine gun recovered from a single stop would be recorded as "a" pistol and "a" machine gun recovered. In this chart, the maximum items a single stop could derive is four as there are four categories of weapons that can be checked by the reporting officer.

Figure 10. Total NYPD Firearm Arrests Compared to Stop & Frisk Guns Recovered, 2008–2012

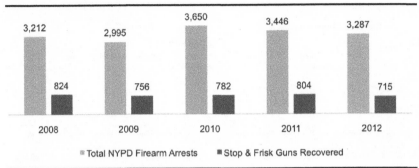

Data Sources: NYPD Stop, Question and Frisk Report Database, 2003–2012 (http://www.nyc.gov/html/nypd/html/analysis_and_planning/stop_question_and_frisk_report.shtml); NYPD annual *Crime and Enforcement Activity in New York City* reports, 2008–2012 (http://www.nyc.gov/html/nypd/html/analysis_and_planning/crime_and_enforcement_activity.shtml). Note: The "stop and frisk guns recovered" represents the amount of stops that led to one or more guns recovered.

(840 guns from 540,302 stops, twenty-one more guns than in 2011 when the number of stops was at 685,724). Though stops decreased by 22% in 2012, the number of guns recovered was closest to the number of guns recovered in 2004 when the documented stops were 313,523 (729 vs. 745). The gun recovery numbers are not consistent with greater productivity due to increased stops nor do they show the steady decline that would be consistent with claims that individuals are leaving their guns at home.

Figure 10 compares the total firearms arrests for each year from 2008 to 2012 to the number of firearms recovered from stop and frisk for those same years. Three quarters or more of firearm arrests each year do not stem from a stop and frisk encounter.

Figure 11 shows that officers are more likely to recover contraband other than weapons during stops. Although the UF-250 provides a space for officers to specify the type of non-weapon contraband found, this portion of the form is not always filled in; and, the information that is available could not be analyzed by the authors in a timely manner. Some studies, conducted by others on this topic, suggest that such contraband is primarily drugs, and specifically marijuana.[7]

From 2003–2011, the number of stops have more than quadrupled, however the recovery of guns has, with small fluctuations from year to year, remained relatively the same. This means that the yield of guns per stop has declined considerably as the number of stops have increased (see Figure 12). Figure 12 also

Figure 11. Recovery of Weapons and Contraband, 2003–2012

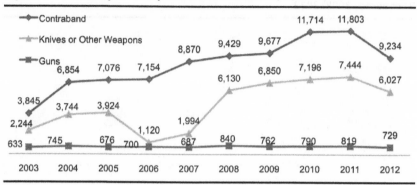

Data Source: NYPD Stop, Question and Frisk Report Database, 2003–2012 (http://www.nyc.gov/html/ nypd/html/analysis_and_planning/stop_question_and_frisk_report.shtml). Note: The number of "knives and other weapons" recovered in a stop was derived by adding whether either a "knife" and/or "other weapon" was found on a suspect. UF-250 forms do not record the quantity of items found, e.g. 3 knives and 2 other weapons recovered in a single stop would be recorded as "a" knife recovered and "an" other weapon. In this instance the maximum a single stop could derive is two items as there are two categories of weapons that can be checked by the reporting officer.

reveals that the yield of contraband, knives (or other weapons) and guns is very low in comparison to the annual number of stops.

As the number of stops has increased and the yield from stops has remained low, complaints to the Civilian Complaint Review Board (CCRB) involving stop incidents have been substantial. As Figure 13 shows, between a quarter and a third of all complaints to the CCRB in the years 2004–2011 involved at least one allegation concerning a police stop.

Figure 12. Recovery of Weapons and Contraband Relative to Total Stops, 2003–2012

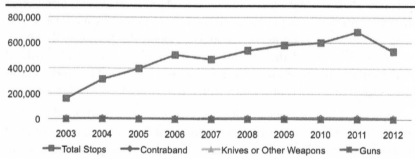

Data Source: NYPD Stop, Question and Frisk Report Database, 2003–2012 (http://www.nyc.gov/html/ nypd/html/analysis_and_planning/stop_question_and_frisk_report.shtml).

Figure 13. Number of CCRB Complaints Involving Stop, Question, Frisk, or Search Police Practices, 2003–2011

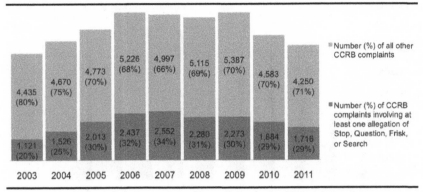

Data Source: CCRB Annual Reports: 2003-2007 (http://www.nyc.gov/html/ccrb/pdf/ccrbann2007_A. pdf); 2006–2010 (http://www.nyc.gov/html/ccrb/pdf/ccrbann2010.pdf); 2011 (http://www.nyc.gov/html/ccrb/pdf/ccrbann2011.pdf).

IX. Who Gets Stopped

Form UF-250 includes six possible categories for describing the "race" of the person stopped: White, Black, White Hispanic, Black Hispanic, Asian/Pacific Islander, or American Indian/Alaskan Native. Because skin color is a more immediately apparent personal characteristic than ethnicity, or even language until words are exchanged, the authors of this Primer grouped Black Hispanics with Blacks for the purpose of statistical analysis. Black Hispanics represented 11.2% (35,772) of all total stops in this combined "Black" category for 2012.

As Figure 14a shows, for each year 2003 through 2012, Blacks and Hispanics make up a substantial majority of persons stopped. In 2011, when stops were at their highest, Blacks (399,181) and Hispanics (175,302) combined were stopped 9 times more than Whites (61,805) and 11 times more than Asian/Others (49,426).[8] For 2012, Blacks made up 320,001 of those stopped. Stops involving (non-Black) Hispanics totaled 129,368. Stops of Whites numbered 50,366. Asian/other stops totaled 33,176.

Police in other cities also stop more Blacks than Whites. A report issued by the ACLU of Southern California in 2008 shows that Blacks were nearly three times more likely to be stopped than Whites.[9] A 2010 article in the *Toronto Star* reports that Blacks are three times more likely than are Whites to be stopped by the Toronto police.[10] Among young males between the ages of 15 and 24, Blacks are stopped 2.5 times more than Whites.[11] On the international front, Black

Figure 14a. Persons Stopped by Race/Ethnicity, 2003–2012

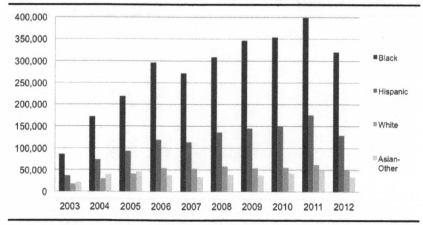

Data Source: NYPD Stop, Question and Frisk Report Database, 2003–2012 (http://www.nyc.gov/html/nypd/html/analysis_and_planning/stop_question_and_frisk_report.shtml).

people in England and Wales are nearly 30 times more likely to be stopped and searched than are white people, even in predominantly white areas. The exact figure is that Blacks were 29.7 times more likely to be stopped than Whites in 2011. This was up from a 2010 figure of 26.6.[12]

Figure 14b shows the number of innocent stops across racial categories for 2012. Rounding, the number of innocent stops involving Blacks was 2.5 times that of innocent Hispanics; close to 6.5 times that of innocent Whites, and more than 9.5 times that of innocent Asian-Others. The number of innocent Blacks

Figure 14b. "Innocent" Stops by Race/Ethnicity, 2012

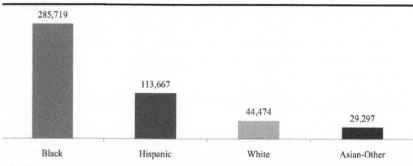

Data Source: NYPD Stop, Question and Frisk Report Database, 2012 (http://www.nyc.gov/html/nypd/html/analysis_and_planning/stop_question_and_frisk_report.shtml).

stopped was nearly 300,000, compared to roughly 114,000 (non-black) Hispanics, less than 45,000 Whites and just under 30,000 Asian/Others.

Though not shown in a figure, the vast majority of stops are of males. From 2003–2011, the percentage of male stops across race was 90% for Whites, 93% for Blacks, 93% for Hispanics and 92% for Asians/Others. This trend continued through 2012, where the percentage of male stops across race was 89% for Whites, 92% for Blacks, and 92% for Hispanics. Notably, the percentage of male stops for Asian/Others in 2012 was 78%. This low percentage of male stops is in part due to the large number of stops in this racial/ethnic category where the sex of the suspect was marked as not known (4,901). Over the nine-year period, 2003 to 2011, Black men and boys represented 59% (2,266,470) of the stops where the suspect was male. Another 25% of male stops involved Hispanics as suspects (962,530). This was also true for 2012, where Black men and boys represented 60% (296,366) of the stops where the suspect was male. Hispanic men and boys accounted for 24.5% of male stops in 2012.

X. What Occurs During Stops and Outcomes for Persons from Different Racial/Ethnic Groups

As shown in Figure 15, the raw number of Blacks and Hispanics stopped by police, frisked, and subject to force substantially exceeds the number of Whites and Asians/Other who have similar experiences. Similarly in Figure 16, the raw numbers of arrests and summonses that occur during stops involving Blacks and Hispanics are also substantially greater than in stops involving Whites and Asian/Others (not shown).

Figure 15. Stops, Frisks, and Physical Force by Race/Ethnicity, 2012

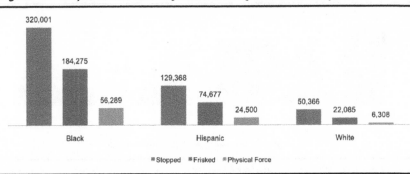

Data Source: NYPD Stop, Question and Frisk Report Database, 2012 (http://www.nyc.gov/html/nypd/html/analysis_and_planning/stop_question_and_frisk_report.shtml).

Figure 16. Arrests & Summonses Issued By Race/Ethnicity, 2012

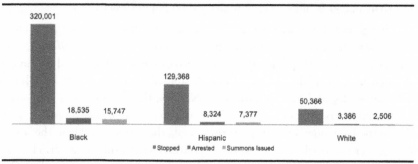

Data Source: NYPD Stop, Question and Frisk Report Database, 2012 (http://www.nyc.gov/html/nypd/html/analysis_and_planning/stop_question_and_frisk_report.shtml).

A look *proportionally* at what occurs during stops for members of each group (Figure 17) shows that the percentage of stops involving Blacks and Hispanics that led to frisks and the use of physical force are almost identical. Members of both groups are more likely than Whites and Asians/Other to be frisked (58% and 57% compared to 44% and 49%) and be subjected to physical force (17% and 19% compared to 12.5% and 15%) during the stops.

Figure 18 shows that the proportional percentage of stops involving Whites that led to arrests are slightly higher (6.7%) as compared to Blacks, Hispanics and Asians/Other (5.8%, 6.4%, and 6.2% respectively). Whites and Hispanics are slightly more likely to be issued a summons (both similar at 5.0% and 5.7% respectively) as compared to Blacks and Asians/Other (4.9% and 5.4% respectively).

Figure 17. Frisks and Use of Force by Race/Ethnicity (%), 2012

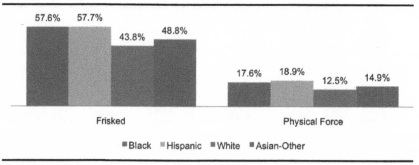

Data Source: NYPD Stop, Question and Frisk Report Database, 2012 (http://www.nyc.gov/html/nypd/html/analysis_and_planning/stop_question_and_frisk_report.shtml).

Figure 18. Arrests and Summonses Issued by Race/Ethnicity (%), 2012

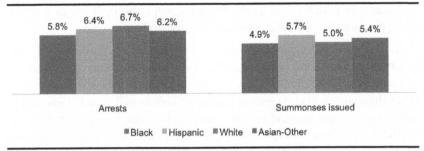

Arrests   Summonses issued

■ Black ▓ Hispanic ▣ White ■ Asian-Other

Data Source: NYPD Stop, Question and Frisk Report Database, 2012 (http://www.nyc.gov/html/nypd/
html/analysis_and_planning/stop_question_and_frisk_report.shtml).

To address the issue of whether the large raw number racial/ethnic disparity in stop, question and frisk practices may be warranted based on differences in criminal behavior, Figure 19 combines Blacks and Hispanics and compares outcomes from their stops with the outcomes of stops involving Whites. *Proportionally*, the outcomes for Whites, who comprise the smallest number of persons stopped of the three, are strikingly similar to those for Blacks and Hispanics (combined), the highest number of persons stopped. As Figure 19 shows, 6.72% of all Whites stopped in 2012 were arrested as compared to 5.98% of Blacks and Hispanics. It should be noted that the proportion of Whites arrested was consistently slightly larger than the proportion of Blacks and Hispanics arrested in every year from 2003–2012 with the exceptions of 2008 and 2010. By contrast, stops of Blacks and

Figure 19. Stop Outcomes by Race/Ethnicity (%), 2012

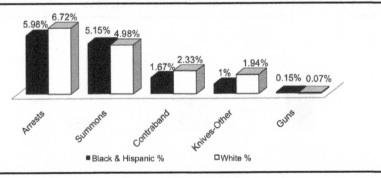

■ Black & Hispanic %   ▫ White %

Data Source: NYPD Stop, Question and Frisk Report Database, 2012 (http://www.nyc.gov/html/nypd/
html/analysis_and_planning/stop_question_and_frisk_report.shtml).

Hispanics (combined) have consistently resulted in a slightly higher proportion of summonses (5.15% versus 4.98% in 2012; down from 6.55% versus 5.79% in 2008, for examples), with the exceptions of 2003 and 2011.

In terms of recovering weapons and other contraband in 2012, stops of Whites yielded a greater share, proportionally, of contraband—other than weapons (2.33% versus 1.67%). The difference in the recovery of knives and weapons—other than guns is slightly greater among Whites as well (1.94% compared to 1.0%). In terms of recovering guns, the situation is reversed: proportionally, stops of Blacks and Hispanics were slightly more likely than stops of Whites to result in the recovery of a gun (0.15% versus 0.07%), but this difference is extremely small (0.08 percentage points).

When calculations are made that take into account the larger number of Blacks and Hispanics (combined) who were not only stopped but also frisked in 2012, as compared to the fewer number of Whites frisked, there is an increase in the differences between the groups for the recovery of weapons and other contraband. As shown in Figure 20, the percentage of Black and Hispanic frisks that recovered contraband in 2012 was 2.9 as compared with 5.3 for Whites. The percentage of frisks that recovered knives and weapons—other than guns for Blacks and Hispanics was 1.7 as compared to 4.4 among Whites frisked. The gun recovery percentage, which is extremely low for both groups, was slightly greater among Blacks and Hispanics frisked compared with Whites (0.30% versus 0.20%).

Examining data from 2011, when documented stops had reached their height, another way to look at the weapons recovered during frisks is that for every 1,000 Black individuals frisked, 2.4 guns were found; the equivalent return for Whites was 1.6 guns, and for Hispanics, 1.2 guns. Frisks were somewhat more efficient

Figure 20. Frisk Outcomes by Race/Ethnicity (%), 2012

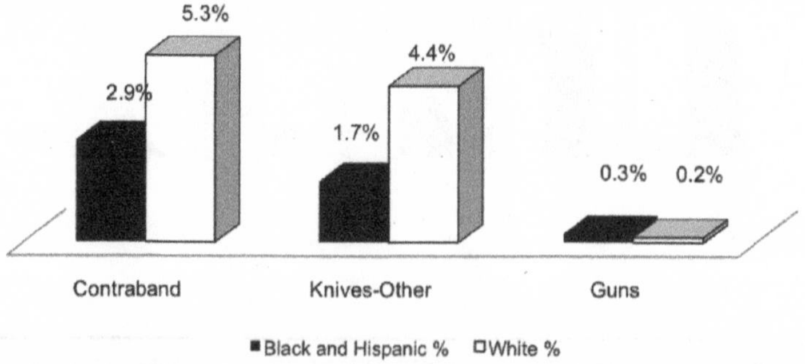

■ Black and Hispanic %   □ White %

Data Source: NYPD Stop, Question and Frisk Report Database, 2012 (http://www.nyc.gov/html/nypd/html/analysis_and_planning/stop_question_and_frisk_report.shtml).

in recovering other types of weapons and contraband, especially among Whites. For every 1,000 White individuals frisked in 2011, officers recovered 36.3 knives or other nonfirearms. The equivalent return for Hispanics and Blacks was 17.9 and 14.8, respectively. Similarly, for every 1000 White individuals frisked in 2011, contraband was found on 45.1 of them as compared to 25.2 for Blacks and 24.5 for Hispanics.

In total raw numbers, out of 399,181 stops of Black individuals in 2011, 596 guns were recovered; out of 175,302 stops of Hispanic individuals, 124 guns were recovered; and out of 61,805 stops of White individuals, 48 guns were recovered. As already mentioned, these returns are small in the context of the vast number of individuals stopped by police in 2011. For Blacks they represent .14% of stops resulting in a gun recovery. For Hispanics they represent .07% of stops resulting in a gun recovery and .08% for Whites.

Recent discussions have attempted to justify Black disproportionality in stops by using the percentage of crime suspects that are identified as Black. Noting that the NYPD has a written policy against racial profiling (see Appendix D), Figure 21 shows the numerical disparity in the total number of Blacks stopped, compared to the number of "innocent stops" for Blacks and their reported numbers as suspects in crime for 2012.

Figure 21. Black Stops, "Innocent" Stops, and Violent Crime Suspects, 2012

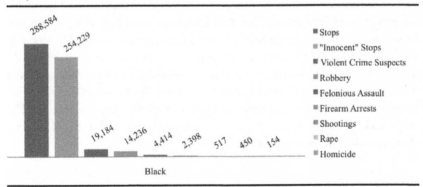

Data Sources: NYPD Stop, Question and Frisk Report Database, 2003–2012 (http://www.nyc.gov/html/nypd/html/analysis_and_planning/stop_question_and_frisk_report.shtml); NYPD annual *Crime and Enforcement Activity in New York City* report, 2012 (http://www.nyc.gov/html/nypd/html/analysis_and_planning/crime_and_enforcement_activity.shtml).

Note: For this figure, Black Stops are as reported in the 2012 *Crime and Enforcement Activity in New York City*. This number does not include Black Hispanics. The "Innocent" stops figure was calculated using this Black stop number. Crime suspect numbers are as listed in the "suspects" category of the report for each offense, with the exception of illegal firearm possession, which is reported as firearm "arrests" across racial/ethnic categories.

Using the reported NYPD data for 2012, 88% of Blacks stopped were innocent, that is their stops did not result in an arrest or summons. The number of Blacks stopped and the number of innocent Blacks stopped substantially exceeds all figures related to Black suspects or arrests for serious violent crimes. The use of percentages instead of raw numbers in the *Crime and Enforcement Activity in New York City* report is misleading. For "Violent Crime Suspects" Blacks are identified as 66% of suspects (which equates to 19,184) and 54.8% (which equates to 288,584) of stops. This represents a difference of 269,400 between alleged Black "suspect" activity and the number of Blacks experiencing documented stops. In other words, Blacks were stopped more than 15 times greater than their number among violent crime suspects.

This disparity gets larger as the number of Black suspects or arrestees diminish across offense categories. For example, the difference between the number of Blacks arrested for possessing firearms (2,398) and the number of Blacks stopped is 286,186, nearly 120 times greater than their firearm arrest number. As shootings suspects (517) compared to their number of stops, the difference for Blacks begins to approach 300,000 (288,067) or almost 560 times the recorded number of Black shooting suspects. Finally, while the *Crime and Enforcement Activity in New York City* report for 2012 lists Blacks representing 53.7% of homicide suspects, that percentage equates to 154 Black suspects compared to 288,584 Black stops or nearly1875 times more stops than suspects.

If stops were distributed neutrally across race/ethnicity,[13] one could expect that the percentage of stops involving members of each race/ethnicity would resemble the percentage of the overall New York City population each group represents. Figure 21 makes this comparison between the race/ethnicity of police stop percentages in 2012 and the 2010 NYC demographics. While Whites make up 33% and Asians/Other 15% of the total NYC population, they were only 9.5% and 6.2% of the total police stops in 2012. Conversely, Blacks are 23% of the NYC population but represent the majority (53.3%) of all the 2012 police stops. The stops made of Hispanics in 2012 (31%) were much closer, though still higher, than their demographic proportion (29%).

XI. Some Highlights from Stops during the 1st Quarter of 2013

At the time this publication was being prepared, data on stops had been issued by the NYPD for the first quarter of 2013:[14]

- **Decline in the number of stops:** Police made 99,788 stops in January, February, and March of 2013 which represents a 51% decrease from the number of police stops in 2012 over the same months.

- **A continuation of the low return rates for stops:** For the first three months of 2013, 6.2% of stops resulted in an arrest and 3.5% of stops resulted in the issuance of a summons.

- **"Furtive Movements" continues to be the leading reasons for stopping people:** Furtive movements were listed as a reason in 50% of stops for the first three months of 2013. Sixty percent of stops were justified on the basis of the additional circumstance of high-crime area[15] in the first three months of 2013. "Fits description" was listed as a reason in 6.3% of stops.

- **Continued focus on stopping Blacks and Hispanics:** In the first three months of 2013 approximately 86% of stops were of Blacks and Latinos.

XII. LEGAL CHALLENGES

Though *Terry v. Ohio* authorized police use of stop, question and frisk practices, there are two major federal constitutional questions that have resulted in litigation around the use of *Terry*-stops, which in New York City are also currently being called, "reasonable suspicion"-stops. The first is related to the Fourth Amendment's requirement for "reasonable" searches and seizures and *Terry's* requirement of "reasonable" suspicion before conducting a stop. The case law is clear that suspicion alone is not legally sufficient to support a stop. Because the NYPD data indicates that nearly 90% of the time officers are inaccurate when they suspect a person of potential criminality, the "reasonableness" of their suspicions is called into question. Police action based on mere suspicion or hunches are not covered by *Terry* and are prohibited by the federal constitution. Police stops for the purpose of merely exploring whether someone might be thinking about engaging in crime are also prohibited and have been termed "suspicionless" stops in current litigation against the NYPD.

The second major legal question involves the Fourteenth Amendment's guarantee of "equal protection" of the law. The amendment was enacted to insure that regardless of racial identity,[16] individuals would not be treated differently by government agencies. While the police have an obligation to protect the public, precedent legal cases have determined that legitimate governmental goals must be achieved by the "least intrusive means" (that is, by means that interfere as little as possible with the rights of the people); and, that anytime racial discrimination is alleged in relation to governmental action, such action must be examined carefully (given "strict scrutiny") so as not to unnecessarily and improperly restrict the rights of individuals in one or more racial groups compared to others.

Litigation over the NYPD's use of stop, question and frisk practices pre-date 1999.

Major cases include:

Daniels, et al. v. The City of New York, a class action lawsuit brought by the Center for Constitutional Rights (CCR) in 1999, which resulted in the requirement that the NYPD make stop and frisk data available to the New York City Council on a quarterly basis and the requirement that the NYPD establish a written policy prohibiting racial profiling (see Appendix D).[17] The suit made 4th and 14th Amendment claims as discussed above.

In the Matter of New York Civil Liberties Union v. New York City Police Department, the New York Civil Liberties Union (NYCLU) filed suit under the Freedom of Information Law (FOIL), and was granted the right to access the NYPD's full electronic databases concerning stop and frisk, with identifying information removed.[18]

Ligon, et al. v. The City of New York, a class action lawsuit brought by NYCLU, decided in February 2013.[19] The case was decided in favor of the plaintiffs who were complaining about stops being made by police outside private residential buildings enrolled in the City's Trespass Affidavit Program. The judge's decision noted that the NYPD acted with "deliberate indifference" to the complaints made against their stop and frisk practices and that their training materials for stop and frisk were constitutionally inaccurate. The case is awaiting a final hearing and decision on the remedies to be imposed. The judge's full 157 page opinion can be accessed on-line.

Floyd, et al. v. The City of New York, a class action lawsuit filed by CCR in 2008 went to trial in March of 2013.[20] The trial ended on May 20, 2013. The case is pending a decision. The suit raised the 4th and 14th Amendment claims discussed previously by individuals who were stopped as pedestrians on New York City streets.

Davis, et al. v. The City of New York, a class action lawsuit brought by the Legal Aid Society and NAACP Legal Defense Fund on behalf of individuals stopped and cited for trespass in public housing developments, is awaiting trial in October 2013.[21]

[...]

CONCLUSION

The data presented in this Primer show that after stopping people in New York City in increasing numbers for nine years, the number of police stops were decreased by more than 22% and overall, crime did not increase. In fact, the decrease in stops in 2012 accompanied the City's reporting of the lowest number of homicides in recent history. There were nearly 153,000 fewer stops in 2012 compared with 2011, in contrast to the quadrupling of stops that occurred since 2003. The trend of decreased stops has continued into the first quarter of 2013. It is duly noted that these data only reflect stops that officers record on a departmental form; an unknown number of stops take place without documentation.

The data on documented stops show that the yield from these hundreds of thousands of encounters between police officers and pedestrians is small in comparison. For example, on average, for every 100 people officers stopped in 2011, when stops were at their highest, they found contraband of some kind (including guns, knives, other weapons, or illegal drugs) on approximately three people. Prior to 2012, as the annual number of stops increased sharply, the annual rate of return declined.

The data continue to show that stops tend to be concentrated in a handful of police precincts and that the vast majority of people stopped are Black or Hispanic. The reasons officers list for stopping people vary, but "carrying a suspicious object in plain view" and *"engaging* in a violent crime" are less commonly documented reasons compared to "furtive movements" or "high crime area"[22]—reasons that are highly ambiguous, undefined and susceptible to personal biases.

Suspect descriptions have little or no direct relationship to stops, with "fits description" being checked off as a reason for making a stop in only 15% of stops in 2011 and 16% of stops in 2012. In 2012, persons who are Black were 15 times likelier to be stopped than they numbered among violent crime suspects. The data also show that, during stops, Blacks and Hispanics are more likely than Whites and Asians/Other to be subjected to frisks and to physical force beyond the pat-down itself. Finally, even though Blacks and Hispanics combined are stopped in far greater numbers than Whites, the arrest and summons outcomes, proportionately are roughly the same. When differential rates of frisking are taken into account, Whites are more likely to be found in possession of contraband and a weapon that is not a firearm. The proportional difference in recovery of a firearm is extremely small.

The many statistics in this Primer are beyond debate, though the interpretation of them have been the source of both plentiful and heated pronouncements and discussions. Numbers alone cannot capture how individuals feel when stopped by police, especially when they are not engaged in criminal conduct. The numbers also cannot capture the consequences of those feelings, particularly among innocent people who are stopped multiple times. Research is needed to determine the individual and social costs as well as the public benefits of stop, question, and frisk policing practices in New York City, beyond speculation, intuition and isolated accounts. Ongoing litigation is poised to resolve questions about whether these police practices are legally justified or whether they infringe upon certain liberties enshrined in U.S. law. But, the police, lawyers, politicians, academics and media should not decide these issues alone, without a robust public debate and discussion that include the diverse voices of the many people of the City of New York, especially those most directly affected by the practice. Collaborative efforts seem essential to shaping stop, question and frisk policies into police practices that are both demonstratively more effective and recognizably more equitable.

APPENDIX A: DEMOGRAPHIC BREAKDOWN FOR TEN HIGHEST STOPS

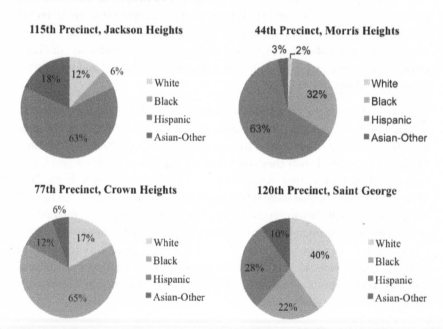

115th Precinct, Jackson Heights

44th Precinct, Morris Heights

77th Precinct, Crown Heights

120th Precinct, Saint George

23rd Precinct, Upper East Side

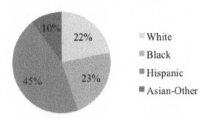

- White 22%
- Black 23%
- Hispanic 45%
- Asian-Other 10%

40th Precinct, Mott Haven / Melrose

2% 2%

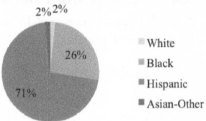

- White 2%
- Black 26%
- Hispanic 71%
- Asian-Other

103rd Precinct, Jamaica

2%

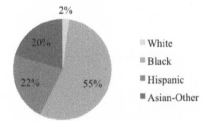

- White 55%
- Black 22%
- Hispanic 20%
- Asian-Other

79th Precinct, Bedford - Stuyvesant

5%

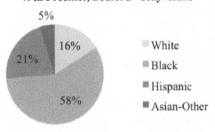

- White 16%
- Black 58%
- Hispanic 21%
- Asian-Other

73rd Precinct, Ocean Hill - Brownsville

3% 1%

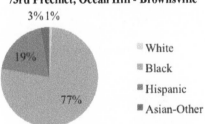

- White
- Black 77%
- Hispanic 19%
- Asian-Other

75th Precinct, East New York

2%

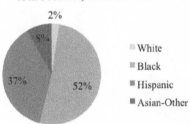

- White 8%
- Black 52%
- Hispanic 37%
- Asian-Other

Data Source: U.S. Census 2010 (http://www.Infoshare.org)

APPENDIX B: DEMOGRAPHIC BREAKDOWN FOR TEN LOWEST STOP PRECINCTS

Note: No Census Data is available for the 22nd precinct, Central Park, because it is largely non-residential.

17th Precinct, Midtown

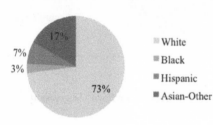

1st Precinct, Tribeca / Wall Street

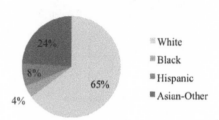

94th Precinct, Greenpoint

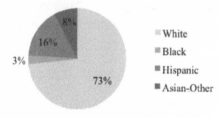

123rd Precinct, Tottenville

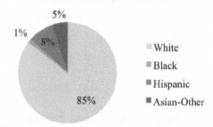

78th Precinct, Park Slope

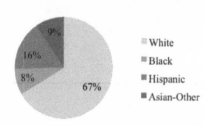

68th Precinct, Bay Ridge

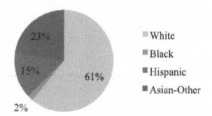

50th Precinct, Riverdale

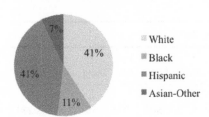

- White
- Black
- Hispanic
- Asian-Other

5th Precinct, Chinatown / Little Italy

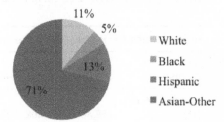

- White
- Black
- Hispanic
- Asian-Other

18th Precinct, Midtown North

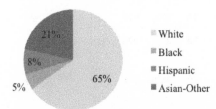

- White
- Black
- Hispanic
- Asian-Other

Data Source: U.S. Census 2010 (http://www.Infoshare.org)

APPENDIX C: INDEX CRIMES FOR HIGHEST AND LOWEST STOP PRECINCTS, 2012

Index Crimes for Highest Stop Precincts, 2012

Precinct	Stops 2003–12	Stops 2012	Hom.	Rape	Rob.	Fel. Ass.	Burg.	Gr. Lar.	G.L. Auto
East New York (75)	258,465	24,408	18	75	847	908	657	988	281
Ocean Hill–Brownsville (73)	196,898	22,148	15	35	578	663	316	489	155
Bedford–Stuyvesant (79)	142,827	15,294	11	18	476	515	325	469	99
Jamaica (103)	139,681	12,986	10	34	439	376	309	494	175
Mott Haven / Melrose (40)	134,060	18,276	12	26	480	392	159	479	78
Upper East Side (23)	126,799	11,095	2	29	270	262	103	320	26
Saint George (120)	124,659	12,368	7	39	290	474	401	492	165
Crown Heights (77)	101,501	9,934	10	20	358	338	309	411	115
Morris Heights (44)	93,335	15,414	8	33	451	668	291	598	151
Jackson Heights (115)	92,978	8,068	5	40	338	329	336	548	171
		Index Crimes Totals	80	274	3,680	4,017	2,549	4,300	1,135

Index Crimes for Lowest Stop Precincts, 2012

Precinct	Stops 2003–12	Stops 2012	Hom.	Rape	Rob.	Fel. Ass.	Burg.	Gr. Lar.	G.L. Auto
Midtown North (18)	25,438	2,978	4	14	123	127	171	1,826	44
Chinatown / Little Italy (5)	25,092	2,782	3	12	121	156	137	549	21
Park Slope (78)	24,220	3,281	1	3	175	86	178	546	53
Bay Ridge (68)	23,553	2,557	1	16	111	109	202	396	113
Riverdale (50)	23,022	1,832	6	10	146	131	178	420	100
Tottenville (123)	22,502	1,940	1	5	29	60	88	182	31
Tribeca / Wall Street (1)	20,956	3,053	1	10	81	110	187	985	42
Greenpoint (94)	20,776	2,092	—	12	134	88	211	417	90
Midtown (17)	13,380	1,331	2	10	47	80	135	724	24
Central Park (22)	7,802	592	—	1	15	7	2	76	—
	Index Crimes Totals		**19**	**93**	**982**	**954**	**1,489**	**6,121**	**518**

Data Source: NYPD Compstat Precinct Crime Statistics, 2012. http://www.nyc.gov/html/nypd/html/crime_prevention/crime_statistics.shtml

[...]

Notes

1. These percentages do not directly derive from adding up arrests and summons because in some cases an arrest and summons were both recorded in the same stop.

2. NYCLU Press Release. http://www.nyclu.org/issues/racial-justice/stop-and-frisk-practices

3. Two percent of UF-250 forms list "furtive movement" as the sole reason for the stop. See also testimony of Dr. Jeffrey Fagan at *Floyd et al. v. City of New York*. Fagan, Jeffery 2010. Expert Report, *Floyd v. City of New York*, 08 Civ. 01034 (SAS). http://www.ccrjustice.org/floyd. Fagan, Jeffery 2012. Second Supplemental Report, *Floyd v. City of New York*, 08 Civ. 01034 (SAS). http://www.ccrjustice.org/floyd.

4. NYS Attorney General Report, 1999, pp.58. (See list of resources for full citation).
5. NYS Attorney General Report, 1999, pp. 53. (See list of resources for full citation).
6. See note that follows Figure 9 for explanation of how "guns recovered" was calculated from the available data.
7. Golub et al., 2007; Harcourt and Ludwig, 2007; Levine and Small, 2008. (See list of references and resources for full citations).
8. Calculated by adding the number of Hispanics and Blacks stopped (399,181+175,302) divided by the number of Whites stopped, 61,805.
9. Long, Colleen. "Police stop more than 1 million people on the street." *Associated Press.* Oct. 8, 2009. http://www.msnbc.msn/com/id/33230464/ns/us_news-crime_and_courts/
10. Rankin, Jim. "Race Matters: Blacks documented by police at high rate." *Toronto Star.* Feb. 6, 2010. http://www.thestar.com/specialsections/raceandcrime/article/761343—race-matters-Blacks-documented-by-police-at-high-rate
11. Ibid.
12. Townsend, M. "Stop and Search 'racial profiling' by police on the increase claims study," *The Guardian.* January 14, 2012.
13. Though crime is not distributed randomly across the City, research has confirmed that areas with similar crime rates but different residential populations are not experiencing the same level of stops and that Blacks and Hispanics who appear in locations where the residents are not predominantly Black and Hispanic are experiencing substantial stop activity, see Gelman, Fagan, and Kiss, 2007, p.6. (See list of references and resources for full citation) and Gardiner, Sean, "NYPD Stops Affect Young Minority Men." *Wall Street Journal,* May 9, 2012. http://online.wsj.com/article/SB10001424052702304070304577394464041545288.html
14. NYPD *New York City Police Department Stop Question & Frisk Activity,* Jan 1–March 31, 2013. http://www.nyclu.org/files/2013_1st_Qtr.pdf
15. Actual wording: "area has high incidence of reported offense of type under investigation".
16. Discriminatory treatment by government agencies on the basis of factors other than race are also covered by the amendment.
17. Visit www.ccrjustice.org for details of the case.
18. Visit www.nyclu.org for details of the case.
19. Visit www.nyclu.org for details of the case.
20. Visit www.ccrjustice.org for details of the case.
21. Visit www.naacpldf.org for details of the case.
22. See Note 52 and UF-250 form.

REFERENCES AND RESOURCES

Center for Constitutional Rights—Report: Racial Disparity in NYPD Stop and Frisks
http://ccrjustice.org/learn-more/reports/report:-racial-disparity-nypd-stop-and-frisks

Center for Constitutional Rights—Summary of *Daniels v. City of New York*
http://ccrjustice.org/ourcases/past-cases/daniels%2C-et-al.-v.-city-new-york

Center for Constitutional Rights—Summary of *Floyd v. City of New York*
http://ccrjustice.org/ourcases/current-cases/floyd,-et-al.-v.-city-new-york,-et-al.

Daniels Stipulation of Settlement December, 2003
http://ccrjustice.org/files/Daniels_StipulationOfSettlement_12_03_0.pdf

Bailey Consent Decree June 21st 2011
    http://www.aclupa.org/downloads/Baileyconsentdecree.pdf

Butler, Paul, "Long Step down the Totalitarian Path: Justice Douglas's Great Dissent in Terry V. Ohio, A." Mississippi Law Journal, Vol. 79, No. 9, 2009 pp. 9-33.

Fagan, Jeffrey, "Shattering Broken Windows: An Analysis of San Francisco's Alternative Crime Policies," Center on Juvenile and Criminal Justice, October, 1999.

Fagan, Jeffrey and Garth Davies, "Street Stops and Broken Windows: Terry, Race, and Disorder in New York City," Fordham Urban Law Journal, Vol. 28, No. 2, 2000 pp. 456-504.

Gelman, Andrew, Jeffrey Fagan, and Alex Kiss, "An Analysis of the New York City Police Department's 'Stop-and-Frisk' Policy in the Context of Claims of Racial Bias," Journal of the American Statistical Association, Vol. 102, No. 479, 2007, pp. 813-823. As of February 24, 2010: http://www.stat.columbia.edu/~gelman/research/unpublished/frisk7.pdf

Golub, Andrew. Bruce D. Johnson, and Eloise Dunlap, "The Race/Ethnicity Disparity in Misdemeanor Marijuana Arrests in New York City." Criminology and Public Policy Vol. 6, 2007, pp. 131-164.

Golub, Andrew. Bruce D. Johnson, and Eloise Dunlap. "Smoking marijuana in public: The spatial and policy shift in New York City arrests, 1992-2003." Harm Reduction Journal, Vo. 3, 2006, pp. 22-45.

Harcourt, Bernard E. and Jens Ludwig. "Reefer Madness: Broken Windows Policing and Misdemeanor Marijuana Arrests in New York City, 1989-2000." Criminology and Public Policy Vol. 6, 2007, pp. 165-182.

Howell, Babe. "From Page to Practice and Back Again: Broken Windows Policing and the Real Costs to Law-abiding New Yorkers of Color, N.Y.U. Rev. L. & Soc. Change , Vol. 34, 2010, pp. 439-461.

Levine, Harry G. and Deborah Peterson Small. "Marijuana Arrest Crusade: Racial Bias and Police Policy in New York City, 1997-2007." NYCLU, 2008. As of February 28th, 2009: http://www.nyclu.org/files/MARIJUANA-ARREST-CRUSADE_Final.pdf

La Vigne, Nancy, Pamela Lachman, Andrea Matthews, and S. Rebecca Neusteter (eds). *Key Issues in the Police Use of Pedestrian Stops and Searches: Discussion Papers from an Urban Institute Roundtable.* Urban Institute, 2012. http://www.urban.org/UploadedPDF/412647-Key-Issues-in-the-Police-Use-of-Pedestrian-Stops-and-Searches.pdf

New York City Civilian Complaint Review Board (CCRB), Status Reports: 2003-2007 (http://www.nyc.gov/html/ccrb/pdf/ccrbann2007_A.pdf); 2006-2010 (http://www.nyc.gov/html/ccrb/pdf/ccrbann2010.pdf); 2011 (http://www.nyc.gov/html/ccrb/pdf/ccrbann2011.pdf).

New York Civil Liberties Union (NYCLU)—Stop and Frisk Practices
    http://www.nyclu.org/issues/racial-justice/stop-and-frisk-practices

NYPD Stop, Question, and Frisk Report Database
    http://www.nyc.gov/html/nypd/html/analysis_and_planning/stop_question_and_frisk_report.shtml

NYS Attorney General's Report: *The New York City Police Department's Stop and Frisk Practices: A Report to the People of the State of New York from the Office of the Attorney General*, New York: Civil Rights Bureau, December 1, 1999.
    http://www.ag.ny.gov/bureaus/civil_rights/pdfs/stp_frsk.pdf

RAND Report: Ridgeway, Greg. *Analysis of Racial Disparities in the New York Police Department's Stop, Question, and Frisk Practices*, Santa Monica, CA: RAND Corporation, 2007. http://www.rand.org/pubs/technical_reports/2007/RAND_TR534.pdf

Stoudt, Brett G., Michelle Fine, and Madeline Fox. "Growing Up Policed." UC Davis Law Review, Vol. 34, 2001, pp. 1005.

Zamani, Nahal. *Stop and Frisk: The Human Impact.* CCR, July 2012. http://stopandfrisk.org/the-human-impact-report/

Cases Cited

Adams v. Williams, 407 U.S. 143 (1972).

Alabama v. White, 496 U.S. 325 (1990).

Bailey v. City of Philadelphia, C.A 10-5952 (2011).

Daniels v. City of New York, 99 Civ. 1695 (SDNY) (2003).

Davis et al v. City of New York 10 Civ. 0699 (SDNY) (pending).

Floyd v. City of New York, 08 Civ. 01034 (SDNY) (pending decision).

Hiibel v. Sixth Judicial District Court of Nevada, 542 U.S. 177 (2004).

Illinois v. Wardlow, 528 U.S. 119 (2000).

In the Matter of New York Civil Liberties Union v. New York City Police Department, 866 N.Y.S.2d 93 (2008).

Ligon et al v. City of New York 12 Civ. 2274 (SAS)(HBP) (2013).

Minnesota v. Dickerson, 508 U.S. 366 (1993).

Terry v. Ohio, 392 U.S. 1 (1968).

People v. DeBour, 40 N.Y. 2d 210 (1976).

Related Resources

Consortium for Police Leadership in Equity (CPLE)—is a research consortium that promotes police transparency and accountability by facilitating innovative research collaborations between law enforcement agencies and world-class social scientists. The Consortium seeks to improve issues of equity—particularly racial and gender equity—in policing both within law enforcement agencies and between agencies and the communities they serve. To learn more about CPLE visit www.policingequity.org.

Marijuana Arrest Research Project—is a research initiative studying race, public policy, and the growing number of arrests for marijuana possession and other victimless crimes in large U.S. cities, especially New York City. Their publications rely on public data, and on the first-hand knowledge of current and former police officers, public defenders, judges, assistant district attorneys, and others who work daily in the criminal justice system. For more information visit their website at: http://marijuana-arrests.com/index.html

Public Science Project (PSP)—is based at the CUNY Graduate Center and collaborates with academics, community organizations, schools, prisons, and public institutions to design, conduct, and support research and practice aimed at interrupting injustice. They have or are currently conducting projects related to stop and frisk including Polling for Justice, the Morris Justice Project and the Researcher for Fair Policing Project. For more information visit their website at: www.publicscienceproject.org.

Communities United for Police Reform (CPR)—is a campaign to end discriminatory policing practices in New York, bringing together a movement of community members, lawyers, researchers and activists to work for change. The partners in this campaign come from all 5 boroughs, from all walks of life and represent many of those unfairly targeted the most by the NYPD. This campaign is fighting for reforms that will promote community safety while ensuring that the NYPD protects and serves all New Yorkers. For general information visit their website at: www.changethenypd.org.

*Delores Jones-Brown is a professor in the department of law, police science, and criminal justice administration at John Jay College of Criminal Justice, City University of New York. She is the founding director of the John Jay College Center on Race, Crime and Justice, where she currently serves as faculty research fellow.

Brett G. Stoudt is an assistant professor with a joint appointment in the psychology department and the gender studies program at John Jay College of Criminal Justice.

Brian Johnston and **Kevin Moran** are doctoral candidates at the City University of New York Graduate Center.

Jones-Brown, Delores, Brett G. Stoudt, Brian Johnston, and Kevin Moran. 2013. "Stop, Question and Frisk Policing Practices in New York City: A Primer (Revised)." Report. New York: Center on Race, Crime and Justice at John Jay College, City University of New York. June 2013: 1–46. This text has been shortened. Passages left out are indicated by [...].

Growing Up Policed in the Age of Aggressive Policing Policies

by Brett G. Stoudt, Michelle Fine, and Madeline Fox*

I. Introduction

Spray-painted atop an old tenement building in the East Village of Manhattan is a large fossilized graffiti image of a tyrannosaurus rex that reads: "NYC EATS ITS YOUNG." With its ribs exposed and mouth open, this image represents symbolically what many young people in the neighborhood already know intimately and have experienced: New York City (NYC) is not an easy place to grow up. Their social safety nets are being dismantled and the public institutions they rely on every day often fail them. In NYC, public school budgets are being slashed each year even though the high school dropout/push-out rates are far too high. Neighborhoods are fast becoming gentrified as the ever-rising cost of rent makes it increasingly difficult for the working class and poor to raise families anywhere in the city. A truly comprehensive health system in the United States is still only a future hope, while countless N YC young people are without adequate healthcare; the logic of the welfare state is forever being attacked. And then there is the mounting police presence. It is this public institution—the New York City Police Department (NYPD), its aggressive policing policies, and how these policies are related to youth experience—that we will take up here. In this article we will explore what it is like to grow up policed in NYC.

Since 1994, aggressive policing policies have been put into place by the NYPD and former NYC Mayor Rudolph W. Giuliani (and continued by Mayor Michael R. Bloomberg). The driving principles of these policies come from a theory of criminal behavior and crime reduction known as the " broken windows" theory. The theory argues that close police surveillance and well-ordered maintenance of high-crime urban environments reduce criminal activity. Having zero tolerance for low-level crime (e.g., panhandling, public urination, public drunkenness, loitering) and quickly mending visual representations of criminal activity such as broken windows or graffiti are thought to prevent further defacement and an escalation to more serious crimes. The theory holds that a well-maintained environment signals law-abiding order and a sense of responsibility to the neighborhood. Therefore, people who formerly retreated from community life out of fear will now feel safe to actively participate and to promoting a secure and positive environment.[1]

The resulting NYPD policing tactics that have derived from this theory have become known as order-maintenance policing (OMP) or zero tolerance policing (ZTP).[2] The NYPD's expression of broken windows requires heavy police surveillance of high-crime communities. Neighborhood "needs" are determined through a problem-focused management approach in conjunction with a real-time mapping database known as CompStat. Frequent street stops are targeted at people suspected of committing crimes, with particular focus on uncovering weapons.[3] This type of policing leads to large numbers of arrests and summons for low-level crimes, rendering vast amounts of people vulnerable to the criminal justice system. Misdemeanor rates have skyrocketed, particularly for marijuana possession.[4]

NYPD's version of broken windows rests upon a policing strategy known as "stop, question and frisk" ("stop and frisk"). Police authority to stop, question, and frisk citizens was held to be constitutional in 1968 in *Terry v. Ohio*.[5] The Fourth Amendment protects citizens against "unreasonable searches and seizures."[6] Before *Terry*, police officers needed probable cause to detain, question, and frisk citizens.[7] As a result of the *Terry* decision however, police officers— provided they can point to "specific and articulable facts" and not " inarticulate hunches"[8] may temporarily detain a citizen to ask questions. They may do so without a warrant or "probable cause" if they have "reasonable suspicion"[9] that a crime has been, or is about to be, committed. If during the stop the police officer reasonably believes he or others are in immediate danger, the officer may pat-down, or frisk, the person's outer clothing and conduct a search if the frisk reveals what the officer suspects to be a weapon.[10]

The *Terry* decision sought to protect police officers and enhance their ability to do an effective job. "*Terry* stops" were initially intended as exceptions to the rule and to be used only when obtaining a warrant was impractical or put the officer or others in danger.[11] Whether it is constitutionally justified remains debatable.[12] Since this landmark decision, a series of cases have further defined just what "reasonable suspicion" means, and the original ruling looks conservative in comparison.[13]

The power of police officers to stop citizens today far exceeds that of 1968. "Reasonable" justifications for a stop now include nearly all minimal indications of criminal activity: living in high-crime areas, the time of day, ambiguously evasive or suspicious behavior, appearing like a criminal, moving in and out of shadows, wearing heavy clothes in summer weather, fitting the description of a reported suspect, and exchanges with people in an area known for drug activity.[14] Nearly any behavior or circumstance can be articulated as reasonable suspicion if it can be attached to the potential for criminal activity. What this ultimately means is that people of color living in poor, generally high-crime urban neighborhoods who are behaving in a manner that can be perceived as "furtive" or "evasive" are perpetual police suspects.[15] Indeed, the legacy of *Terry* for many is that it laid the groundwork for the increasing legalization of racially biased policing.[16]

From the NYPD's standpoint, aggressive policing policies were the impetus behind the significant decline in crime, and provide a number of other valuable advantages such as general deterrence of criminal activity and basic intelligence-gathering at the street level.[17] While it must be acknowledged that zero-tolerance policing has indirectly, to a small degree, contributed to lowering crime, its direct contributions alone have been found to be exceedingly minor compared to other factors such as structural disadvantage.[18] Whatever negligible impact frequent police stops may have on reducing crime, the collateral damages may be too great and even criminogenic, exacerbating the poor police-community relations of some neighborhoods, increasing mistrust of police, heightening the perception of racial discrimination by police, diminishing the viability of community safety, and making effective crime-fighting unsustainable.[19]

[. . .]

II. Incidence and Frequency of NYPD Stops Involving Youth

Stop and frisk has continued to rise since zero tolerance policing policies were implemented in NYC.[21] Although crime in New York City has remained relatively low and stable since 2003, stops have more than tripled since then and nearly all those stopped are neither arrested nor given a summons.[22] Thus, these stops are increasingly less effective and their purpose has become even more suspect.[23] In this section we will examine—from the perspective of the police and then from the perspective of NYC youth, the general, radicalized, and spatialized occurance and frequencies of police stops on young people during a two-year period.

A. From the Perspective of the NYPD

When it comes to police stops, it is important to recognize that youth in NYC are disproportionally targeted as compared to other age groups. We examined the NYPD Stop, Question and Frisk dataset for the years 2008 and 2009. These data were derived from the UF-250 report worksheets that police officers fill out after a large portion of the stops.[24] In order to examine the experiences of NYC youth specifically, this dataset was further broken down for only those stops involving a person between the ages of fourteen and twenty-one. During this two-year period, 1,121,470 New Yorkers were stopped. Of these stops, 37% (or 416,350) were targeted at youth between the ages of fourteen and twenty-one. Indeed, more than a third of the stops recorded occurred during this seven-year age range. Yet, this age range only represents approximately a tenth of the city's population.[25] Though seldom made explicit, stop and frisk is a policy heavily focused on the younger citizens in NYC.

[...]

III. RACIAL DISPARITIES IN NYPD
CONTACT WITH YOUNG PEOPLE

In *Terry*, the Supreme Court Justices were acutely aware of how their decision might affect race relations;[61] records suggest that they were careful not to make this court case about race. The NAACP Legal Defense and Education Fund lawyers were denied time during oral arguments to present their evidence that black people were disproportionately affected by stop and frisk laws.[62] The Court's decision was written, with but a few exceptions, to be largely race-neutral.[63] Although the Court held that the officer making the stop "must be able to point to specific and articulable facts .... [not] inarticulate hunches,"[64] many have argued that elements of racial bias or profiling, at least in part, often enter into the decision making of police and that ambiguous—though articulated—reasons for a stop leave room for articulated hunches that are to some greater or lesser degree—and to some acknowledged or unacknowledged extent—due to racial stereotypes.[65] Generally, evidence has consistently emerged that racial disparities exist—in the initiation of police stops, what occurs during the stops, and in the outcome of stops—between black and Hispanic people as compared to white people.[66] However, the extent of these differences, and the circumstances in which they occur, tend to differ depending on the analytical approach and the benchmarks used.[67]

According to the NYPD's official policy on profiling, officers may not use race (or other demographic characteristics such as gender and sexual identity) as a factor in stopping someone *unless* the suspect matches a specific description in which race (or gender, sexual identity, etc.) is noted.[68] Much of the discussion of racial profiling is concerned with police officers' intent to be racially biased. Yet, it is important to recognize that, as Ridgeway and MacDonald make clear, "[e]ven if police decisions[about] whom to stop, search, and detain are not intentionally biased, they may be structurally discriminatory. Patrolling differently in high-crime neighborhoods may place a disparate burden on minorities but may not reflect actual bias in police decision making."[69]

Whether stops are racially (or sexually) motivated, we cannot know definitively from this data. We cannot tell to what extent racial or sexual profiling is occurring intentionally. Instead, we use the term "differential stops" to focus on what our data can actually reveal.[70] We assume that some police officers are biased, but that most are trying to do their jobs with honor and competence. A serious public policy concern emerges, however, once we examine the systematic and systemic burden that disproportionally lands on some marginalized youth, with nearly all of them innocent. Similar to the previous section, we will start from the perspective of the NYPD and then move to the youth perspective.

A. From the Perspective of the NYPD
[...]

1. Reasons for Stops

Earlier in this article we examined two concerning reasons police officers initiated a stop on youth: the ambiguous furtive movements and contextual factors that have little to do with characteristics of the young person.[73] Both were common reasons used by police officers in combination with other reasons; however, we also focused specifically on when these were the *only* reasons given for initiating a stop. We explored these reasons further by combining them into a single category; a slightly more inclusive look at what Harris called " location *and* evasion" cases.[74] Sixteen percent of the time, young people were stopped for "furtive movements only," "contextual factors only," or " furtive and context only." This analysis uncovered disproportional racial differences.[75] White and Asian/Pacific Islander youth were less likely to be stopped for the combination of these two vague reasons as compared to black and Latino youth.

2. Stops Inside Housing

Disproportional racial differences were uncovered when we examined where stops occurred. The majority of the youth stops occurred outside in public (324,195 or 78%); however, 22% (92,155) of the stops occurred inside. Closer examination of these inside stops revealed that black and Hispanic youth were far more likely to be stopped inside *housing* as compared to those who were white and Asian.[76] These data suggest that black and Latino youth are less likely than white and Asian youth to be able to enjoy the comfort and privacy of their homes free from police interference. Operation Clean Halls is a New York City program that allows police to "vertically patrol " public housing and likely contributes heavily to these results.[77]

Table 5. Police Stop and Post-Stop Activities by Demographics. % (f)

	Context and/or furtive	Frisked	Physical Force	Stopped inside housing	No arrests or summons	No weapons or contraband
Gender						
Female	21.8% (6,074)	31.8%* (8,874)	15.6% (4,340)	43.6% (4,420)	86.2% (24,033)	98.1% (27,368)
Male	15.7% (59,871)	63.5% (242,157)	27.1% (103,261)	41.4% (33,398)	89.8% (342,716)	97.4% (371,739)
Race/Ethnicity						
Black or African American	17.8% (38,864)	62.4% (136,248)	27.0% (59,016)	48.6% (28,366)	90.0% (196,495)	97.7% (213,232)
Latino/a or Hispanic	15.7% (20,207)	64.5% (83,146)	28.1% (36,221)	32.0% (8,412)	88.8% (114,577)	97.2% (125,400)
Other	16.0% (2,480)	57.6% (8,953)	25.2% (3,920)	33.4% (888)	91.1% (14,152)	98.2% (15,261)
Asian or Pacific Islander	10.1% (1,339)	55.9% (7,445)	20.5% (2,735)	16.3% (236)	89.2% (11,871)	97.3% (12,951)
White	10.3% (4,126)	48.0% (19,333)	18.9% (7,607)	12.7% (439)	89.4% (35,979)	97.1% (39,054)

*These numbers represent the percentage of those youth within each demographic category (row) and their recorded experiences with police (columns). For example, of those females stopped by police between 2008 and 2009, 31.8% were frisked as compared to 63.5% of the males who were stopped.

3. Physical Contact

An examination of stops that escalate to physical contact by police revealed proportional differences between race *and* gender. Males who were stopped were more likely to experience physical force by police and more than twice as likely to be frisked by police as compared to females. White and Asian youth were less likely to be frisked and to experience physical force as compared to black and Hispanic youth.

4. Legal Outcomes

Despite disproportional racial and sometimes gender differences, no meaningful differences were uncovered in analyzing legal outcomes. Youth stopped by police were equally likely to be innocent regardless of their race or gender. Youth stopped by police were equally unlikely to be found in possession a weapon and/or contraband, regardless of their race or gender.

The race of suspects in this dataset was determined by the police officer filling out the form. We cannot tell from this data the suspect's own racial identity (or gendered identity for that matter), nor do we have indication of youth who identify as multiracial. We also do not have information about sexual identity. For these important distinctions, we explore our PFJ data and, with it, a look at proportional disparity from multiple demographic standpoints as well as multiple categories of police contact.

B. From the Perspective of NYC Youth

1. Race and Gender

The aggregated and disaggregated experiences with police from the PFJ data were examined by gender and race.[78] Though the PFJ questions were designed to capture youth-police engagement more broadly than police stops only, our results showed comparable, but not always identical, and sometimes additional, results to the NYPD data. Like the NYPD data, the PFJ data suggested that males were proportionally more likely to have negative (*and also* positive) contact with police. Males were more likely to report negative verbal contact and three times more likely to report physical contact with police in the last six months than females. Similarly, Asian and white young people were proportionally less likely to have negative police experiences as compared to Latino, African American, and multi-racial youth.

Unlike the NYPD data, male respondents who took the PFJ survey were nearly twice as likely to report legal issues. It is also important to note from the PFJ data that young people who identified as multi-racial (not a category in the NYPD data) had the most negative contact with police over the disaggregated categories (they also had the most positive contact). Additionally, unlike the NYPD data, Asian youth rather than white youth tended to have the lowest amount of negative (or positive) contact with police. Finally, while the NYPD data for those who were identified as Hispanic tended to be similar to and sometimes proportionally higher than black youth, in the PFJ data those who identified themselves as Hispanic tended to appear proportionally not too different from white youth. The complexity of racial identity and a police officer's perception of race (e.g., light-skin Hispanic versus dark-skin Hispanic) make these distinctions important to consider.

Table 6. Young people's experiences with police by demographics. % (*f*)

	Negative Legal Police Experience	Negative Verbal Police Experience	Negative Sexual Police Experience	Negative Physical Police Experience	Negative Police Contact	Positive Police Experience
Gender						
Female	16.8%* (107)	33.0% (210)	11.3% (72)	8.6% (55)	41.9% (267)	29.7% (189)
Male	32.2% (113)	52.4% (178)	12.9% (44)	28.5% (97)	58.1% (370)	43.5% (148)
Race/Ethnicity						
Asian, South Asian, Pacific Islander	11.7% (19)	21.5% (35)	7.4% (12)	7.4% (12)	26.4% (43)	26.4% (43)
White	21.0% (17)	37.0% (30)	14.8% (12)	11.1% (9)	43.2% (35)	29.6% (24)
Latino/a or Hispanic	24.2% (75)	38.7% (120)	9.0% (28)	16.1% (50)	47.4% (147)	34.8% (108)
Black, African American, African Caribbean	24.3% (78)	46.7% (150)	14.3% (46)	17.8% (57)	55.1% (177)	34.3% (110)
Multi-Racial	29.5% (31)	55.2% (58)	17.1% (18)	24.8% (105)	62.9% (66)	47.6% (50)
Sexual Orientation						
Straight	21.3% (189)	38.9% (345)	10.2% (90)	15.1% (134)	46.5% (412)	35.1% (311)
LGBQ	34.3% (37)	53.7% (58)	27.8% (30)	24.1% (26)	61.1% (66)	28.7% (31)

*These numbers represent the percentage of those youth within each demographic category (row) and their police experiences (column). For example, of those females in the PFJ sample, 16.8% reported having a negative legal experience with police in the last six months as compared to 32.2% of the males in the sample.

2. Sexual Orientation

The aggregated and disaggregated experiences with police from the PFJ data were also examined by self-defined sexual orientation.[79] This was a category not included in the NYPD data. Of great surprise and concern are the differences that emerged between those youth who identified as lesbian, gay, bisexual, or questioning (LGBQ) compared to straight youth. The LGBQ youth who took our survey were much more likely to have negative experiences with police (and slightly less likely to report positive experiences). LGBQ youth were proportionally more likely to have negative legal contact, verbal contact, physical contact, and, most concerning, more than twice as likely to report negative sexual contact with police in the last six months. These results led us to conduct a series of data-driven focus groups to learn more about their experiences.

In these focus groups, young people who identified as lesbian, gay, bisexual, queer, questioning, or transgendered were asked to interpret, for and with us, the PFJ data. As the participants poured over findings about negative interactions between youth and police, they discussed their anger in response to experiences like getting ticketed on the subway for putting their feet on a seat, sitting in a playground after dark, or getting harassed for wearing the wrong clothes ("gay wear") in the wrong neighborhood. Some young people described feeling disrespected by police. Others described police as a normalized part of their every day. A focus group participant explained that they might not speak up about their experiences due to anticipated heterosexism: "Let's say I'm walking out on the street with my girlfriend and a cop grabs me inappropriately, how would that sound?... Like how would that sound if I told somebody?... It's gonna stop right there. You were walking down the street with your *girlfriend?*" The participants discussed their critique of these realities, their desire for safer spaces, and greater acceptance from friends, families, teachers, and communities.[80]

IV. THE SOCIAL PSYCHOLOGY OF GROWING UP POLICED

In *Terry*, the Supreme Court rejected the perspective that being stopped and detained against a person's will was a generally inconsequential experience. Instead, the Court was very clear that "[i]t is a serious intrusion upon the sanctity of the person, which may inflict great indignity and arouse strong resentment, and it is not to be undertaken lightly."[81] The Court acknowledged the possibility of psychological impact, explaining that "[e]ven a limited search of the outer clothing for weapons constitutes a severe, though brief, intrusion upon cherished personal security, and it must surely be an annoying, frightening, and perhaps humiliating experience."[82] Strong police-community relationships are fundamental to safe, democratic, participatory communities and to effective crime-fighting. These moments of severe intrusion can be traumatic and have the potential to harm community relationships with police, particularly among marginalized communities and communities of color.

The importance of this issue has led to a great deal of research on people's attitudes towards police, their willingness to support police, and their overall sense of legitimacy towards police.[83] These are complex relationships that are not simply marked by blanket hatred or blind endorsement. There are multiple factors that contribute to attitudes towards police, including cumulative experiences, context, socioeconomic status, and, of course, race.[84] Growing up policed is a developmental issue that threatens to fray the threads of our fragile democracy inherited by youth who may feel less, not more, safe with heavy police presence on the streets, in the subways, in their public housing, and in their schools. It is indeed vital to examine the psychological impact of aggressive surveillance on young people in NYC.

This section will explore the factors influencing the social psychology of heavily policed youth including race, sexual identity, and the quality of direct as well as indirect contact with police. We address these factors in two ways. Using the questions from the PFJ survey asking about interaction with police, four categories were created: young people who have had no contact with police in the last six months; young people with only positive contact; young people with both positive and negative contact; and finally, young people who only had negative contact with police in the last six months. These categories were then compared to four indicators asking about youth attitudes and emotions towards police and the criminal justice system. In addition, Brunson has argued for the importance of examining the individualized experiences and specific narratives of youth-police relationships as opposed to most studies that tend to be focused on the aggregated numbers alone.[85] Therefore, we thematically analyzed young people's responses to an open-ended question in our survey, "[t]ell us about a time when you witnessed or experienced an injustice/unfairness that upset you."

A. Racial and Sexual Identity

We used the PFJ data to begin exploring four indicators by asking about youth attitudes and emotions towards police and the criminal justice system. The majority of the young people who took the PFJ survey reported never feeling stressed or worried about the police or the criminal justice system, only a fifth reported feeling comfortable turning to police when having a problem or hard time, and about half agreed that "the police in NYC protect people like me." A concerning trend occurred when considering race.

One particularly influential factor commonly reported in the literature is racial identity. People of color, especially those who identify as black and Latino, tend to perceive police more unfavorably as compared to those who identify as white.[86] The data from PFJ support these general findings. Indeed, white and Asian youth (61% and 63%, respectively) were more likely to agree that "police in NYC protect young people like me" as compared to Latino (52%), black (41%), and multi-racial youth (40%). This might be expected since the probability of police contact—as previously revealed by the NYPD data—and the subsequent risk of entering the criminal justice system tends to be far greater for black and Latino youth as compared to white and Asian youth. Yet surprisingly, black (74%) and Latino youth (75%) were more likely to report they are never stressed about the criminal justice system as compared to white youth (58%) and to a smaller degree, Asian youth (68%).[87]

Similarly, our focus groups also revealed a sense of normalization. For example, one young person explained police stops as just part of living in NYC: "It's like an everyday life in the city. It's like cops are mean, we just have to deal with because it's really like, there's really not much I can do with arguing with a cop." This sense of powerlessness can blunt young people's sense of outrage (though not their sense that something is wrong): "So it gets to the point where . . . it's not as shocking to us anymore. It just goes away after a while, you know, you walk it off, you watch TV, take a shower, and then it's like, okay, just another day in New York City." We both speculate and worry about the potential normalization and desensitization for marginalized youth, youth of color, or youth living in those communities that share the greatest burdens of aggressive policing.

Of particular noteworthiness, and a valuable contribution to this literature, are the attitudes in our sample expressed by those youth who identified as LGBQ. More than half of the sample of LGBQ youth reported feeling stressed or worried to some extent by police, as compared to straight youth. Not surprisingly, straight youth were nearly twice as likely to express feeling comfortable to some degree turning to police (21%), as well as feeling the police "protect young people like me" (53%), compared to youth who identified as LGBQ (12% and 26%, respectively). These findings, in combination with the results reported earlier by LGBQ youth, reveal a seldom researched but highly concerning trend for this marginalized community of NYC young people. Our data suggest that greater attention is needed on this issue.

B. Quality of Direct Contact

While race and other demographic factors contribute to attitudes towards police, researchers have also produced evidence that the quality of recent and direct contact with police contributes heavily to attitudes.[88] Certainly direct and negatively perceived police contact has an impact on unfavorable attitudes;[89] however,

Table 7. Attitudes towards police by quality of contact with police in the last six months. % (f)

	No Contact with Police	Positive Contact with Police Only	Both Positive and Negative Contact with Police	Negative Contact with Police Only
Percent of respondents who reported they were never stressed or worried about police.*	81.8% (162)	84.8% (39)	62.5% (85)	56.6% (60)
Percent of respondents who reported they were never stressed or worried about the criminal justice system.*	84.8% (168)	76.1% (35)	68.4% (93)	56.6% (60)
Percent of respondents who agreed that "in general, the police in NYC protect young people like me."	61.3% (257)	68.2% (58)	40.3% (102)	**31.4% (69)
Percent of respondents who felt comfortable, to some degree, turning to police (or school safety agents) when having a problem or hard time.	18.1% (76)	27.9% (24)	25.4% (63)	16.2% (35)

*These questions were only asked in the long-form edition of the PFJ survey and therefore have smaller sample sizes.

**These numbers represent the percentage of youth within each police contact category (column) and their attitudes towards police (row). For example, of those young people who experienced only negative contact with police in the last six months, 31.4% agreed that "in general, the police in NYC protect young people like me."

researchers also found data that direct and positively perceived experiences can have favorable effects on attitudes.[90] Furthermore, there may be a difference between direct contact—not only through personal experience but also observing police activity in the neighborhood or hearing about police activity from friends and family—and no contact at all where attitudes are more likely to be derived from abstract social representations (e.g., media).[91]

The PFJ survey helped us examine how attitudes towards police might be connected with the type of contact young people have had with police in two ways. Table 7 illustrates how the quality of recent contact with police may be associated with anxiety towards the police and the criminal justice system. The majority of the sample of young people who took the PFJ survey reported never feeling stressed or worried about the police. However, those who had no contact with police in the last six months were more likely to share this sentiment (82%) than their peers who had negative but also positive contact with police (63%), and even more so than those young people who reported only negative contact with police in the previous six months (57%). The youth least likely to report never feeling stressed about police were those who had only positive contact with police in the last six months. A similar pattern was revealed when youth were asked about the criminal justice system. Most reported not feeling stressed or worried about the criminal justice system, but this sentiment was more likely to be felt by those who had no contact with police (85%) in the last six months, and increasingly less likely depending on their positive or negative contact with police.

The PFJ survey also asked youth about the extent to which they believed the NYPD protected young people and whether they felt comfortable turning to police when having a problem or hard time.[92] Youth who reported no contact with police in the last six months were more likely to agree that "police in NYC protect young people like me" (61%) as compared to youth who reported both positive and negative contact with police (40%) and youth who reported only negative contact with police in the last six months (31%). Young people who had *only* positive contact with police were the most likely to perceive the NYPD as protecting young people like them (68%). An interesting pattern was revealed for the degree to which young people felt comfortable turning to police (or school safety agents) when having a problem or hard time. Most young people reported not feeling comfortable turning to police. However, those who had positive contact with police in the last six months were more likely to feel comfortable as compared to those young people who had no contact or only negative contact with police.

In the PFJ survey, we asked young people to "[t]ell us about a time when you witnessed or experienced an injustice/unfairness that upset you." There were a variety of open-ended responses (778 responses in total). Some young people expressed frustration that clerks and security guards assumed them to be criminals because of their race or religion or age. For example, an eighteen-year-old African American male respondent wrote, "A doorman in a convenience store accused me of stealing a bag of chips, because of my race, clothes, and due to the fact that I had a book bag, when in fact I took nothing." Some wrote of being followed around stores, such as this sixteen-year-old Latina, who said, " When I walked into a Verizon store the security guard followed me around." Still others, like this seventeen-year-old American female of Southeast Asian descent, witnessed a pattern of heavy surveillance at the airport: "My mother was searched thoroughly in the airport because she wore a hijab." And of course, young people expressed feeling criminalized by the NYPD, such as this young female immigrant: "cops all over the Bronx [are] *always* looking at groups of youth as if we're about to make trouble." What are the developmental and societal implications of young people growing up " fitting the description" of a criminal; to be so interchangeable that they are suspected of committing a crime simply because of how they look, where they live, or where they shop?

A little more than a third (35.1% or 273) of those who responded to our question about witnessing or experiencing injustice specifically provided narratives referencing police. It was the largest single thematic category. Reading these narratives helped us to catch a firsthand glimpse of the psychosocial experiences connected with growing up aggressively policed, particularly from *but not only* from youth of color. For example, a young white male described feeling both harassed and embarrassed by his contact with police: "A group of friends and I were stopped by a police officer who searched us all and called our parents to verify that we were not running away (even though we didn't have luggage and we were on our way to bowling). It was needless, unprovoked harassment and embarrassing."

Police contact can seem unexpected and confusing for young people who did nothing to warrant a stop except fitting a description. A seventeen-year-old black female living in the Bedford Park neighborhood of the Bronx wrote of being stopped by police with her two friends while walking to get something to eat: "A police car pulled up and they demanded ID. But we were so confused. They then told us that we had fit the description of three girls that got into a fight. We were standing in the cold for about a half an hour." The confusion, the fear, the embarrassment, and, of course, the anger felt from what many young people commonly perceive as police harassment are not held individually for long. They quickly become shared experiences that vibrate across the young person's network of friends and family, and even strangers and acquaintances.

C. Vicarious Experiences

Some of the stories young people told, like those in the last section, referenced their own personal experiences (these emerged in 28.2% or 77 of the open-ended responses referencing injustice with police). However, while direct experiences are certainly an important factor, research has shown that indirect vicarious experiences can have equal or even greater impact on attitudes towards police.[93] Other young people in our sample provided narratives of police injustice towards their friends (24.2% or 66 responses) and families (9.5% or 26 responses). Take as an example this black female living in the Bay Ridge area of Brooklyn. She described her frustration, not over her own experience with police, but with her brother's: "My lil ' brother was harassed and searched by the police for wearing the color red because they thought he was in a gang. And he's so sweet and innocent. . . . I was highly pissed off when I had found out he had been harassed."

Slightly more than a third (33.7% or 92 responses) of the young people in our sample specifically provided narratives of police injustice not towards themselves, friends or family, but towards others—strangers—in their neighborhood, on the street, inside their buildings, at school, etc. For example, a sixteen-year-old African American female living in Central Harlem explained that she was simply tired of "watching kids my age get stopped on the streets by cops suspecting them to commit a crime." Or this nineteen-year-old female living in Queens: "I've seen kids of color stopped from leaving the school building by security guards to check their IDs (when they were done for the day and were permitted to leave the school)." Her self- awareness allowed her to reflect upon who of her peers were more likely to be suspected of wrongdoing: "Whereas I, as a white student, was questioned only once when leaving the building and have walked out of the building (past security guards) on several occasions when I should have been in class."

Attitudes towards police are not only informed by one's own experience, stories told by friends and family, and witnessing activity in the neighborhood; attitudes are also informed by the media.[94] Many youth responded to the question about witnessing and experiencing injustice by simply stating, "Sean Bell." Sean Bell was shot in 2006 on the evening of his bachelor party by a group of undercover police officers firing fifty times. During the time of our PFJ study, three of the five officers brought up on charges were acquitted. This high-profile story affected youth attitudes even if they never experienced or witnessed injustice firsthand. For example, this sixteen-year-old black female stated, "I never experienced injustice, but the Sean Bell case affected me."

This thematic analysis demonstrates the multiple sources from which young people can feel injustice and, in this case, generate attitudes about police. It reinforces the very public impact of frequent police stops that occur largely out in the open and in ways that can echo across communities, particularly poor communities of color. These stops are individually felt, yes, but they also are felt across social and media networks—from uncles at the dinner table, friends at recess, the local news, or simply walking home from school and witnessing yet one more person being frisked by police. Our fear is that, in some communities, youth are not only growing up policed, but also growing up as relatively helpless witnesses to police harassment. In contrast to the familiar "see something, say something," these young people are learning that when the police are involved, trying to help friends, family, or strangers is a dangerous business and they risk arrest themselves. However, not all stops are police initiated. What about when young people need the police?

D. Seeking Police Help

Young people's relationships to police are complicated. While their contact with police is often unsolicited, there are times when young people want and need help from the police.[95] However, the narratives we collected suggest that these points of contact can be unsatisfying. Take, for example, this nineteen-year-old Latino who lives in the Bronx: "I got robbed last year in front of a school. After thirty minutes, I called the cops and I told them, but all they did was take me in and ask me questions. They did nothing else to help me. I felt it wasn't fair." A sixteen-year-old Asian female who lives in Queens found the police to be unresponsive: "Our car was stolen and we called the police and the police ended up coming after two hours when police should come in one minute, as soon as the call was made, but that they ended up coming late and we never found our car."

In times of need, some felt the police were racially biased and assumed the young person's guilt. A sixteen-year-old Asian male who lived in Queens offered this example from when he and his mother were in a car accident: "The other car was at fault to anyone on the street. We were the ones hit by the other car. The police arrived about five minutes later and went straight to the other car. The officer talked with the 'white' people in the vehicle." He remembered his mother's reaction: "My mom got very angry because the police officer didn't come to the car that was hit and told her to get her license and all out without even asking if she was okay." Experiences like these can lead young people to determine that involving the police is more likely to escalate the problem than resolve it. For example, during a serious scuff le between groups of adults and youth, despite needing police assistance, one of the young people, trying to defend a friend in need, ran away as police arrived because he knew "from past history the cops don't really treat [him] well."

E. Lack of Legitimacy and Insecurity

Given how often stops occur and how frequently those stopped are innocent, it is understandable that some young people, such as this Latino immigrant, felt that police are above the law and that "cops get away with everything." Given the high rates of physical police contact, it is not surprising that some young people like this seventeen-year-old Asian immigrant listed the NYPD's use of excessive physicality as his example of injustice: "Police officers using extreme force to put down civilians who just wanted to speak out." A general sense that police are racially discriminatory was a commonly referenced theme among young people of color such as this black female: "Often in NYC you find officers who racially profile." A fifteen-year-old female Pakistani immigrant wrote, "I saw a white policeman abusing a black man for no reason! And that was not right. It pissed me off. It made me think that they can do it to me too or anyone from my race." Youth perceptions of legitimacy towards police activity, and feelings of insecurity rather than safety when police are around, deserve further exploration.

Young people, particularly young people in heavily policed neighborhoods, are not unsophisticated about their assessment of police. They do not dismiss police outright and they see the value and necessity of police.[96] However, the perception of police legitimacy and the desire to cooperate with police are dependent on interpreting the police as procedurally just. Young people need to see the police as a racially unbiased organization that is fair, neutral, and consistent in their surveillance. They need to view police practices as essentially effective at stopping criminal activity and as having the best interest of the community and its citizens in mind. Furthermore, they need to perceive the police as treating them with respect and in a way that allows them to live a life of dignity. This includes feeling heard—being able to express grievances or their side of the story without feeling devalued.[97]

Suzanne Meiners speculated that aggressive policing tactics might undermine young people's trust in police, more likely expose them to the justice system, and, in the process, fray the very fabric of our democracy. [98] Our data lends support to this fear. The heavy police surveillance on young people and the lack of legitimacy and security towards the police and the criminal justice system generally, as perceived by certain young people in our sample, may in fact facilitate criminal activity to the extent that police officers need to partner with people in the community to effectively fight crime.[99] This is even more concerning when considering that nearly all of the young people stopped are innocent. We are particularly worried about the potential normalization that aggressive policing may have on some young people in heavily policed communities. However, an interesting relationship emerged between positive contact with police and attitudes towards police. Though cause and effect cannot be determined and further exploration is needed, it is worth noting and potentially speculating about the more favorable associations positive contact with police had, even as compared to having no contact with police.

V. CONCLUSION

Young people living on the economic and unfortunately racialized and sexualized margins of society are particularly vulnerable to the ebbs and flows of public institutions; they are, however, seldom included in the discussion about policy: what needs to change and in what ways those changes should happen. Young people in our city have an enormous amount of expertise to share. Polling for Justice was a project designed to create spaces, through research and advocacy, for young people to share their knowledge and inform debates about School Safety Agents, sex education, and community policing, to name a few. In the process, youth told us what it was like growing up policed in NYC. The NYPD dataset and the PFJ dataset—borne of very different perspectives—confirm each other in significant ways. At its most sweeping, these data cumulatively reveal that young people between the ages of fourteen and twenty-one during 2008 through 2009 experienced a great deal of largely negative police contact with implications well beyond the police stop itself. More particularly, we gained insight into what it means for many youth in NYC to grow up as perpetual suspects because of their age, how they look, or where they live. Our analysis supports several tentative conclusions:

Young people in NYC are growing up policed. Many young people are in contact with police on the streets, in their apartment buildings, and even in their schools. The quality of contact varies and can be positive, but too often it escalates into negative experiences with, for example, verbal, physical, and sometimes even sexual contact. Yet, according to the NYPD, nearly all of the young people stopped were not arrested, given a summons, or found to be in possession of a weapon or other contraband. In other words, nearly all of these young people were innocent.

Some groups and communities are disproportionally burdened with police surveillance. Young people of color, males, and youth who identify as LGBQ were more likely to have contact with police. Young people in largely poor, under-educated communities of color were also more likely to deal with aggressive policing. It makes sense that these communities would have more police presence because they also tend to be the communities with higher violent crime rates. Yet, the stop and frisk strategy seems largely unsuccessful at directly stopping those young people committing crimes.

Momentary detainment with police extends longer than the experience itself. Young people's attitudes towards police and the criminal justice system are complicated. Many want to have reliable and fair police officers to depend on. They are not unquestionably opposed to police presence. Yet, for many of the young people, what they witness or experience in practice are over-surveillance, harassment, excessive aggressiveness and discrimination. Most of the young people, particularly young people of color or LGBQ youth—do not feel comfortable seeking out a police officer for help. Indeed, some said they feared seeking help from police because the situation too often escalated in undesirable ways. Contact with police is not usually private, but witnessed by neighborhoods and shared with family and friends. Attitudes are derived not only from the quality of experience during a direct contact, but also from the vicarious, indirect experiences and observations of others.

Justice Douglas, the sole dissenting voice in the *Terry* decision, argued that, "To give the police greater power than a magistrate is to take a long step down the totalitarian path."[100] The data revealed in this article, in combination with a large amount of scholarship produced on this issue, supports Justice Douglas's foresight. For some young people in some neighborhoods, it appears that totalitarianism does exist. We believe the *Terry v. Ohio* decision—now more than forty years old—has set legal precedence for policing practices that are too heavily against personal liberty. We interpret the current aggressive policing policies as too ineffective to warrant the continued and frequent harassment of young people in New York City. The direct and collateral damages are too great, the costs too severe, borne disproportionally by marginalized groups and communities of color.

We have now had nearly a decade's experiment with broken windows policing tactics and the evidence is in. We need to consider whether the current practices of aggressive policing warrant the costs—of liberty, of insecurity, of mistrust. Perhaps the individual police officers do not *intend* to discriminate. Yet large numbers of young and innocent New Yorkers, particularly marginalized young people living in poorer communities of color, are growing up heavily policed. The question of intent should be reframed. Do we as a nation *intend* to collectively consider the evidence, or will we exercise the collective *intent* to ignore the evidence? On behalf of our youngest citizens, a public and political debate is deserved and long overdue.

[...]

NOTES

1. See Jeffrey Fagan, *Policing Guns and Youth Violence*, 12 FUTURE CHILD 133, 140–42 (2002); George L. Kelling & James Q. Wilson, *Broken Windows: The Police and Neighborhood Safety*, THE ATLANTIC, Mar. 1982, at 29–38, *available at* http://www.theatlantic.com/magazine/archive/1982/03/brokenwindows/4465/.

2. See M. Chris Fabricant, *War Crimes and Misdemeanors: Understanding "Zero-Tolerance" Policing as a Form of Collective Punishment and Human Rights Violation*, 3 DREXEL L. REV. 373, 375–401 (2011); Fagan, *supra* note 1, at 140 –42.

3. *See* Fagan, *supra* note 1.

4. *See* Fabricant, *supra* note 2, at 378–90; Harry G. Levine & Deborah Peterson Small, NYCLU, Marijuana Arrest Crusade: Racial Bias and Police Policy in New York City 1997–2007, at 4 (20 08), http://www.nyclu.org/files/MARIJUANA-ARREST-CRUSADE _Final.pdf.

5. 392 U.S. 1, 30 –31 (1968) (holding that a limited search of the outer clothing of persons who may pose a threat to police officers and others nearby is a reasonable search under the Fourth Amendment).

6. U.S. Const. amend. IV ("The right of the people to be secure in their persons, houses, papers, and effects, against unreasonable searches and seizures, shall not be violated . . . .").

7. Nicholas R. Alioto, Note, *Unreasonable Differences: The Dispute Regarding the Application of Terry Stops to Completed Misdemeanor Crimes*, 83 St. John's L. Rev., 947–51 (2009).

8. *Terry*, 392 U.S. at 21–22.

9. *Id.*; *see also* L. Darnell Weeden, *It is Not Right Under the Constitution to Stop and Frisk Minority People Because They Don't Look Right*, 21 U. Ark. Little Rock L. Rev. 829, 834 (1999).

10. *Terry v. Ohio* marks the minimum constitutional standard to which states must adhere. *See* 392 U.S. at 31. However, *People v. De Bour* mandated, in theory, a more restrictive four-tiered standard for police stops in New York. 40 N.Y.2d 210 (1976); *see also*, e.g., Kent Roach & M.L. Friedland, *Borderline Justice: Policing in the Two Niagaras*, 23 Am. J. Crim. L., 316–17 (1996).

11. *See* Alioto, *supra* note 7, at 950–51.

12. *See* Bill Ross, *Stop and Frisk: Invasion of Privacy Without Probable Cause*, 4 U.S.F. L. Rev. 284 (1969).

13. *See*, e.g., Bd. of Educ. v. Earls, 536 U.S. 822 (2002); Illinois v. Wardlow, 528 U.S. 119 (2000); Whren v. United States, 517 U.S. 806 (1996); United States v. Cortez-Galaviz, 495 F.3d 1203 (10th Cir. 2007); United States v. McKoy, 428 F.3d 38 (1st Cir. 2005). 1333

14. *See* Paul Butler, *A Long Step Down the Totalitarian Path: Justice Douglas's Great Dissent in* Terry v. Ohio, 79 Miss. L.J. 9, 26–29 (2009); Fabricant, *supra* note 2, at 375–401; James J. Fyfe, *Stops, Frisks, Searches, and the Constitution*, 3 Criminality & Pub. Pol'y 379, 384–90 (2004); David A. Harris, *Factors for Reasonable Suspicion: When Black and Poor Means Stopped and Frisked*, 69 Ind. L.J. 659 (1994); Weeden, *supra* note 9, at 836–41.

15. *See* Delores Jones-Brown et al., Stop, Question & Frisk Policing Practices in New York City: A Primer 8 (John Jay College Center on Race, Crime, & Justice, 2010); Harris, *supra* note 14; Gregory H. Williams, *The Supreme Court and Broken Promises: The Gradual but Continual Erosion of* Terry v. Ohio, 34 How. L.J. 567 (1991).

16. *See* Delores Jones-Brown & Brian A. Maule, *Racially Biased Policing: A Review of the Judicial and Legislative Literature*, in Race, Ethnicity, and Policing: New and Essential Readings 140 (Stephen K. R ice & Michael D. White eds., 2010); Harris, *supra* note 14; Weeden, *supra* note 9.

17. *See* Hope Corman & Naci Mocan, *Carrots, Sticks, and Broken Windows*, 48 J.L. & Econ. 235, 262 (2005); Ross, *supra* note 12.

18. *See* Bernard E. Harcourt, *Reflecting on the Subject: A Critique of the Social Influence Conception of Deterrence, the Broken Windows Theory, and Order-Maintenance Policing New York Style*, 97 Mich. L. Rev. 291, 308–31 (1999); Bernard E. Harcourt & Jens Ludwig, *Broken Windows: New Evidence from New York City and a Five-City Social Experiment*, 73 U. Chi. L. Rev. 271, 314–16 (2006); Richard Rosenfeld et al., *The Impact of Order-Maintenance Policing of New York City Homicide and Robbery Rates: 1988–2001*, 45 Criminology 355, 377–79 (20 07); Robert J. Sampson & Stephen W. Raudenbush, *Systematic Social Observation of Public Spaces: A New Look at Disorder in Urban Neighborhoods*, 105 Am. J. Sociology 603, 637–39 (1999).

19. *See* Fabricant, *supra* note 2; K. Babe Howell, *Broken Lives from Broken Windows: The Hidden Costs of Aggressive Order-Maintenance Policing*, 33 N.Y.U. Rev. L. & Soc. Change 271, 271–315 (2009).

[...]

21. *See* Andrew Gelman et al., *An Analysis of the NYPD's Stop-and-Frisk Policy in the Context of Claims of Racial Bias*, 102 J. AM. STATISTICAL ASS'N 813, 813–23 (2007); DELORES JONES-BROWN ET AL., *supra* note 15, at 3–5.

22. JONES-BROWN ET AL., *supra* note 15.

23. *See* Jeffrey Fagan et al., *Street Stops and Broken Windows Revisited: The Demography and Logic of Proactive Policing in a Safe and Changing City*, in RACE, ETHNICITY AND POLICING: NEW AND ESSENTIAL READINGS 337–39 (Stephen K. Rice & Michael D. White eds., 2010); JONES-BROWN ET AL., *supra* note 22.

24. The UF-250's are the standardized forms that police officers fill out to record what occurred during a stop and frisk encounter. *See* JONES-BROWN ET AL., *supra* note 22. Under NYPD policy, police officers are required to fill out the U F-250 forms only under certain conditions. However, analyses have confirmed that the data do a reasonably good job at representing the population of NYC stops. *See* Gelman et al., *supra* note 21.

25. 10.7% was calculated from the 2010 Census *available at* infoshare.org.

[...]

61. *See* John Q. Barret, *"Stop and Frisk" in 1968: Deciding the Stop and Frisk Cases: A Look Inside the Supreme Court's Conference*, 72 ST. JOHN'S L. REV. 749, 769–72 (1998); Anothony C. Thompson, *Stopping the Usual Suspects: Race and the Fourth Amendment*, 74 N.Y.U. L. REV. 956, 962–83 (1999).

62. *See* Barret, *supra* note 61, at 771–72; Thompson, *supra* note 61, at 965–66.

63. *See* Barret, *supra* note 61, at 771–72; Thompson, *supra* note 61, at 964.

64. Terry v. Ohio, 392 U.S. 1, 21–22 (1968).

65. *See* generally Harris, *supra* note 14; Sherri Lynn Johnson, *Race and the Decision to Detain a Suspect*, 93 YALE L.J. 214 (1983); Lerner, *supra* note 27; Maclin, *supra* note 27; David Rudovsky, *Law Enforcement by Stereotypes and Serendipity: Racial Profiling and Stops and Searches Without Causes*, 3 U. PA. J. CONST. L. 296 (2001); Adina Schwartz, *"Just Take Away Their Guns": Hidden Racism of Terry v. Ohio*, 23 FORDHAM URB. L.J. 317 (1996); Thompson, *supra* note 61; Weeden, *supra* note 9.

66. *See* STOP AND FRISK PRACTICES, *supra* note 60, at 14–16; CENTER FOR CONSTITUTIONAL RIGHTS, RACIAL DISPARITY IN NYPD STOP-AND-FRISKS: THE CENTER FOR CONSTITUTIONAL RIGHTS PRELIMINARY REPORT ON UF-250 DATA FROM 2005 THROUGH JUNE 2008, at 4 (2009); Fagan, *supra* note 23, at 310; Andrew Gelman et al., *supra* note 21; JONES-BROWN ET AL., *supra* note 15, at 14–20.

67. *See* GREG RIDGEWAY, RAND CORP., ANALYSIS OF RACIAL DISPARITIES IN THE NEW YORK POLICE DEPARTMENT'S STOP, QUESTION, AND FRISK PRACTICES 1–50 (20 07); Greg Ridgeway & John MacDonald, *Methods for Assessing Racially Biased Policing*, in RACE, ETHNICITY, AND POLICING: NEW AND ESSENTIAL READINGS 180, 180–99 (Stephen K. Rice & Michael D. White eds., 2010).

68. N.Y. POLICE DEP'T, NEW YORK POLICE DEPARTMENT OPERATIONS ORDER: DEPARTMENT POLICY REGARDING RACIAL PROFILING (2002).

69. Ridgeway & MacDonald, *supra* note 67, at 199.

70. Meaghan Paulhamus et al., State of the Science in Racial Profiling Research: Substantive and Methodological Considerations, in RACE, ETHNICITY, AND POLICING: NEW AND ESSENTIAL READINGS 239, 249 (Stephen K. Rice & Michael D. White eds., 2010).

[...]

74. Harris, *supra* note 14, at 672–75.

75. *See infra* Table 5.

76. *See infra* Table 5.

77. Operation Clean Halls is a program where police officers conduct "vertical patrols" through the hallways, stair wells, and rooftops of residential buildings in search of the sale and use of drugs as well as non-residents who are loitering or trespassing. New York City Housing Authority (NYCHA) buildings are automatically enlisted in this program. Landlords of private buildings can request to be included as well. See Adam Carlis, Note, *The Illegality of Vertical Patrols*, 109 COLUM. L. REV. 2002, 2003 (2009).

78. *See infra* Table 6.

79. *See infra* Table 6. 1350

80. Kendra Brewster et al., LGBTQ Youth Experiences with Police in and Around Schools, QuER I Graduate Student Round Table (Nov. 2010), http://www.queeringeducation.org/research/2010-2011conference- presentations.

81. Terry v. Ohio, 392 U.S. 1, 17 (1967).

82. *Id.* at 24–25.

83. *See generally* Yolander G. Hurst & James Frank, *How Kids View Cops: The Nature of Juvenile Attitudes Toward the Police*, 28 J. CRIM. JUST. 189 (2000); Patrick J. Carr et al., *We Never Call the Cops and Here is Why: A Qualitative Examination of Legal Cynicism in Three Philadelphia Neighborhoods*, 45 CRIMINOLOGY 445 (2007); Tom R. Tyler, *Enhancing Police Legitimacy*, 593 ANNALS AM. ACAD. POL. & SOC. SCI. 84 (2004).

84. *See* Rod K. Brunson, *"Police Don't Like Black People": African-American Young Men's Accumulated Police Experiences*, 6 CRIMINOLOGY & PUB. POL'Y 71 (2007); Ronald Weitzer, *Race and Policing in Different Ecological Contexts*, in RACE, ETHNICITY, AND POLICING: NEW AND ESSENTIAL READINGS 118 (Stephen K. R ice & Michael D. White eds., 2010); Ronald Weitzer & Stephen A. Tuch, *Perceptions of Racial Profiling: Race, Class, and Personal Experience*, 40 CRIMINOLOGY 435 (2002).

85. *See* Brunson, *supra* note 84, at 72; Rod K. Brunson, *Beyond Stop Rates: Using Qualitative Methods to Examine Racially Biased Policing*, in RACE, ETHNICITY, AND POLICING: NEW AND ESSENTIAL READINGS 221 (Stephen K. Rice & Michael D. White eds., 2010).

86. Hurst & Frank, *supra* note 83; Fine et al., *supra* note 20; Carmen Solis et al., *Latino Youths' Experiences with and Perceptions of Involuntary Police Encounters*, 623 ANNALS AM. ACAD. POL. & SOC. SCI. 39 (2009).

87. *See* Dennis P. Rosenbaum et al., Attitudes Toward the Police: The Effects of Direct and Vicarious Experience, 8 POLICE Q. 343, 360 (2005). 1353

88. *See id.*; Brunson, *supra* note 84; Carr et al., *supra* note 83.

89. Beth M. Heubner et al., *African American and White Perceptions of Police Services: Within- and Between-group Variation*, 32 J. CRIM. JUST. 123 (2004); Hurst & Frank, *supra* note 83.

90. Amie M. Schuck & Denn is P. Rosenbaum, *Global and Neighborhood Attitudes Toward the Police: Differentiation by Race, Ethnicity and Type of Contact*, 21 J. QUANTITATIVE CRIMINOLOGY 391, 412 (2005); Ben Bradford et al., *Contact and Confidence: Revisiting the Impact of Public Encounters with the Police*, 19 POLICING & SOC'Y 20, 24–25 (2009); Tom R. Tyler & Jeffrey A. Fagan, *Legitimacy and Cooperation: Why Do People Help the Police Fight Crime in their Communities?*, in RACE, ETHNICITY, AND POLICING: NEW AND ESSENTIAL READINGS 94 (Stephen K. Rice & Michael D. White eds., 2010).

91. Schuck & Rosenbaum, *supra* note 90, at 441.

92. Polling for Justice, *supra* note 50; *see also infra* Table 7.

93. *See* Brunson, *supra* note 84; Hurst & Frank, *supra* note 83; Rosenbaum et al., *supra* note 87.

94. Ronald Weitzer, *Incidents of Police Misconduct and Public Opinion*, 30 J. CRIM. JUSTICE 397 (2002).

95. *See* Rosenbaum, *supra* note 86; Fine et al., *supra* note 20; Hurst & Frank, *supra* note 83.

96. *See* Carr et al., *supra* note 83.

97. Tyler, *supra* note 83; Jason Sunshine & Tom R. Tyler, *The Role of Procedural Justice and Legitimacy in Shaping Public Support for Policing*, 37 L. & SOC'Y REV. 513 (2003).

98. Suzanne Meiners, A *Tale of Political Alienation of Our Youth: An Examination of the Potential Threats on Democracy Posed by Incomplete "Community Policing" Programs*, 7 U.C. DAVIS J. INT'L L. & POL'Y 161, 177, 182 (2003).

99. Howell, *supra* note 19, at 278–79; Tyler, *supra* note 83, at 90.

100. Terry v. Ohio, 392 U.S. 1, 38 (1968).

*Brett G. Stoudt is an assistant professor with a joint appointment in the psychology department and the gender studies program at John Jay College of Criminal Justice.

Michelle Fine is a professor of psychology at the Graduate Center at the City University of New York.

Madeline Fox is a doctoral student in social-personality psychology at the Graduate Center of the City University of New York.

Stoudt, Brett G., Michelle Fine, and Madeline Fox. "Growing Up Policed in the Age of Aggressive Policing Practices" *New York Law School Law Review* 56 (2011/12): 1331–70. This text has been shortened. Passages left out are indicated by [...].

Used by Permission.

Profiling Mexican American Identity: Issues and Concerns

by Adalberto Aguirre Jr.*

Racial profiling is a repressive social practice that uses group characteristics to individualize stereotypic behavior for minorities in American society. The practice of racial profiling victimizes minority persons to support a White hegemonic structure that promotes White values and beliefs as superior. The harmful effects of racial profiling on Mexican American social identity are discussed in this article. Several court cases are reviewed to illustrate how "Hispanic identity" is used by law enforcement agencies to profile Mexican Americans as either drug smugglers or undocumented aliens.

Have you ever had the feeling that you're being watched? Or, have you felt employees' eyes following every movement you make while you shop? Or, you're driving on the interstate or on a city street and you feel the prying eyes of police officers as they drive past you? I know, it sounds like paranoid thinking. But, what if the way you look, dress, or talk makes you more noticeable to people around you? It causes people around you to watch you. Maybe it's not even you that people are watching. Maybe it's just what they think you might do that makes them watch you.

I use the preceding statements to create a mindset for students in my sociology classes regarding the interfacing of race and ethnicity with the social construction of identity in American society. The mindset asks students to consider the saliency of racial and ethnic identity in structuring social relations for persons that challenge the Anglo Saxon core in American society. The Anglo Saxon core is the social construction of a racial ideology that views White society and its values as superior to racial and ethnic minorities[1] (Horsman, 1997; Vargas, 1998). The mindset also asks students to consider the utility to American society from making some persons more noticeable than others.[2] In particular, I ask students to use the mindset as an interpretive tool for understanding the social relations that construct social contexts for racializing the social identity of racial and ethnic minority persons. To enhance the mindset's purpose as an instructional tool, I tell students to label the mindset as *racial profiling*.

The purpose of this article is to discuss racial profiling and its implications for the Mexican American population in the United States. The intent of this article is to use one's sociological imagination to discuss the effects of racial profiling on the social relations that characterize the Mexican American population in the United States. As a result, this article is not designed to be a comprehensive review of the racial profiling literature.[3] For the purpose of discussion, I use the term *Mexican American* to identify Mexican-origin persons born in the United States. Quite possibly, the term could be expanded to include persons born in Mexico who immigrated to the United States at a very young age and who as a result became accustomed to American cultural values and behavior. Keep in mind, my definition of *Mexican American* only situates persons in the discussion, it is not designed to mute discussion of who else could be included in the definition.

RACIAL PROFILING

Racial profiling is a term used to identify law enforcement practices that use race to make discretionary judgments. In general, race is used in public life to profile racial and ethnic minority persons, especially as shoppers (Graves, 2001; Main, 2000–2001). The idea of profiling persons on the basis of race has become popularized into the phrase *driving while Black* (DWB). The phrase has been extended in its application to also include Mexican Americans—driving while brown. The identifiability of Black or brown persons as either drivers of automobiles or as passengers in automobiles is used by law enforcement personnel as a basis for profiling minority persons. For example, Black and Hispanic motorists stopped by the police are more likely than White motorists to have their vehicle searched, 11% versus 5%, respectively, and to undergo a physical search, 8% versus 4%, respectively (Bureau of Justice Statistics, 2001). In addition, Black and Hispanic persons are more likely to be victims of force used against them by police. In general, law enforcement agencies rationalize their use of race as a profiling tool by arguing that minorities commit more crimes than Whites, the social impact of crimes committed by minorities is greater than those committed by Whites, and minorities are more likely than Whites to possess weapons and illegal contraband (Rudovsky, 2002).[4]

Although racial profiling is usually linked with the activities of law enforcement agencies, one can find its application to other areas in the public lives of minorities. For example, in *City of Chicago v. Morales* (1999), the Supreme Court ruled that a gang loitering ordinance enforced by the city of Chicago was overly broad and vague. The Chicago city council passed a gang loitering ordinance in June 1992 empowering police to disperse groups of two or more persons if they were standing in public space, such as a sidewalk or street corner, and if the police suspected gang activity. Persons refusing to disperse were subject to arrest and 6 months in prison. According to Roberts (1999), the ordinance was written in language that was "deliberately expansive to allow the police to clean up the streets based on their suspicions of gang membership rather than waiting for a crime to take place" (p. 775). The gang loitering ordinance was in effect for 3 years and resulted in more than 40,000 arrests. The majority of the persons arrested were either Black or Latino residents of inner-city neighborhoods in Chicago.

Racial profiling can also be used as a tool for excluding minority persons from certain areas in public life, such as retail stores (Austin, 1994). In *Robinson v. Town of Colonie* (1995), employees of a T.J. Maxx clothing store called police to remove a "suspicious" Black couple, Mr. and Mrs. Robinson, from the store. Their behavior became suspicious to store employees because they were trying on clothes. When Mrs. Robinson asked the police why they were being asked to leave the store, a police officer replied, "They don't need a reason. If you don't want to leave you will be arrested for trespass" (Fennessy, 1999, p. 550). Although there was no evidence showing that the Robinsons had shoplifted, a police officer testified in court that a series of prior shoplifting incidents involving Black persons made store employees suspicious of the Robinsons. The police officer also testified that store employees felt that the Robinsons had been involved in the prior shoplifting incidents. No evidence was presented showing the Robinsons' involvement in the prior shoplifting incidents.[5]

Finally, on October 10, 2000, the publisher of the *Sacramento Valley Mirror*, Tim Crews, created a stir when he revealed the contents of a U.S. Forest Service memo. According to the memo, U.S. Forest Service officers were directed to detain Hispanics driving through Mendocino National Forest as possible drug smugglers. The memo stated, "If a vehicle stop is conducted and no marijuana is located and the vehicle has Hispanics inside at a minimum we would like all individuals FI'd (field interrogated)" (Bulwa, 2000, p. A4). The association of drug smuggling with Hispanic identity served as the basis for U.S. Forest Service officers to suspect Hispanics driving through Mendocino National Forest of transporting drugs.[6]

The preceding examples illustrate the precarious position of minority persons in American society when race is used to profile their presence in society. Although one might argue that it makes sense to target those persons more likely to commit crimes, it asks one to set aside concerns regarding the harmful effects of racial profiling. Consider how quickly the U.S. government targeted *Middle Eastern* appearance as a descriptor of potential terrorists without regard to the harmful effects it might have on American citizens who simply appear to look Middle Eastern (Akram & Johnson, 2002; Ashar, 2002). Racial profiling only works because it targets racial and ethnic minorities in American society and because they are less likely to occupy positions of power and influence that shield them from aggressive and intrusive public scrutiny. Despite the Enron and WorldCom financial scandals and their harmful effects on the American economy, American society is still unwilling to profile White male corporate executives as criminals or at least to increase public scrutiny over their management of financial resources. The point is that White males are not profiled as suspicious characters in the corporate world.

In accepting the logic underlying the practice of racial profiling that minorities are more likely than Whites to commit deviant acts, one fails to consider that the structuration of social relations for minorities in American society is designed to fabricate deviant images of minority persons. That is, the social relations characterizing the life experience of minority persons in American society are shaped by social forces, such as prejudice and discrimination, responsible for constraining their participation to social contexts, such as poor crime-ridden neighborhoods, that impute their social identity with deviant images (Aguirre & Turner, 2000; Appiah, 2000). For example, the depiction of Black and Latino youth by the television and movie industry as inner-city gang members whose only form of economic activity is to sell drugs criminalizes their social identity in American society. Denzin (1998) argued that the "hood and barrio" movies of the 1990s created an image of violent minority youth that served to privilege Whiteness in American society. In this context then, racial profiling is both the means and end for legitimating the deviant images associated with minority group identity. For an example of how racial profiling affects the quality of life of minority persons and their communities, see Romero (2001).

The deviant images reinforce the structuration of minority group social relations in society by creating a set of expectations for minority group behavior. These expectations create interpretative assumptions that racialize the behavior of minority persons by providing interpretive filters that target as significant only behavior that is profiled as deviant. That is, the behavior is racialized because the assumptions are rooted in the deviant images attributed to minority persons; as a result, minority behavior can only be interpreted as minority behavior. Ironically, interpretive assumptions are often used to construct explanatory models, such as those used to explain intelligence differences between racial groups, that identify intelligence differences as rooted in biological structures, such as genes, that are racial in their origin. However, because interpretive assumptions are social constructions, their use in explanatory models renders description or interpretation a social construction. As such, intelligence differences between racial groups are social constructions rather than a scientific description of innate biological differences between the groups.

Consider the expectations for minority group behavior as a thick layer of description for the social construction of stereotypes. I have constructed an interpretive framework for discussing how expectations operate in the application of racial profiling by using the following observational statements.[7]

    a. Status characteristics, such as sex, race, ethnicity, age, and so on, are markers of a person's identity.

    b. Status characteristics are assigned expectation states in the construction of social relations between persons.

    c. The expectation states are either positive or negative.

Status characteristics are an agent in the construction of interpretative filters for social relations in society. By assigning expectation states to status characteristics, one can observe the differentiation of social relations into positive or negative events. For the purpose of discussing racial profiling, we need to consider additional observational statements.[8]

    d. Status characteristics that are noticeably different from those of the dominant social group are assigned negative expectation states.

    e. Racial and ethnic minority persons are noticeably different from the dominant social group, such as White persons.

    f. Racial and ethnic minority persons are assigned negative expectation states in the construction of social relations.

As a status characteristic, racial and ethnic identity is associated with expectations that are assigned a negative expectation state in social relations. In the conduct of social relations, negative expectations promote perceptions that racial and ethnic identity violates social norms and as a result requires control and supervision. In terms of racial profiling, racial and ethnic identity is associated with negative expectations and perceptions that legitimate the profiling of minorities in society. For example, the expectation that minorities are more likely to commit a crime than Whites legitimates profiling as a practice that seeks to control the violation of social norms by controlling and supervising minorities, for example, those most likely to violate social norms. In everyday language, racial profiling is thus packaged as an explanation for maintaining order in society, "We profile them to prevent them from doing something wrong."[9]

PROFILING MEXICAN IDENTITY

Racial profiling is situated in popular thinking as something that only happens to Black persons. However, there are at least two reasons why one should not assume that racial profiling only happens to Black persons. First, by thinking that racial profiling affects only Black persons, one fails to consider how it affects the life experience of other racial and ethnic minority groups.[10] In particular, one fails to consider how the general application of racial profiling affects the quality of life for minorities in American society. For example, consider how quickly after the September 11th tragedy in New York City Middle Eastern looking persons were profiled as potential terrorists at U.S. airports (Thornton, 2001). As such, racial profiling became a rational means for controlling terrorism in the United States.[11] Not surprisingly, the overwhelming majority of Americans support racial profiling as a weapon against terrorism (Fetto, 2002).

Second, thinking that racial profiling only affects Black persons ignores its victimization of Mexican American persons in the United States. Proposition 187 for example was fueled by the belief that Mexican immigrants were a threat to the social and economic well-being of the White population in California (Aguirre, 2002b). Proposition 187 profiled all Mexican-origin persons in California as immigrants seeking to deprive White persons of social and economic opportunity. One harmful effect of Proposition 187 was its portrayal of Mexican-origin persons as immigrants or foreigners that were out of control in California society. As such, their ethnic identity, Mexican, was associated with negative expectations, such as the abuse of social welfare programs, promoting perceptions that they needed to be controlled by deporting them back to Mexico. The negative expectations associated with Mexican identity became more severe after September 11, 2001, as the American public increased their suspicions that terrorists were making their way into the United States from Mexico (Susswein, 2002).

The profiling of Mexican-origin persons as immigrants or foreigners increases the likelihood that they will be associated in popular thinking with social problems, such as drug smuggling or undocumented immigration, that threaten social norms in American society (Johnson, 1997). The profiling of Mexican-origin persons as immigrants or foreigners in turn criminalizes the population's identity in popular thinking. According to Johnson (2000), the profiling of Mexican-origin persons as foreigners in the United States

> deserves special scrutiny because it disproportionately burdens persons
> of Latin American ancestry in the United States, the vast majority
> of whom are U.S. citizens or lawful immigrants. Generally speaking,
> whether they are U.S. citizens, lawful immigrants, or undocumented
> aliens, persons of Latin American ancestry or appearance are more likely
> than other persons in the United States to be stopped and interrogated
> about their immigration status. (pp. 677–678)

Racial profiling as a result harms Mexican American persons because it assumes that they are immigrants; that is, their status as American citizens is suspect. Consider the following examples involving Mexican American persons.

The Federal Judge

Filemon B. Vela, a federal judge, was driving with three of his aides on an isolated road on their way to Laredo, Texas. The geographical area they were driving through was considered by the U.S. Border Patrol as a corridor for smugglers bringing drugs from Mexico into the United States. A Border Patrol agent stopped the judge's car because he suspected him of being an illegal alien.

When Judge Vela asked the agent why he made him stop, the agent replied that there were too many people in the car (Pinkerton, 2000; Yardley, 2000).

The Mayor

Pomona Mayor Eddie Cortez was driving his late model pick-up truck when he was stopped by U.S. Border Patrol agents in the city of Pomona. The agents stopped him because they suspected he was an illegal alien. According to Mayor Cortez,

> The real reason for the Border Patrol stopping me, and the agent was very frank with me, is the "profile." I said, "If I was driving my Cadillac or my Corvette, would you be asking me all these questions?" And he said, "No. You would not fit the profile." (Romney, 1993, p. J1)

The Lawyer

Sylvia Baez, a lawyer, was driving with her family on a San Diego freeway. She was pulled over by a U.S. Border Patrol agent. When she asked the agent the reason for stopping her, she recalls the agent saying, "You look Mexican, and you were driving with a Chula Vista license plate" (Sanchez, 2000, p. A1).

The preceding examples suggest that Mexican identity is profiled regarding its immigration status. The profiling of Mexican identity as immigrant results in a negative expectation state that depicts the person as an undocumented alien or drug smuggler. The immigration stop supports the perception that Mexican-origin persons are foreigners and the perception that they are likely to be drug smugglers or undocumented aliens. As such, the social identity of Mexican-origin persons is suspect in the eyes of law enforcement agencies. It becomes a target of opportunity for these agencies because it allows them to initiate actions that reinforce the perception that Mexican-origin persons are a threat to public life in the United States.

To understand the nexus of Mexican-origin social identity and racial profiling in the United States, one must examine *United States v. Brigoni-Ponce* (1975). *Brigoni-Ponce* is crucial to understanding the social construction of Mexican-origin identity as suspect in public life by social institutions, in this case the U.S. Supreme Court.

United States v. Brigoni-Ponce (1975)

On the evening of March 11, 1973, U.S. Border Patrol agents operating a checkpoint on Interstate 5 south of San Clemente, California, pursued and stopped a suspicious vehicle. The agents questioned the defendant and his two passengers about their citizenship. The agents learned that the two passengers had entered the United States illegally. The defendant was arrested for transporting illegal immigrants, and the passengers were arrested for illegal entry into the United States. At trial, the agents testified that they labeled the vehicle as *suspicious* because the occupants appeared to be of Mexican descent.

The U.S. Supreme Court ruled that the stop of the defendant's vehicle violated the Fourth Amendment because Border Patrol agents based their reason for stopping the vehicle only on the "perceived" Mexican ancestry of the vehicle's occupants. The court noted that Border Patrol agents may stop persons "only if they are aware of specific attributable facts, together with rational inferences from the facts, that reasonably warrant suspicion that the vehicles contain aliens who may be illegally in the country" (*United States v. Brigoni-Ponce*, 1975, p. 884). In his writing of the court's opinion, Justice Powell constructed the context for using social identity as a basis for profiling Mexican-origin persons: "The likelihood that any given person of Mexican ancestry is an alien is high enough to make Mexican appearance a relevant factor, but standing alone it does not justify stopping all Mexican-Americans to ask if they are aliens" (*United States v. Brigoni-Ponce*, 1975, pp. 886–887).

Despite its ruling that Mexican ancestry or Mexican identity alone is not sufficient to justify stopping Mexican Americans, the court did suggest in *United States v. Brigoni-Ponce* (1975) that there is a "likelihood" that Mexican-origin persons are aliens. Based on a review of immigration cases after *Brigoni-Ponce*, Johnson (2000) argued that *Brigoni-Ponce* opened the door for the U.S. Border Patrol to increase its use of Mexican appearance as the sole basis for stopping Mexican-origin persons. Important to our discussion is the fact that *Brigoni-Ponce* serves as a tool that legitimates the processing of Mexican identity by organizations that are instrumental in constructing and promoting perceptions of people based on group characteristics in public life. In this case, the Supreme Court created the opportunity for the U.S. Border Patrol to use Mexican identity as a tool for profiling Mexican-origin persons. In turn, actions resulting from the profiling activities serve to legitimate public perceptions that Mexican-origin persons are likely to be aliens and also likely to be drug smugglers.[12]

Thus, the dilemma posed by *United States v. Brigoni-Ponce* (1975) is that it identifies social contexts, such as immigration stops, in which Mexican identity can be used to classify suspects. According to Strauss (1995), *Brigoni-Ponce* ruled that

> law enforcement officers may use Mexican American ancestry as a "relevant factor"... in determining whether there is reasonable suspicion that a person is an undocumented alien... it seems reasonably clear that *Brigoni-Ponce* represents a category of cases in which the courts would allow race or national origin to be used as a basis for classification.... Thus the prohibition on the use of racial generalizations is not as absolute as the cases suggest. (p. 9)

The ruling in *Brigoni-Ponce* creates an overinclusive category for Mexican Americans that is premised on the expectation that "Mexican ancestry" is associated with a negative evaluation outcome, for example, undocumented alien.

Twenty-five years after *United States v. Brigoni-Ponce* (1975), the generalized use of Mexican ancestry in establishing reasonable suspicion stops by law enforcement agencies remains a legal controversy in the courts (Romero, 2000; Sterngold, 2000). Ruling in a case similar to *Brigoni-Ponce*, the 9th Circuit Court of Appeals ruled in *United States v. Montero-Camargo* (2000) that the U.S. Border Patrol could not consider "Hispanic appearance" in making immigration stops.[13] The Appeals Court argued that population changes had taken place in the Southwestern states in the United States since *Brigoni-Ponce* resulting in the noticeable presence of Mexican-origin persons. The Appeals Court noted that in some areas of California and Texas, Mexican-origin persons had become the single largest group. As a result, the court noted in its ruling that "in an area in which a large number of people share a specific characteristic, that characteristic casts too wide a net to play any part in a particularized suspicion determination" (p. 1134). In other words, the increased number of Mexican-origin persons in the U.S. population makes Hispanic appearance of little use to law enforcement agencies in their efforts to determine who is an undocumented alien. As a result, the court wrote in its ruling, "Hispanic appearance is, in general, of such little probative value that it may not be considered as a relevant factor where particularized or individualized suspicion is required" (p. 1135).[14]

The 9th Circuit Court of Appeals ruling in *United States v. Montero-Camargo* (2000) is especially interesting because it identifies the harm of profiling persons simply on the basis of Hispanic appearance. For example, the court noted in its ruling that

stops based on race or ethnic appearance send the underlying message to all our citizens that those who are not white are judged by the color of their skin alone. Such stops also send a clear message that those who are not white enjoy a lesser degree of constitutional protection—that they are in effect assumed to be potential criminals first and individuals second. It would be an anomalous result to hold that race may be considered when it harms people, but not when it helps them.(p. 1135)

The court appears to be making a significant statement about institutional practices and social relations that result in some persons being treated less equally or equitably than others.

The court's statement in *United States v. Montero-Camargo* has the following implications for Mexican Americans in the United States. First, profiling persons on the basis of Hispanic identity marginalizes Mexican Americans because it makes them vulnerable to expectations associated with negative evaluations. That is, the suspicion that Hispanic appearance identifies one as an alien robs Mexican Americans of their identity as Americans. Second, profiling Mexican American persons as suspect on the basis of Hispanic identity increases their exposure to repressive and depersonalizing institutional practices, such as immigration queries or deportation. As a result, Mexican Americans are subjected to greater scrutiny in public life than other groups, especially White persons, in American society. Third, profiling Mexican Americans solely on their Hispanic appearance trivializes their citizenship status. In particular, it enhances their precarious position in U.S. society by showing how easily their citizenship status can be brought into question.[15]

CONCLUDING REMARKS

Racial profiling is a repressive social practice that uses group characteristics to individualize stereotypic behavior for racial and ethnic minorities in American society. Racial profiling is fueled by the operation of interpretive assumptions that impute the behavior of minority persons with negative expectation states. Not unsurprisingly, racial profiling attacks those persons most vulnerable in public life, especially those persons whose behavior can be labeled as *suspect* in public life. Racial profiling uses racial and ethnic minorities as targets of opportunity for constructing deviant images in society. Racial profiling is thus a product of a White hegemonic structure intent on exploiting the social identity of racial and ethnic minorities in American society.

The inference in racial profiling that Hispanic identity identifies a person as a potential drug smuggler or undocumented alien harms Mexican Americans. It harms Mexican Americans because it silences them in society by subordinating their social identity in public life. Racial profiling challenges Mexican Americans to defend themselves against deviant images to assert an identity, that of American citizen, that situates them in the social fabric of American society. As a result, racial profiling harms Mexican Americans because it marginalizes their presence in American society. More important, racial profiling enhances the precarious position of Mexican Americans in American society by silencing their voice and tainting their social identity with negative expectations that constrain their pursuit of opportunity in American society.

NOTES

1. I use the term *ideology* in reference to an organized set of values that structure social reality in society. Broadly conceived, ideology structures social reality in order for persons to interpret the social relations that situate them in social structure; that is, ideology provides persons with a social and cultural map for their social relations in society. The idea of racial ideology posits that persons occupying superordinate positions in the social structure are able to racialize the social relations for persons occupying subordinate positions in the social structure. For example, the exploitation of non-White populations, namely, Native Americans, Mexicans, and Blacks, by White immigrant groups shaped a hegemonic relationship between White persons and superiority in social relations. One result is that White persons have been able to structure their social relations into a historical framework that depicts them as always having been in power, for example, superordinate positions in society. My notion of racial ideology may seem overly broad and generalized. However, the point is to think of minority status as a structural position in society and one that is racialized by White cultural values and beliefs about racial and ethnic minorities.

2. A person's everyday life is mostly situated within formal organizations. As such, a person's behavior in everyday life is governed by social processes that allow formal organizations to function in a rational manner; that is, a person's behavior is tied to the rational goal-seeking activities of the organization. A person's social identity has utility to formal organizations because organizations use social identity to determine the parameters of a person's participation in organizational activities. For example, social identities typified by sex, race, ethnicity, or social class background are used by formal organizations to pattern a person's behavior (Aguirre, 2002a; Carbado & Gulati, 2000; Kanter, 1977). As a result, one may observe that access to organizational resources, such as career opportunities, can be typed on the basis of a person's sex, race, ethnicity, or social class background. Comparatively speaking, one would

observe the following associations regarding social identity and access to resources in formal organizations: Men have more access than women, White persons have more access than racial and ethnic minority persons, and a high social class background results in greater access than a low social class background. In this sense, social identity has utility in society.

3. A comprehensive analysis of the racial profiling literature is found in the following: Engel, Calnon, and Bernard (2002); Jernigan (2000); Lyle (2001); Russell (2001); Sklansky (1997); General Accounting Office (2000); and Weitzer and Tuch (2002).

4. According to a Harris opinion poll, most White persons (55%) do not oppose racial profiling, whereas most (55%) minority persons oppose it (Fetto, 2002). One interpretation of the Harris poll is that White persons do not oppose racial profiling because they do not perceive themselves as likely to become victims of racial profiling. If this is the case, then it fits the argument that White persons interpret Whiteness as a safeguard and as a derivative of their superordinate position in society against the social forces that victimize minority persons (e.g., see Bell, 1995; Mahoney, 1997; Wildman, 1996).

5. According to a Gallop poll, half of the Black persons surveyed reported that they had suffered some form of discrimination while shopping during the past 30 days. In particular, the poll shows that Black persons are more likely to experience discrimination from store employees while shopping than from the police (O'Connell, 2001).

6. The profiling of the suspect in the Samantha Runnion case as an "Americanized Hispanic" made most Hispanic men "suspicious." Rather than focus on specific features of the suspect—such as, accented English or Spanish language use, skin tone, or eye color—to construct a realistic composite portrait of the suspect, the Orange County law enforcement authorities decided to identify ethnicity as the suspect's primary descriptor (Salinas, 2002). Similarly, rumors that Danielle Van Dam had been spotted in Tijuana led to speculation that she had been smuggled into Mexico as part of a child prostitution ring (Hughes, 2002). As a result, Mexican men became suspects in the eyes of law enforcement agencies.

7. The observational statements are a synthesis of ideas I have extrapolated from the research literature. The notion that status characteristics are associated with expectation states that pattern the social interactions between persons is drawn from Berger, Cohen, and Zelditch (1966). The idea that expectation states are integral to the construction of parameters for governing social relations between persons in society I adapted from Blau (1977).

8. The negative evaluations assigned to minority persons in the United States are the outcome of a history in which Whites have exploited and oppressed minority persons and their communities (Perea, Delgado, Harris, & Wildman, 2000; Takaki, 1993).

9. In an ironic twist, Pre-Paid Legal Services Inc. in Ada, Oklahoma, specializes in representing Black and Hispanic motorists who are potential victims of racial profiling. Pre-Paid Legal Services markets a plan called *Legal Shield* that provides telephone access to a lawyer 24 hours a day. Clients are provided with a card they can present to a police officer. The card tells the officer, "If it is your intention to question, detain or arrest me, please allow me to call an attorney immediately" (O'Brien, 2000). The strategy behind Legal Shield is that law police officers will be less likely to detain persons on the basis of racial profiling if they know that persons have immediate access to an attorney. Since its inception in 1999, Legal Shield has enrolled more than 100,000 members.

10. Racial profiling is a generalized phenomenon for racial and ethnic minority persons because it focuses on perceived group characteristics instead of individual characteristics. For example, Vincent Chin, a Chinese American, was misidentified by a group of drunken, unemployed White autoworkers as a "Jap" that was responsible for the loss of jobs in the U.S. auto industry. Vincent Chin was beaten to death by the White autoworkers (Aguirre & Turner, 2000). Black persons with "African sounding" names are often targeted by the U.S. Immigration and Naturalization Service as "suspect aliens" (see *Orhorhaghe v. INS*, 1994). Eisenman (2001) argued that because racial profiling is based on group data instead of individual characteristics, more Black schoolchildren than White schoolchildren are identified for services regarding academic and physical health problems. Hamilton Bank, a predominantly Hispanic-owned bank in Miami, filed suit against the Office of the Comptroller of the Currency (OCC) arguing that

it had been the victim of racial profiling by the OCC. According to Hamilton Bank officials, the OCC employed tactics in its review of the bank that attacked the ethnic background of bank employees. According to Hamilton Bank's lawsuit,

> The OCC has regulated Hamilton under a presumption of guilt based on the OCC's stereotype of Hamilton's customers that as Hispanics living in South Florida and South and Central America, these individuals and entities are more likely to be engaged in money laundering. (Rosenberg, 2001, p. A1)

In short, racial profiling is a generalized social phenomenon for minority persons because it reinforces group characteristics that individualize stereotypic images for the general public.

11. The profiling of Jews by Nazi Germany is a classic example of how group characteristics became a useful strategy for rationalizing repressive social practices to protect Germans from antisocials (Black, 2001). Similarly, identifying terrorists as "people who look different" is a repressive social practice because it creates an overly inclusive category that identifies suspects where none may exist. That is, any person having some similarity with the suspect characteristics increases their chances of being subjected to repressive social practices, such as incarceration without due process or legal counsel.

12. Thirty years ago, Jorge Bustamante (1972) used labeling theory to illustrate how the U.S. Border Patrol created the *wetback* as a social identity in American society. Prior to the Border Patrol's creation, Mexican immigrants had been entering the United States as seasonal laborers via a fairly open U.S.-Mexico border. However, after the Border Patrol's creation, institutional interventions, such as work permits, were employed to label Mexican immigrants not meeting the Border Patrol's rules as *wetbacks*; that is, as persons here illegally. In a certain sense, the Border Patrol created a deviant social identity, wetback, to legitimate its institutional identity and practices.

13. On October 15, 1996, a driver passing through a Border Patrol checkpoint in El Centro, California, told agents that two cars with Mexicali license plates had made U-turns to avoid passing through the checkpoint. Two Border Patrol agents following up on the driver's tip encountered two vehicles with Mexicali plates about a mile from the checkpoint. The agents pursued the vehicles because the drivers and passengers appeared to be Hispanic. After stopping the vehicles, the agents searched the vehicles and found marijuana and a loaded handgun.

14. The court employed the notion of "reasonable suspicion calculus" in its ruling. In the court's view, reasonable suspicion requires that a particular person being stopped has committed or is about to commit a crime. Using a broad profile, such as Hispanic identity, does not support reasonable suspicion because it is based on group behavior rather than on individual activity.

15. I have noted in this article that Proposition 187 was a noticeable use of profiling to muster support for anti-immigrant initiatives. The most serious harm of Proposition 187 was its labeling of Mexican Americans as *foreigners*—as persons not deserving of citizenship in American society. For a discussion of how nativism has challenged the notion of citizenship for immigrants and minorities in American society, see Delgado (1999).

REFERENCES

Aguirre, A., Jr. (2002a). Propositions 187 and 227: A nativist response to Mexicans. In C. Hohm & J. Glynn (Eds.), *California's social problems* (2nd ed., pp. 303–324). Thousand Oaks, CA: Pine Forge Press.

Aguirre, A., Jr. (2002b). Social class in the workplace. In C. Harvey & M. J. Allard (Eds.), *Understanding and managing diversity* (2nd ed., pp. 141–148). Englewood Cliffs, NJ: Prentice Hall.

Aguirre, A., Jr., & Turner, J. (2000). *American ethnicity: The dynamics and consequences of discrimination* (3rd ed.). New York: McGraw-Hill.

Akram, S., & Johnson, K. (2002). Race, civil rights, and immigration law after September 11, 2001: The targeting of Arabs and Muslims. *New York University Annual Survey of American Law, 58*, 295–355.

Appiah, K. A. (2000). Stereotypes and the shaping of identity. *California Law Review*, 88, 41–53.

Ashar, S. (2002). Immigration enforcement and subordination: The consequences of racial profiling after September 11. *Connecticut Law Review*, 34, 1185–1199.

Austin, R. (1994). A nation of thieves: Securing Black peoples' rights to shop and sell in White America. *Utah Law Review*, 1994, 147–177.

Bell, D. (1995). Property rights in Whiteness—Their legal legacy, their economic costs. In R. Delgado (Ed.), *Critical race theory: The cutting edge* (pp. 75–83). Philadelphia: Temple University Press.

Berger, J., Cohen, B., & Zelditch, M., Jr. (1966). Status characteristics and expectation states. In J. Berger, M. Zelditch, Jr., & B. Anderson (Eds.), *Sociological theories in progress* (Vol. 1, pp. 29–46). Boston: Houghton Mifflin.

Black, E. (2001). *IBM and the holocaust: The strategic alliance between Nazi Germany and America's most powerful corporation.* New York: Crown Publishers.

Blau, P. (1977). *Inequality and heterogeneity: A primitive theory of social structure.* New York: Free Press.

Bulwa, D. (2000, October 13). Memo: Interrogate Hispanics. *The San Francisco Examiner*, p. A4.

Bureau of Justice Statistics. (2001). *Contacts between police and the public: Findings from the 1999 national survey.* Washington, DC: U.S. Department of Justice.

Bustamante, J. (1972). The wetback as deviant: An application of labeling theory. *American Journal of Sociology*, 77, 706–718.

Carbado, D., & Gulati, M. (2000). Working identity. *Cornell Law Review*, 85, 1259–1308.

City of Chicago v. Morales, 119 S. Ct. 1849 (1999).

Delgado, R. (1999). Citizenship. In R. Torres, L. Miron, & J. Inda (Eds.), *Race, ethnicity, and citizenship* (pp. 247–252). Cambridge, MA: Blackwell.

Denzin, N. (1998). Reading the cinema of racial violence. *Perspectives on Social Problems*, 10, 31–60.

Eisenman, R. (2001). Demographic profiling. *Policy Evaluation*, 7, 4–11.

Engel, R., Calnon, J., & Bernard, T. (2002). Theory and racial profiling: Shortcomings and future directions in research. *Justice Quarterly*, 19, 249–273.

Fennessy, J. (1999). New Jersey law and police response to the exclusion of minority patrons from retail stores based on the suspicion of shoplifting. *Seton Hall Constitutional Law Journal*, 9, 549–608.

Fetto, J. (2002). The usual suspects: Americans are divided on the issue of racial profiling. *American Demographics*, 24, 14.

General Accounting Office. (2000). *Racial profiling: Limited data available on motorist stops.* Washington, DC: Government Printing Office.

Graves, M. (2001). Purchasing while Black: How courts condone discrimination in the marketplace. *Michigan Journal of Race and Law*, 7, 159–194.

Horsman, R. (1997). Race and manifest destiny: The origins of American racial Anglo-Saxonism. In R. Delgado & J. Stefancic (Eds.), *Critical White studies: Looking behind the mirror* (pp. 139–144). Philadelphia: Temple University Press.

Hughes, J. (2002, March 10). 900 tips received in search for Danielle. *San Diego Union-Tribune*, p. B1.

Jernigan, A. (2000). Driving while Black: Racial profiling in America. *Law and Psychology Review*, 24, 127–138.

Johnson, K. (1997). Some thoughts on the future of Latino legal scholarship. *Harvard Latino Law Review*, 2, 101–144.

Johnson, K. (2000). The case against race profiling in immigration enforcement. *Washington University Law Quarterly*, 78, 675–736.

Kanter, R. (1977). *Men and women of the corporation.* New York: Basic Books.

Lyle, P. (2001). Racial profiling and the Fourth Amendment: Applying the minority victim perspective to ensure equal protection under the law. *Boston College Third World Law Journal*, 21, 127–138.

Mahoney, M. (1997). The social construction of Whiteness. In R. Delgado & J. Stefancic (Eds.), *Critical White studies: Looking behind the mirror* (pp. 330–333). Philadelphia: Temple University Press.

Main, A. (2000–2001). Racial profiling in places of public accommodation: Theories of recovery and relief. *Brandeis Law Journal*, 39, 289–316.

O'Brien, T. (2000, December 8). Novel legal service: Racial profiling insurance. *The Recorder*, p. 3.

O'Connell, T. (2001, April). Retail racism: Caught red handed. *Security Magazine*, pp. 9–10, 12, 14.

Orhorhaghe v. INS, 38 F.3d 488, 498, 9th Cir. (1994).

Perea, J., Delgado, R., Harris, A., & Wildman, S. (2000). *Race and races: Cases and resources for a diverse America.* St. Paul, MN: West Group.

Pinkerton, J. (2000, October 1). Border Patrol twice stops judge on way to court. *Houston Chronicle*, p. A1.

Roberts, D. (1999). Race, vagueness, and the social meaning of order-maintenance policing. *Journal of Criminal Law & Criminology*, 89, 775–836.

Robinson v. Town of Colonie, 878 F. Supp. 387, 392 N.D.N.Y. (1995).

Romero, M. (2001). State violence, and the social and legal construction of Latino criminality: From El Bandido to gang member. *Denver University Law Review*, 78, 1081–1118.

Romero, V. (2000). Racial profiling: "Driving while Mexican" and affirmative action. *Michigan Journal of Race & Law*, 6, 195–207.

Romney, L. (1993, September 2). Over the line? Citing questioning of mayor, activists say border patrol targets all Latinos. *Los Angeles Times*, p. J1.

Rosenberg, S. (2001, December 14). Biased regulators? Hispanic owned Hamilton Bank claims racial profiling at root of crackdown on international lending practices. *Broward Daily Business Review*, p. A1.

Rudovsky, D. (2002). Breaking the pattern of racial profiling. *Trial*, 38, 29–36.

Russell, K. (2001). Racial profiling: A status report of the legal, legislative, and empirical literature. *Rutgers Race & the Law Review*, 3, 61–81.

Salinas, M. (2002, July 30). Will all Hispanic men be suspect? *Seattle Post-Intelligencer*, p. B5.

Sanchez, L. (2000, July 24). Latinos complain of racial profiling: Complaints mount against immigration and police officers. *The San Diego Union–Tribune*, p. A1.

Sklansky, D. (1997). Traffic stops, minority motorists, and the future of the Fourth Amendment. *Supreme Court Review*, 1997, 271–328.

Sterngold, J. (2000, April 13). Appeals court voids ethnic profiling in searches. *The New York Times*, p. A20.

Strauss, D. (1995). Affirmative action and the public interest. *Supreme Court Review*, 1995, 1–43.

Susswein, G. (2002, June 29). A town torn in two. *Austin American Statesman*, p. A1.

Takaki, R. (1993). *A different mirror: A history of multicultural America.* Boston: Little, Brown.

Thornton, K. (2001, September 23). Racial profiling debate lands in airports. *The San Diego Union–Tribune*, p. A1.

United States v. Brigoni-Ponce, 422 U.S. 873 (1975).

United States v. Montero-Camargo, 208 F.3d 1122, 9th Cir. (2000).

Vargas, S. (1998). Deconstructing homogeneous Americanus: The White ethnic immigrant narrative and its exclusionary effect. *Tulane Law Review*, 72, 1493–1596.

Weitzer, R., & Tuch, S. (2002). Perceptions of racial profiling: Race, class, and personal experience. *Criminology*, 40, 435–456.

Wildman, S. (1996). *White privilege*. New York: New York University Press.

Yardley, J. (2000, January 26). Some Texans say Border Patrol singles out too many Hispanics. *The New York Times*, p. A17.

*Adalberto Aguirre Jr. is professor of sociology at the University of California, Riverside. His research interests are in the areas of social inequality, race and ethnic relations, and critical race theory. He is the author of *American Ethnicity: The Dynamics and Consequences of Discrimination, Women and Minority Faculty in the Academic Workplace,* and *Structured Inequality in the United States*.

Perceptions of Consumer Racial Profiling and Negative Emotions: An Exploratory Study

by George E. Higgins and Shaun L. Gabbidon*

Profiling is a technique that has typically been used by law enforcement to quickly identify offenders or potential offenders of criminal activity. However, race has been introduced into the profiling equation. With the inclusion of race, law enforcement has used this tool to implement disparate and discriminatory practices in the criminal justice system. To date, a growing body of literature examines the effect of racial profiling in the context of traffic stops and searches that illustrate disparate and discriminatory practices (D. A. Harris, 2002; Withrow, 2006).

Racial profiling is not bound only to law enforcement. The practice has also migrated into retail environments, where it is referred to as consumer racial profiling (CRP; Gabbidon, 2003). To date, very little research has focused on CRP or perceptions of CRP. A few studies have uncovered evidence showing that some people perceive that they have been victims of discriminatory practices in retail environments due to CRP (Crockett, Grier, & Williams, 2003; Feagin, 1991). However, no research in criminology or criminal justice has examined the strain implications of the perception of CRP.

Although no study in criminology or criminal justice has examined the strain implications of the perception of this discriminatory practice, the strain theory literature does contain studies that have examined the role of discrimination within the context of Agnew's (1992, 2001, 2006) general strain theory. Some scholars have shown that negative emotions occur after an individual perceives that he or she has been a victim of discrimination. Unfortunately, this research does not include perceptions of CRP. Therefore, a gap exists in the empirical literature concerning the psychological implications of perceived CRP.

CRIMINAL PROFILING

Profiling is a technique that is used to improve the probability of identifying and apprehending a suspect (Meeks, 1999). This dynamic process includes the use of a number of factors or some combination of physical, behavioral, or psychological factors. Typically, profiles are used to focus the attention of an investigation away or toward a specific person or group of people.

Profiles can take several interconnecting forms. On one hand, profiles can be institutional (i.e., a profile that has been settled on by a specific organization such as the police, DEA, and FBI). On the other, a profile can be targeted at the individual level. That is, an individual has derived a specific profile that has been developed from personal experiences. Withrow (2006) discussed these types of profiles as formal (i.e., institutional) and informal (i.e., individual). From these perspectives, profiles can be applied to several different areas.

Profiles can be applied to a range of criminal activity, including possession and distribution of illegal substances. In particular, criminal profiling provides an outline of the type of individual who is likely to have committed a specific crime. For instance, Holmes and Holmes (2002) indicate that criminal profiling is very productive in serial murder cases. The technique has been equally productive in drug activity. However, the use of criminal profiles may subject innocent individuals to scrutiny. For example, some psychologists and other researchers argue that such profiles are not accurate, with several showing that profiles are marginal in identifying offenders (Alison, Bennell, Mokros, & Ormerod, 2002; Alison, Smith, & Morgan, 2003). Two meta-analyses on criminal profiling have shown that the practice is inaccurate even in predicting offense behaviors (Snook, Eastwood, Gendreau, Googin, & Cullen, 2007).

Racial Profiling

Withrow (2006) shows profiling has been especially productive in identifying drug couriers, but race has been a key feature in these profiles. In particular, African Americans were targeted in these profiles in the 1980s and 1990s. Race in profiles may seem logical to use because of the statistical realities of African Americans having higher rates of misdemeanor, violent, and victimization activity than any other racial group. However, this practice has some pejorative implications. That is, the use of racial profiles may be the result of a self-fulfilling prophecy. For example, the use of profiles might result in the persistence of higher rates of misdemeanors, violence, and victimization. This could be the case because the individuals see profiling as discriminatory, and this forces them to withdraw from conventional society to avoid the scrutiny of the discrimination (Anderson, 1999).

Given the potential self-fulfilling prophecy and innocent individual arguments, many states and local governments have become more conscious of the use of racial profiling. To show communities that they are paying attention to the problem of racial profiling, many states and local governments have begun enacting initiatives in order to understand the issue. Many states have mandated that data be collected (primarily through traffic stops) and analyzed to uncover racial profiling as well as to understand its practice and accuracy.

The criminological and criminal justice literature has grown with regard to racial profiling studies. These studies have examined racial profiling in areas such as traffic stops, traffic searches, and airport searches (Gaines, 2006; Grogger & Ridgeway, 2006; D. A. Harris, 1999, 2002; Lange, Johnson, & Voas, 2005; Onwudiwe, 2005; Ramirez, McDevitt, & Farrell, 2000; Reitzel & Piquero, 2006; Rice, Reitzel, & Piquero, 2005; Ruiz & Woessner, 2006; Schafer, Carter, Katz-Bannister, & Wells, 2006; E. L. Smith & Durose, 2006; M. R. Smith & Alpert, 2002; Weitzer & Tuch, 2002, 2005; Withrow, 2006). However, less empirical research has been produced in the area of CRP.

CRP

As noted previously, CRP is the discriminatory treatment of racial and ethnic minorities in retail establishments (Gabbidon, 2003; Gabbidon & Higgins, 2007). CRP has been used as an explanation for disparate treatment in stores or shopping malls. According to Fifield (2001), in a 1999 Gallup poll, half (50%) of the 1,001 African Americans in the United States who were polled reported that they had encountered this sort of disparate treatment. In addition, a 2004 Gallup poll of more than 2,000 individuals in the United States revealed that many of these individuals (i.e., 49%) felt that CRP was being practiced. In essence, although many people believe it is being practiced in the United States, very few scholars have given it any attention.

Currently, two streams of literature exist concerning CRP. The first stream of research is concerned with the lack of service due to race. The second stream of research centers on race and suspicion in retail settings. Although these two streams of research seem divergent, they are not mutually exclusive. The research on CRP has used several different methodologies to arrive at results that indicate minorities are not treated very well in retail establishments. For instance, within this literature, there are interviews (Crockett et al., 2003; Feagin, 1991; Henderson, 2001; Lee, 2000; Williams, Harris, & Henderson, 2001), reviews of legal cases (Adamson, 2000; Gabbidon, 2003; A. G. Harris, 2003; A. G. Harris, Henderson, & Williams, 2005; Russell, 1999; Williams, Harris, & Henderson, 2006), and experimental (Asquith & Bristow, 2000) and observational research in the context of shoplifting (Dabney, Dugan, Topalli, & Hollinger, 2006; Dabney, Hollinger, & Dugan, 2004). These studies reveal that disparate treatment of various minority groups does seem to occur in retail settings.

CRP and General Strain Theory

The perception that one is the victim of CRP may have important negative implications. To date, no research has explicitly examined the negative emotions that may arise from the perception of CRP. To best understand the link between CRP and negative emotions, it may be helpful to view perception of CRP as an important stressor or strain. Agnew (1992, 2001) argued that events may occur in an individual's life that develop negative emotions. From this perspective, negative emotions (e.g., self-concept) arise from the presentation of noxious stimulus (Agnew, 1992) and an evaluation that the noxious stimulus is a threat or harm (Agnew, 2001). For example, Agnew (1992) sees events such as physical or general abuse, insults from peers, and treatments of disrespect as stressors. CRP may also be seen as a treatment of disrespect. When the noxious stimulus is evaluated as a threat or harm, then the individual develops negative forms of emotions that may energize the individual to seek some form of corrective action to relieve the noxious stimulus.

Agnew (2006) presented a literature review of the efficacy of strain theory. This literature review shows that life events—including noxious stimuli—have implications in developing negative emotions, and some of the literature indicates that noxious stimuli are important in generating *specific* negative emotions. Some research (Broidy, 2001; Hay, 2003; Hay & Evans, 2006; Mazerolle, Piquero, & Capowich, 2003; Piquero & Sealock, 2004; Sharp, Brewster, & Love, 2005) indicates that noxious stimuli do have a link with general forms of negative emotions. Furthermore, some research shows that discriminatory practices do have a link with negative emotions (Baron, 2004; Eitle, 2002; Eitle & Turner, 2003; Preston, 2006; Walls, Chapple, & Johnson, 2007). To date, the criminological literature is not clear if CRP, as a strain, can have implications for negative emotions. Nor is the criminological literature clear as to the demographic characteristics that have a connection with these negative emotions.

The Present Study

The purpose of this study is to provide an understanding of the negative emotions that perception of CRP develops and the demographic characteristics that have a link with these negative emotions. Two models are necessary to provide this understanding. The first model is a confirmatory factor analysis to determine the psychometric qualities of the measure of negative emotions that may accompany the perception that one has experienced CRP.[1] We expect that the items of the negative emotions measure will coalesce into a single measure, as predicted by

Agnew's (1992, 2001) strain theory. The second is a multiple indicator, multiple cause (MIMIC) model that examines the link between demographic factors (i.e., gender, age, and income) and the negative emotion measure. If the demographic factors have a link with the negative emotion measure, then we can understand the profile of the individuals who perceive that they were victims of CRP. Therefore, we expect that the perception of CRP will develop negative emotions and that the different demographics will have a link with these negative emotions.

This study is important to the racial profiling literature because it expands the racial profiling literature beyond policing issues. Furthermore, this study provides an understanding of an understudied part of racial profiling—negative emotions.

METHOD

This research is based on a telephone survey of Philadelphia residents. Using random-digit dialing, the study was carried out by Penn State Harrisburg's Center for Survey Research, which utilizes VOXCO computer-assisted telephone interviewing (CATI) software. The CATI system accommodated 11 concurrent interviewers and quality control supervisors assisted by VOXCO's monitoring and productivity tools. Before starting the project, each interviewer was trained in proper data collection techniques through a formalized interview training class, which included role-playing and feedback, in addition to the technical methodology of interviewing. Additionally, the interviewers met with the principal investigator to provide further clarification of the project.

Participants

When contacted, the respondent was informed of the nature of the study. The interviewer discussed with the respondents the rights of their participation. That is, the respondent was told that he or she could withdraw at any time and that his or her responses would be anonymous and confidential. The phone interviews were conducted between November 30, 2006, and December 13, 2006. The respondents' telephone numbers were randomly selected from all of Philadelphia's telephone exchanges. To ensure that each member of a sampled household had an equal probability of being interviewed, the last-birthday method of respondent selection was utilized. This was used to eliminate biases that could arise from interviewing the person who answers the phone.

The actual interviewing took place on weekdays from 4 p.m. to 9 p.m., on Saturdays from 10 a.m. to 6 p.m., and on Sundays from 1 p.m. to 6 p.m. Follow-up calls to households that did not answer or that had a busy signal or an answering machine were scheduled at varying times of day and varying days of the week. Because these callbacks are the principal means by which response rates are typically increased, the Center for Survey Research attempted an average of 4.79 contacts to identify a number's actual disposition. This procedure yielded 500 completed and 16 partially completed interviews. Of these, 5 completed interviews were eliminated from the study because the respondents' self-reported zip code fell outside of Philadelphia.

Overall, the survey cooperation rate, which is the total number of completed calls minus the refusals, was 40.2%. The response rate may be due to the data being collected during the heaviest shopping time of the year—November through December. To ensure that the results from the CRP survey were not biased toward any single demographic group or region, the results were checked against the known occurrences of the demographic distribution of Philadelphia's population. Census data were the most accurate and reliable for verifying survey results (U.S. Census Bureau, 2005). Weighting was used so that the sample's demographic profile accurately reflected the population's known properties. The descriptive findings from the research are presented in the next section.

Measures

The measures for this study included demographic characteristics and perceptions of negative emotions that potentially arose due to perceptions of CRP. The demographic characteristics (gender, race, income, and age) were recorded for the residents. Gender was coded as 1 for male and 2 for female. In addition, race was coded so that non-African Americans were 0 and African Americans were 1. Income was coded using nine categories that begin with less than $10,000 and end with more than $150,000. Age was coded as follows: 1 = 18–24, 2 = 25–34, 3 = 35–44, 4 = 45–54, 5 = 55–64, 6 = 65–74, and 7 = 75 years and older.

Negative emotions due to CRP were captured using seven measures (see Table 1 for a complete list of the measures and descriptive statistics). These measures asked the respondents about the emotions attached to their perceptions of the CRP incident. Therefore, our measure of negative emotion assumes that the individual believes that a CRP incident has occurred. The respondents indicated their perceptions using a 4-point Likert-type scale that ranged from 1 (*strongly disagree*) to 4 (*strongly agree*). This means that the scale had a range of 7 to 28. Higher scores on the items indicated more negative emotions.

Table 1. Descriptive Statistics

Measure	Mean	Standard Deviation	Minimum	Maximum
Age	4	2	1	7
Gender	1.64 (i.e., female)	0.48	1	2
Income	40,001 to 60,000	Less than 10,000 to 100,001 to 125,000	Less than 10,000 per year	More than 150,000 per year
Whites	.49	.50	0	1
Blacks	.50	.50	0	1

Analysis

The analysis took place in three steps. Step 1 provided the descriptive statistics for the sample based on the demographics used in this study. Step 2 examined the psychometric properties of the items that made up the negative emotions measure. This examination took place using structural equation modeling (SEM). SEM is a process that examines the hypothetical pathways of a measure. This examination determines the convergent and discriminant validity of a set of items that are hypothesized to make up a measure. Step 3 utilized a MIMIC model that examined the influence of the demographic measures on the negative emotion measure. Step 4 presented the results from simulation models in order to further investigate the stability and tenability of the results. That is, the simulation model was used to test the model for statistical power and bias in estimates (i.e., slope estimates and standard error estimates). In our view, if the model has proper levels of statistical power without biased estimates, then the model has the proper stability, and confidence in the model has been found.

RESULTS

Step 1

The first step provides the descriptive statistics for the sample based on the demographics used in this study. Table 1 presents the demographics, including the individual's age, gender, income, and race. The average respondent for this sample is between the ages of 45 to 54 years. Thirty-five percent of the sample is male. The average income of the sample is between $40,001 and $60,000 per year. Forty-three percent of the sample is White, 45% of the sample is Black, and the remaining individuals are of other races.

Step 2

The second step is to present the results of a SEM to better understand how the items making up negative emotions as a result of the perceptions of CRP come together. A measurement model (a specific form of SEM) is used to arrive at these results. A measurement model allows for the development of factor loadings that can demonstrate proper levels of convergent and discriminant validity. In particular, convergent validity has been found when the measures demonstrate proper fit (see Gibbs, Giever, & Higgins, 2003, for the standards and description of fit indexes), and discriminant validity has been found when the factor loadings are reasonably large. The measurement model for this analysis is derived from the correlation matrix (available from the first author by request).

Table 2 shows the measurement model. The first piece of information to be understood for the measurement model is the fit of the model to the data. The chi-square statistic is statistically significant. This indicates that the model does not fit the data properly (Kline, 2005). Two problems exist in using the chi-square as the sole measure of model fit. First, the chi-square statistic may not be able to be interpreted by researchers. That is, the lower bound of the chi-square statistic is always zero and the upper bound is limitless, reducing the ability of researchers to use standardized means of interpretation (Kline, 2005). Second, the chi-square statistic is sensitive to sample size. This is important because large sample sizes—like those used in the present study—are necessary to interpret chi-square as a significance test. However, the large samples allow chi-square to find statistical significance between the observed model and the hypothesized model even if the covariances have slight differences (Hu & Bentler, 1999). Thus, consulting additional fit indexes that are not sensitive to sample size are necessary to understand model fit. In particular, the confirmatory fit index (CFI) is .99, the root mean square error of approximation (RMSEA) is .08, and the standardized root mean square residual (SRMR) is .01, all indicating that the model is a good fit to the data. Therefore, convergent validity has been found. In addition, all of the factor loadings are well above Kline's (2005) standard of .50 for reasonably large factor loadings, indicating that discriminant validity has been found.

These results also indicate support for our expectation that negative emotions arise due to the perceptions of CRP. Negative emotions are a by-product of the perceptions of CRP and are at a high-level mean of 19. Therefore, these

Table 2. Measurement Model[a]

Item[b]	Mean	Standard Deviation	Minimum	Maximum	Standard-ized Factor Loading
The CRP incident was stressful.	2.75	0.85	1	4	.95*
The CRP incident made me angry.	3.31	0.73	1	4	.96*
I was shocked when I realized I was a victim of CRP.	2.57	1.05	1	4	.90*
The CRP incident made me sad.	2.64	0.93	1	4	.94*
The CRP incident embarrassed me.	2.70	0.97	1	4	.95*
My self-worth was negatively affected as a result of the CRP incident.	2.11	0.94	1	4	.89*
The incident had a negative impact on me.	2.78	0.92	1	4	.94*

a. Model fit measures: χ^2 = 84.03, p= .00; comparative fit index = .99; root mean square error of approximation = .08; standardized root mean square residual = .01.
b. Coding for these measures: 1 = strongly disagree, 2 = disagree, 3 = agree, 4 = strongly agree.
*p = .05.

findings lead us to believe that the perception of CRP is a strain that leads to a negative emotion, supportive of Agnew's (1992, 2001, 2006) version of strain theory. However, the factors of the individuals likely to develop these negative emotions are important.

Step 3

The third step is important for understanding the demographic differences in the negative emotions. Table 3 presents the MIMIC model. This model provides an opportunity to examine the individual characteristics (i.e., age, gender, race, and income) that may develop instances of negative emotions. However, these results begin with a review of the fit of this model to the data. As with the

Table 3. Structural Model of Covariates on Negative Emotions[a]

Covariate	Estimate
White	.43* (.16)
Black	.49* (.18)
Gender	.06 (.02)
Income	2.63* (.94)

a. Model fit measures: χ^2 = 125.90, p= .00; comparative fit index = .99; root mean square error of approximation = .07; standardized root mean square residual = .01.
*p = .05.

measurement model, the chi-square statistic is statistically significant, indicating a misfit between the model and the data. However, the CFI (.99), RMSEA (.07), and SRMR (.01) indicate that the model is a proper fit to the data.

Table 3 shows that all of the factors except gender have distinctive implications for negative emotions from the perceptions of CRP. However, some of the results seem contradictory.

For instance, Whites are likely (B = .155) to have a link with negative emotions, but being Black also has a link with negative emotions (B = .176). The largest connection between the demographic factors and negative effect comes from income (B = .939). Therefore, individuals who are likely to experience negative emotions from the perceptions of CRP have a profile that includes being Black and having higher incomes. These findings support implications drawn from Agnew's (1992, 2001, 2006) strain theory that racial and ethnic minorities and differential incomes are likely to have implications for strain and the development of negative emotions. However, we do not wish to overstate these results and thus seek additional information about the results.

Step 4

The fourth step is the development of simulation models to better understand the results. Specifically, Muthén and Muthén (2002) were clear that simulation models can be used to examine the statistical power and the possibility of Type I errors in results from studies. For instance, through simulation analysis we are able to determine if we have a large enough sample to arrive at these results and reduce the risk of a Type II error. Furthermore, by examining the slope estimates and the standard error estimates, we can determine whether a Type I error is possible in these results. If Type I or Type II errors are not found, Muthén and Muthén (2002) argue, then enough evidence is present to suggest that the results are replicable.

Following the work of Paternoster and Brame (2000), we developed our simulation using a normal distribution and 1,000 repetitions. That is, we had our statistical program develop 1,000 normal distributions and apply our final model in Step 3 for our examination. In this analysis, we found that we had adequate levels of statistical power. That is, our sample size was large enough to properly detect the desired effect. This means that we are not at risk of Type II error. Furthermore, we found that our slope estimates and our standard error estimates were not biased. This evidence suggests that Type I errors were not an issue in these data. Overall, these results suggest that our results are robust and replicable, using the same measures in different samples (a more detailed presentation of the simulation analysis can be obtained from the first author).

In summary, the results show that perception of CRP generates negative emotions. Furthermore, we show that these negative emotions resonate with Whites, Blacks, and those with higher incomes. Our simulation results indicate that we have adequate statistical power with little parameter (i.e., slope) and standard error biases.

DISCUSSION

The purpose of the present study was to examine whether perceptions of CRP generated negative emotions (e.g., "The CRP incident was stressful," "The CRP incident made me angry," "I was shocked when I realized I was a victim of CRP," and "The CRP incident made me sad"). Perception of CRP is an important area of study in the racial profiling arena. Although understudied, CRP should become a more germane topic in criminology and criminal justice research. Furthermore, less is known as to whether negative emotions arise due to this behavior. In addition, less is known about the perceptions of CRP and the demographic factors that have a connection with negative emotions. We cast these issues in the context of Agnew's general strain theory. In particular, Agnew's strain theory purports that negative events are stressors that develop negative emotions and energize individuals into action. Each issue will be discussed in turn below.

The first issue is to determine whether the perception of CRP generates negative emotions. Using SEM's version of a measurement model, we found that CRP does seem to generate negative emotions in our sample. Our results indicate a high level of negative emotions. This is consistent with Agnew's theory that perceptions of individual acts serve as strains that can generate negative emotions.

Given that this behavior is related to perceptions of discriminatory practices, the results are consistent with the research within the strain literature that examines the discriminatory practices. Thus, we have evidence to suggest that individuals who perceive that they have been victims of CRP are likely to develop negative emotions. Although not directly tested in the present study, we speculate that the development of some of these negative emotions is rather severe. Therefore, perceptions of CRP may have very important detrimental effects for society.

The second issue is the determination of the demographic factors that are connected to these negative emotions. Surprisingly, our results revealed that White individuals are likely to develop negative emotions due to perceptions of CRP. In a forthcoming article, the authors found that perceptions of CRP did occur among Whites (Gabbidon & Higgins, in press). This occurs because Whites may view themselves as not fitting the profile of a criminal. Thus, our results here are consistent with this literature. Furthermore, our results should generate more research to determine the extent that perceptions of CRP occur among Whites and what the outcomes of this behavior may entail. In addition, we found that Blacks were also likely to develop negative emotions due to CRP. The effect of CRP on Blacks was larger than the effects on Whites. This suggests that being Black and perceiving CRP is more likely to result in a negative emotion. This is consistent with the literature from Agnew's strain theory, specifically the literature that examined discriminatory practices.

Of the demographics, income has the largest effect on whether an individual will experience a negative emotion. The individuals with greater incomes are more likely to experience a negative emotion. It is important to note that the research revealed that there were no differences by gender when it comes to developing this sort of negative emotion due to the perception of CRP. This is counter to the research on Agnew's strain theory, which suggests that males and females would experience strain and negative emotions differently. We believe that the lack of gender differences occurs because males and females view profiling the same way.

This study does have limitations. First, the results are confined to a cross-sectional sample. This is not a major issue, given that we are exploring a relatively new area of study. Second, we did not include a measure of education because it was shown to be multicollinear with our measure of income. That is, in additional analyses not presented here but available by request from the lead author, income and education in this sample were highly correlated and multicollinear. Therefore, we chose to use the income measure in the present study to be consistent with previous CRP research (Gabbidon & Higgins, 2007). Third, our results come from one location. This is an exploratory study that provides future researchers with instruction for developing a more in-depth understanding. Therefore, we believe that one location is important for these exploratory purposes. Fourth, the measurement of negative emotions was combined with CRP, reducing the opportunity to examine a causal logic between the two issues. The combined measures reduced the explanation beyond our constructs. However, we believe that this allows us to understand how the perceptions of CRP work in developing negative emotions. These would be proper areas for future research.

Despite the limits, the present study provides evidence that race and income are important areas that have implications for the development of negative emotions. In particular, those who have higher incomes and are Black are more likely to experience negative emotions due to the perceptions of CRP. Future studies should reexamine these results using longitudinal data from multiple locations and cleaner measures of negative emotions. For now, the present study supports the premise that CRP has the ability to develop negative emotions and that race and income are relevant in this area.

Note

1. Consumer racial profiling (CRP) could not be substantiated in the present study because the negative emotion items captured the *perception* of CRP, based on an incident the participant had experienced (e.g., being followed by a store employee).

[...]

References

Adamson, J. (2000). *The Denny's story: How a company in crisis resurrected its good name and reputation.* New York: John Wiley.

Agnew, R. (1992). Foundation for a general strain theory of crime and delinquency. *Criminology, 30,* 47–87.

Agnew, R. (2001). Building on the foundation of general strain theory: Specifying the types of strain most likely to lead to crime and delinquency. *Journal of Research in Crime and Delinquency, 38,* 319–361.

Agnew, R. (2006). *Pressured into crime: An overview of general strain theory.* Los Angeles, CA: Roxbury Press.

Alison, L., Bennell, C., Mokros, A., & Ormerod, D. (2002). The personality paradox in offender profiling: A theoretical review of the processes involved in deriving background characteristics from crime scene actions. *Psychology, Public Policy, and Law, 8,* 115–135.

Alison, L., Smith, M. D., & Morgan, K. (2003). Interpreting the accuracy of offender profiles. *Psychology, Crime & Law, 9,* 185–195.

Anderson, E. (1999). *Code of the street: Decency, violence, and the moral life of the inner city.* New York: W. W. Norton.

Asquith, J. L., & Bristow, D. N. (2000). To catch a thief: A pedagogical study of retail shoplifting. *Journal of Education for Business, 75,* 271–276.

Baron, S. (2004). General strain, street youth and crime: A test of Agnew's revised theory. *Criminology, 42*, 457–483.

Broidy, L. M. (2001). A test of general strain theory. *Criminology, 39*, 9–33.

Crockett, D., Grier, S. A., & Williams, J. A. (2003). Coping with marketplace discrimination: An exploration of the experiences of Black men. *Academy of Marketing Science Review, 7*. Available at http://www.amsreview.org/articles/crockett04-2003.pdf

Dabney, D. A., Dugan, L., Topalli, V., & Hollinger, R. C. (2006). The impact of implicit stereotyping on offender profiling: Unexpected results from an observational study of shoplifting. *Criminal Justice and Behavior, 33*, 646–674.

Dabney, D. A., Hollinger, R. C., & Dugan, L. (2004). Who actually steals? A study of covertly observed shoplifters. *Justice Quarterly, 21*, 693–728.

Eitle, D. J. (2002). Exploring a source of deviance-producing strain for females: Perceived discrimination and general strain theory. *Journal of Criminal Justice, 30*, 429–442.

Eitle, D. J., & Turner, R. J. (2003). Stress exposure, race, and young adult male crime. *Sociological Quarterly, 44*, 243–269.

Feagin, J. R. (1991). The continuing significance of race: Antidiscrimination in public places. *American Sociological Review, 56*, 101–116.

Fifield, A. (2001). Shopping while Black. *Good Housekeeping, 233*, 129–136.

Gabbidon, S. L. (2003). Racial profiling by store clerks and security personnel in retail establishments: An exploration of "Shopping while Black." *Journal of Contemporary Criminal Justice, 19*, 345–364.

Gabbidon, S. L., & Higgins, G. E. (2007). Consumer racial profiling and perceived victimization: A phone survey of Philadelphia area residents. *American Journal of Criminal Justice, 32*, 1–11.

Gabbidon, S. L., & Higgins, G. E. (in press). Profiling White Americans: An exploration of "Shopping while White." In M. J. Lynch, E. Britt Patterson, & K. Childs (Eds.), *Racial divide: Racial and ethnic bias in the criminal justice system*. Monsey, NY: Criminal Justice Press.

Gaines, L. K. (2006). An analysis of traffic stop data in Riverside, California. *Police Quarterly, 9*, 210–233.

Gibbs, J. J., Giever, D., & Higgins, G. E. (2003). A test of Gottfredson and Hirschi's general theory using structural equation modeling. *Criminal Justice and Behavior, 30*, 441–458.

Grogger, J., & Ridgeway, G. (2006). Testing for racial profiling in traffic stops from behind a veil of darkness. *Journal of the American Statistical Association, 101*, 878–887.

Harris, A. G. (2003). Shopping while Black: Applying 42 U.S.C. § 1981 to cases of consumer racial profiling. *Boston College Third World Law Journal, 23*, 1–56.

Harris, A. G., Henderson, G. R., & Williams, J. D. (2005). Courting customers: Assessing consumer racial profiling and other marketplace discrimination. *Journal of Public Policy & Marketing, 24*, 163–171.

Harris, D. A. (1999). *Driving while Black: Racial profiling on our nation's highways*. Retrieved January 23, 2001, from http://www.aclu.org/profiling/report/index/html

Harris, D. A. (2002). *Profiles in injustice: Why racial profiling cannot work*. New York: New Press.

Hay, C. (2003). Family strain, gender, and delinquency. *Sociological Perspectives, 46*, 107–135.

Hay, C., & Evans, M. M. (2006). Violent victimization and involvement in delinquency: Examining predictions from general strain theory. *Journal of Criminal Justice, 34*, 261–274.

Henderson, T. P. (2001). Perception that some merchants practice racial profiling generates debate. *Stores, 83*. Retrieved June 2001 from http://stores.org/archives/junoredit.asap

Holmes, R. M., & Holmes, S. T. (2002). *Profiling violent crimes: An investigative tool*. Thousand Oaks, CA: Sage.

Hu, L. T., & Bentler, P. M. (1999). Cutoff criteria for fit indexes in covariance structural analysis: Conventional criteria versus new alternatives. *Structural Equation Modeling, 6*, 1–55.

Kline, R. B. (2005). *Principles and practices of structural equation modeling* (2nd ed.). New York: Guilford Press.

Lange, J. E., Johnson, M. B., & Voas, R. B. (2005). Testing the racial profiling hypothesis for seemingly disparate traffic stops on the New Jersey Turnpike. *Justice Quarterly, 22,* 193–223.

Lee, J. (2000). The salience of race in everyday life: Black customers' shopping experiences in Black and White neighborhoods. *Work and Occupations, 27,* 353–376.

Mazerolle, P., Piquero, A. R., & Capowich, G. E. (2003). Examining the links between strain, situational and dispositional anger, and crime: Further specifying and testing general strain theory. *Youth & Society, 35,* 131–157.

Meeks, K. (1999). *Driving while Black.* New York: Broadway Books.

Muthén, L. K., & Muthén, B. O. (2002). How to use a Monte Carlo study to decide on sample size and determine power. *Structural Equation Modeling, 9,* 599–620.

Onwudiwe, I. D. (2005). Defining terrorism, racial profiling and the demonization of Arabs and Muslims in the USA. *Community Safety Journal, 4,* 4–11.

Paternoster, R., & Brame, R. (2000). On the association among self-control, crime, and analogous behaviors. *Criminology, 38,* 971–982.

Piquero, N. L., & Sealock, M. D. (2004). Gender and general strain theory: A preliminary test of Broidy and Agnew's/GST hypotheses. *Justice Quarterly, 21,* 125–158.

Preston, P. (2006). Marijuana use as a coping response to psychological strain: Racial, ethnic, and gender differences among young adults. *Deviant Behavior, 27,* 397–421.

Ramirez, O., McDevitt, J., & Farrell, A. (2000). *A resource guide on racial profiling data collection systems: Promising practices and lessons learned.* Washington, DC: Department of Justice.

Reitzel, J., & Piquero, A. R. (2006). Does it exist? Studying citizens' attitudes of racial profiling. *Police Quarterly, 9,* 161–183.

Rice, S. K., Reitzel, J. D., & Piquero, A. R. (2005). Shades of brown: Perception of racial profiling and the intra-ethnic differential. *Journal of Ethnicity in Criminal Justice, 3,* 47–70.

Ruiz, J. R., & Woessner, M. (2006). Profiling, Cajun style: Racial profiling and demographic profiling in Louisiana's war on drugs. *International Journal of Police Science & Management, 8,* 176–197.

Russell, K. K. (1999). "Driving while Black": Corollary phenomena and collateral consequences. *Boston College Law Review, 40,* 717–731.

Schafer, J. A., Carter, D. L., Katz-Bannister, A., & Wells, W. M. (2006). Decision making in traffic stop encounters: A multivariate analysis of police behavior. *Police Quarterly, 9,* 184–209.

Sharp, S. F., Brewster, D., & Love, S. R. (2005). Disentangling strain, personal attributes, affective response and deviance: A gendered analysis. *Deviant Behavior, 26,* 133–157.

Smith, E. L., & Durose, M. R. (2006). *Characteristics of drivers stopped by the police, 2002.* Washington, DC: Bureau of Justice Statistics.

Smith, M. R., & Alpert, G. P. (2002). Searching for direction: Courts, social science, and the adjudication of racial profiling claims. *Justice Quarterly, 19,* 673–703.

Snook, B., Eastwood, J., Gendreau, P., Goggin, C., & Cullen, R. M. (2007). Taking stock of criminal profiling: A narrative review and meta-analysis. *Criminal Justice and Behavior, 34,* 437–453.

U.S. Census Bureau. (2005). *Detailed county population estimates. Data provided by Pennsylvania State Data Center.* Washington, DC: Author.

Walls, M. L., Chapple, C. L., & Johnson, K. D. (2007). Strain, emotion, and suicide among American Indian youth. *Deviant Behavior, 28,* 219–246.

Weitzer, R., & Tuch, S. A. (2002). Perceptions of racial profiling: Race, class, and personal experience. *Criminology, 40,* 435–456.

Weitzer, R., & Tuch, S. A. (2005). Racially biased policing: Determinants of citizen perceptions. *Social Forces, 83,* 1009–1030.

Williams, J. D., Harris, A. M., & Henderson, G. R. (2001). Consumer racial profiling: Bigotry goes to market. *New Crisis*, 108, 22–24.

Williams, J. D., Harris, A. M., & Henderson, G. R. (2006, January). Equal treatment for equal dollars in Illinois: Assessing consumer racial profiling and other marketplace discrimination. *Law Enforcement Executive Forum*, 83–104.

Withrow, B. L. (2006). *Racial profiling: From rhetoric to reason.* Upper Saddle River, NJ: Prentice Hall.

*George E. Higgins is a professor in the Department of Justice Administration at the University of Louisville. His most recent publications appear or are forthcoming in the *Journal of Criminal Justice, Deviant Behavior, Criminal Justice and Behavior, Youth and Society*, and the *American Journal of Criminal Justice*.

Shaun L. Gabbidon is Distinguished Professor of Criminal Justice in the School of Public Affairs at Penn State, Harrisburg. His most recent books include *Race and Crime* (3rd edition; 2012, SAGE) and the co-authored book, *A Theory of African American Offending* (2011; Routledge). He is the coauthor of the recently published book, *A Theory of African American Offending: Race, Racism, and Crime* (Routledge, 2011). He currently serves as the founding editor of the SAGE journal *Race and Justice: An International Journal*.

Disputed Definitions and Fluid Identities: The Limitations of Social Profiling in Relation to Ethnic Youth Gangs

by Rob White*

INTRODUCTION

This article draws upon a national study of youth gangs in Australia in order to illustrate the limitations of risk analysis and social profiling. Specifically, the paper argues that, based on available information about youth group formations and group behaviour, youth gang intervention premised upon particular gang identifiers can in effect create the very problem allegedly being addressed. That is, the intervention itself can serve to consolidate and concretize gang formation and gang identity. This is especially so if accompanied by aggressive forms of policing and street regulation.

A major reason why 'gangs' as such cannot be easily profiled is because of the complexities of social belonging and social identity pertaining to how young people live their lives. The notion of 'fluid identities' refers to the fact that young people have multiple identifications, and can be simultaneously gang members and non-gang members. This means that if the latter become part of the 'profile', then 'innocent' young people are wrongly identified as being members of gangs. It is the multilayered nature and dynamics of youth associations and affiliations that make a gang-targeting exercise difficult and problematic.

Alternatively, it needs to be reiterated that gang identity is fluid; that identity, and action based upon identity, depends upon specific context, and that identity counts in terms of prevalence and types of violence. These are important aspects of social belonging and social action insofar as each is very much shaped by 'external' factors such as media images and law enforcement interventions. The impact of these factors is especially powerful in relation to so called 'ethnic youth gangs', that is, groups of (generally) young men who are identified as deviant on the basis of ethnic affiliation as much as specific criminal activities. Moreover, if 'gangs' are seen as the central problem, a focus that is reinforced by particular kinds of social profiling, then less attention tends to be provided to other crucial issues such as youth violence. Indeed, one could well argue that it is youth violence, across different kinds of youth group formations, including gangs, that poses the greatest challenges vis-a-vis safe streets and peaceful communities.

The paper is divided into three interrelated elements. The first part explores issues surrounding social belonging and social identity. This section draws upon a recent national study of youth gangs in Australia (see for example, White, 2006, 2007a, 2007b). The next section briefly describes nine key propositions about the nature of gangs, gang membership, gang activity and gangs as a 'problem'. It illustrates the complexities and disputed definitions associated with empirical research into gangs as a social phenomenon. The final section examines how risk analysis, as a form of social research, gets translated into specific kinds of social profiling when applied to subjects such as gangs. The article concludes with some observations regarding the implications of profiling for anti-gang strategies.

The issue of youth gangs has come to the fore in many jurisdictions worldwide, and the question of how best to respond to gang activities has generated considerable attention from academics, policy makers and law enforcement services in recent years (see for example, Klein et al., 2001; Short and Hughes, 2006). The often central place of 'race' and ethnicity in gang members' identities, a phenomenon apparent in many different national contexts, has also been acknowledged (see, for example, Hagedorn, 2007; van Gemert et al., 2008). While this article is principally based upon Australian research, the subject matter finds wider application in the similar social processes, policy responses and law enforcement practices evident across many industrialized countries. The issues and problems identified below, therefore, are not unique; nor should they be unfamiliar to those engaged with youth justice systems in many different national and regional contexts.

SOCIAL BELONGING AND SOCIAL IDENTITY

To understand gang formation and gang activities, we first need to appreciate the nature of group dynamics. Gang members are simultaneously members of particular gangs and of diverse social groups, and there is overlap between the two. How different groups relate to each other has implications for how gangs are formed, the nature of gang membership and the kinds of violence associated with different gangs. Group membership hinges upon shared ethnicity, language and culture. It also very much depends upon locale, age and activities. In part, this simply reflects family connections and basic commonalities such as 'speaking the same language'—both literally, and figuratively vis-a-vis religion, origins, and shared understandings of manners, honour and relationships.

How best to categorize people and experiences in ways that provide accurate and sensitive portrayals of social life, is part of an ongoing conundrum for social research. This is especially evident in research and scholarship addressing phenomena such as youth gangs. Several recent edited volumes (see Short and Hughes, 2006; Hagedorn, 2007; van Gemert et al., 2008), for instance, have each in their own way affirmed the complicated intersections between the ongoing projects of the 'self' (constructions of personal identity), the importance of specific local contexts (material resources and social histories), and wider global social, economic and cultural processes (globalization) as these pertain to youth gangs. Group formations such as gangs are located in particular spaces at particular times, and they engage in particular kinds of activities. The collective and the personal—in terms of identities and well-being—are fused in the praxis of group formation and group dynamics.

Furthermore, research has demonstrated that the complexities of social life frequently pivot around the lynchpin of ethnicity, and that ethnic identification, too, is dynamic, historical and multidimensional as is evidenced in the research being considered here. As part of a national youth gangs study, interviews with up to 50 young people in each capital city of Australia including Canberra were arranged (White, 2006). The main subjects of the study were young people who claimed to be, or who were identified by local youth and community workers as being, members of youth gangs. In other words, the sample was entirely contingent upon the selection of local groups that were identified as gangs, not on ethnicity as such. However, in virtually every location around the country, ethnicity turned out to be central as to which groups were deemed to be 'gangs' and who were in turn seen as gang members. Ethnicity was also central to relationships at the local level between the gang members and other 'non-gang' youth. Social being—which encapsulates consciousness of self and the ways in which one negotiates everyday life—is thus very much intertwined with ethnic background, as well as class and gender.

Diverse social factors and networks bring young men and women together. In the Australian gang research, it was observed that ethnicity (a distinct cultural identity) often forms the core of social relationships, but then intersects with variables such as geography (specific locality), age (mainly teenagers, but up to mid-twenties), size (sheer number of people who congregate at any point in time), affiliation (with people from similar cultural backgrounds) and familiarity (of one's immediate neighbours, peers and acquaintances).

As part of the national study, 50 young people in the Bankstown area of Sydney were interviewed. Findings derived from these interviews will be briefly discussed in order to illustrate how these young people relate to each other (see White, 2008 for more detailed elaboration). Three main groups of young people were interviewed: Lebanese (Australians), Samoan (Australians), and Vietnamese (Australians). The sample also included a small number of migrant youth from

Figure 1. Connecting to and as a group

Affiliations [connection through given circumstances]	Attractors [connection through choice/preference]
Local area	Group activity
School	Size of group
Ethnic communities	Criminality
Religion	Violence
Class background	Music
Male bonding	Drugs
Friends	Acquaintances
Family	Masculine display

Fiji and Jamaica. Five young women were interviewed as part of the sample. The stories of each main group provided interesting insights into gang formation, group identity, ethnicity and violence (see White, 2008).

As indicated in Figure 1, there were a variety of connections between the young people beyond that of ethnicity as such. *Affiliations* are based upon certain given shared circumstances, which tend to be outside of the young person's immediate control, that bring people together. Social connection is also related to *attractors*, based upon choice and preferences (in relation to music and sport for example), that likewise facilitate shared activity among individuals.

While the primary group connection is to one's specific ethnic group, other connections are also very significant. Some of these are based upon activities, some on simple geography. For example, the Samoan and Lebanese Australian young people generally shared an interest in rap music. Rapping together was OK, and was one activity that was generally inclusive of people regardless of ethnic background.

Living in the same area also was meaningful, even if the young people did not hang around together in the same groups. Many of the youths commented on the 'bad' reputation of the area, yet most were proud to live there and wished to remain there in the future. Identity was in fact often constructed both in terms of ethnicity and in terms of locality. Living in an area of relative economic disadvantage and high levels of unemployment also meant that group membership has specific class dimensions that cut across ethnic belonging. Distinctions were drawn between 'the rich' who were privileged, and those young people who were perceived to be more resilient and stronger because they had to do things the hard way.

Social difference and social belonging was not only constructed in terms of material advantage, however. There were fairly strong antagonisms expressed by the Lebanese and Samoan young people against 'Asian' young people. Each group tended to have particular 'enemies' and potential allies. In some cases these were one and the same. For example, generally speaking, the Vietnamese did not particularly like the Chinese. Yet, on occasion, for example at school, the two groups would get along. The category 'Islanders' includes a wide array of nationalities, yet most of the Samoans interviewed were very antagonistic toward the Tongan young people. This was reflected in gang talk and gang gear—the Bloods [Samoans] wear red, the Crips [Tongans] wear blue, and other Islanders (such as a Fijian young man in the sample) were caught in-between conflicting loyalties.

Specific activities were associated with specific types of group formation. For example, fighting was definitely associated with masculinity. However, hanging out, rapping and music-making allowed for the inclusion of young women. Criminal acts such as armed robbery and assaults, as well as group fights, were pretty much the domain of the young men. Masculinity was very much constructed in terms of 'toughness' and aggressive physicality. It also included notions of loyalty to the group and to each other, to courage and fearlessness, and to mutual protection.

Group membership and friendship networks involve many different points of belonging and connection, which vary according to circumstances and activities. Many of the young people who were interviewed had friends from other ethnic backgrounds. They were all familiar with the other groups who lived in their neighbourhood. Different groups would collaborate or have alliances with each other, particularly the Samoan and Lebanese groups, depending upon what was happening in the neighbourhood at the time. They might share in drug taking (smoking cannabis), in music making (rapping together) or even fighting (combining against a third force). In some instances, the neighbourhood connection was stronger than ethnic identity as such, as when 'outsiders' from a similar group (such as an outside Lebanese gang) entered into the shared geographical area in order to battle it out with local Lebanese youth.

In other cases, as with the Samoan young people, the local 'gangs' are part of larger ethnic networks and sub-groups, incorporating large geographical areas and relationships across distances. For example, there were connections across the city (different groups of 'Bloods' that sometimes had additional local names as well), as well as across the Tasman Sea (back to New Zealand, from where many families had migrated).

In the end, while group membership is exclusive, individual friendship is not. And groups can combine in varying ways to protect territory, reputation and specific individuals. Most of the young people who were interviewed had an active part in fighting and other kinds of 'anti-social behaviour'. Most could be labelled a 'gang member.' All of them said that, first and foremost, it was important to be part of their particular group—which in this case inevitably referred to specific ethnic-background youth formations.

Yet people make sense of their lives in complicated ways. We are all part of wider families and communities than simply those of our immediate friends and colleagues. Consider for example the position of gangs within local communities (White, 2007a):

- there are frequently close ties between gang members and other members of their community, whether through family, religious or cultural linkages.

- gang members do not simply and solely engage in criminal activities, but in a wide range of conventional activities that bring them in close contact with other people in the local community

- gang membership (however loosely defined) may be a continuous feature of some communities, and thus have a measure of traditional legitimacy attached to it.

- gang-related activity may in fact tap into underground or criminal economies that are on the whole beneficial to many ordinary residents in poorer working class neighbourhoods (in that they provide a source of income and purchasing power that allows money to circulate within community agencies and businesses).

- gang membership may be viewed by adult members of a community as an important way in which to protect each other, and to maintain a particular social identity important to the community as a whole (visible expression of ethnic pride and strength).

There are, then, connections between the social circumstances that give rise to gangs, and the community relations that sustain them. Just as these connections are situational and depend upon historical as well as contemporary factors, so too the life of each individual within a gang is multidimensional.

A key aspect to understanding gang formation, gang activity and gang membership is that of social identity. As revealed in the national Australian gangs study, and corroborated in work undertaken by other researchers in places such

---

Figure 2. Complexities of social identity

Identity is:

Chosen

I am who I say I am. People have some choice in how they wish to construct their own ethnicity and identity—as Australian, as hyphenated Australian, as German/Irish descent [agency in choosing identity].

Bestowed

I am who others say I am. Certain stereotypes and ethnic markers are used to construct ethnicity and identity for people—as 'Middle Eastern,' as ethnic gang member, as not-Australian [identities that entrench the sense of being Other].

Simultaneous

I am more than one identity at the same time. I can be Australian *and* Lebanese, Australian *and* Jewish, Australian *and* Spanish-speaking [bi-cultural and transnational identities].

Strategic

I am who I am depending upon the circumstances. I am Lebanese, Lebanese-Australian or Australian depending upon whether I am at home, with my friends, at school or overseas [hybrid identities].

Virtual

I am who I am as shaped by global telecommunications. I can support Manchester United Football club without ever going to England; I can be affected by worldwide portrayals of Muslims, Jews, and Hindus [virtual communities; communities considered through the lens of sameness rather than variation in beliefs, practices and attitudes].

---

as Sydney (see Collins et al., 2000; Poynting et al., 2004), identity is multilayered and complex. Some of this complexity is indicated in Figure 2.

All young people today are growing up in a world that is commonly influenced by phenomena such as globalization, neo-liberal political economy, war and consumerism. The specificity of personal being, however, is shaped not only by epochal and global features but by the mundane experiences of family, friends, neighbourhood, school and community (see White and Wyn, 2008). The global may shape the local, but it is on the streets and in the suburbs that the particularities of social life are constructed and made manifest.

Listening to the stories of the young people in the national study allowed a better appreciation of the temporal dimension of lived experience—the ways in which people and circumstances change over time. The limitations of conventional approaches to the problem of youth gangs, which tend to define people primarily and solely in terms of gang membership, also became apparent. Each of the young men in the case studies was a gang member, and yet much more than this. They were part of ethnic communities, of families, of school groups and of street scenes. Not all of their lives was spent in the 'gang'. Not all of their time was spent doing 'gang stuff'. Many of the young people, during the course of their interview, mentioned how scared they were of the violence, and of the possibility of not having their close friends around them. They are strong and vulnerable at the same time.

DISPUTED DEFINITIONS AND FLUID IDENTITIES

The lived realities of young people who identify with gangs are indeed complicated. It is not surprising then that researchers sometimes struggle with interpreting such complexity. This is partly due to the fact that gang research and the development of appropriate 'anti-gang' strategies are beset by persistent problems relating to definitional issues. They are also made more complex due to the ambiguities and paradoxes of youth group behaviour generally. The key issues surrounding analysis of gangs can be summarized in the form of a series of basic propositions. These are largely based on work undertaken as part of the national youth gangs study, that included an extensive international literature review (White, 2007a). Significant sources for this review included Miller (1992), Decker (1996), Howell (1998), Gordon (2000), Klein et al. (2001), Esbensen et al. (2001), Klein (2002), and Standing (2005), among other writers working in the area.

Proposition 1: US, Canadian, European, Australian and South African research has increasingly emphasized that gang formation is a *social process* involving complex forms of membership, transformation and disintegration.

Proposition 2: The composition of youth gangs is ever changing and there are large differences in how groups are structured, organized and defined (by different organizations, agencies and researchers). This makes 'gangs' as a descriptor even more *ambiguous* and difficult to comprehend.

Proposition 3: Gangs are primarily tangible expressions of *identity*, and identity itself is shaped by intermingling factors such as community recognition of the group as a gang, the group's recognition of itself as a distinct group, and the group's involvement in enough illegal activities to elicit a consistent negative response from law enforcement officials and local people.

Proposition 4: Just as there are problems in defining what a gang is, so too there are major difficulties in trying to establish who a gang member is, since *group membership is a fluid process* and specific individuals have varying degrees and types of association with the gang over time.

Proposition 5: Even where a gang can be said to exist, gang membership is not absolute or fixed, since *gang membership is highly variable and changing,* and there is often no clear dividing line between those who are in a gang and those who are not—there are layers of belonging and connection that vary according to circumstance and activities.

Proposition 6: Many young people who do not identify with gangs may nevertheless engage in gang-like behaviour, such as criminal activity, street fights, drug use and wearing of gang type clothing. *Gang-related behaviour is not the same as gang membership.* Nor do all gangs engage in the full range of gang-like behaviour.

Proposition 7: Not all gang behaviour is necessarily criminal, illegal or 'bad' since a lot of what young people do is simply to hang out together. *Much of the time the gang is not a problem* for nearby residents, for other young people or for themselves

Proposition 8: Where young people themselves claim gang membership, they tend to engage in substantially more anti-social and criminal behaviour than those who do not profess to be gang members. Thus *who young people say they are has implications for what they do and who they do it with.* Group identification is intertwined with group activity.

Proposition 9: Gang membership is heavily tied in with group violence. However, this violence is manifest within a wider *context of social marginalization and exclusion* based upon ethnicity. Antagonisms on the street—between groups of ethnic minority youth and authority figures such as the police, and between diverse groups of young people—are constantly reinforced by negative stereotyping, media-induced moral panics and the day-to-day racism experienced by such young people.

If formal responses to the gang phenomenon are to be appropriate, then it is imperative that they are informed by the above propositions. What should be avoided, however, are responses that ignore the difficulties, challenges and complexities posed by the same propositions in favour of intervention strategies underpinned by more simplistic (even if convenient) analytical models.

RISK ANALYSIS AND SOCIAL PROFILING

The conceptual perspective that is often used to frame 'youth' and youthful 'deviance,' including gang-related activity, is derived from developmental criminology and especially its narrower variant, the 'risk factor' paradigm (Farrington, 1994). This generally involves the 'charting-up' of specific risk and protective factors that are seen to influence how individuals negotiate particular transitions and pathways in their lives (see Developmental Crime Prevention Consortium, 1999). This paradigm has come to assume a prominent position in fields such as health, welfare, criminal justice and education. Multi-factoral analysis is statistically correlated with certain types of behaviour and certain types of people. The implication is that if particular combinations of factors appear deviancy (or pathology) will result.

This kind of forward-looking (actuarial) risk assessment is finding increasing favour in the juvenile justice field (Goldson and Muncie, 2006; Muncie and Goldson, 2006; Priday, 2006; MacDonald, 2006; Case, 2007). It is not simply being used as a diagnostic tool (to pinpoint a person's specific needs and deficits), but it is also being used in a prognostic manner (to determine which young people are most likely to offend). The construction of 'at risk' youth is thus achieved via the formulation of categories based on combinations of risk factors, and the accumulation of information about particular individuals. More generalized profiles are also constructed whereby all young people falling within a certain range of empirical indicators (age group, school record, type of family, previous criminal record) are conceptualized in accordance with the level and nature of 'risk' that they (presumably) pose now and into the future. It is a process of homogenization wherein all people with certain similarities are treated similarly.

By their very nature, these kinds of risk assessment tools fail to capture the historical dynamics of societies. The tools reinterpret certain characteristics as representing the failings of individuals. This is because they are constructed on the basis of individualized data, rather than analysis of, for example, how state policy affects particular groups. The structured formation of specific groups and individuals, as the outcome of inequality, discrimination and the absence of opportunity, is basically lost in such analysis (Cunneen and White, 2006).

Ethnicity is an important component in this process. For example, being an indigenous person is counted as a 'risk' factor in some assessment processes (Palmer and Collard, 1993; Palmer, 1999). When this occurs, one's heritage and community identity is degraded as a contributing factor to youth deviancy (Priday, 2006). From the point of view of gangs research, similar issues are especially apparent. Ethnicity and community ties are frequently construed as core elements of gang membership (as evident in moral panics about 'ethnic youth gangs'). Strong ethnic identification can thus be considered a 'risk factor' when it comes to group deviancy.

Analysis of youth trajectories based upon this kind of risk factor modelling is likely to forgo contextualized individual experience in favour of aggregated data analysis based on individual histories. The quantification of risk and protective factors through manipulation of aggregated data tends to reify positivistic and predictive explanations of deviancy. For example, the combination of poverty, 'poor' parenting, 'bad' schooling and unemployment (as measured on predetermined scales) might be said to equate to deviant behaviour (as defined in conventional criminal justice terms). Such calculations are then utilized to 'read back' into the life circumstances of certain individuals the probable trajectory that they follow. Interventions can then be activated on a pre-emptive basis, before the 'risk' has actually been realized in practice.

The identification of 'at risk' youth typically involves three steps: first, by defining specific indicators of the problem, second, by applying such indicators to identify a target group and, third, by implementing an intervention to bring the target group 'into line' with the 'mainstream'. This popular policy process overlooks the ways in which institutions and policy processes themselves contribute to social problems involving young people, and instead emphasizes the need to change and/or reform individuals. The paradoxical element of this process is that the 'at risk' come to be stigmatized, adding to their sense of difference and marginality (White and Wyn, 2008: 134). Moreover, the phenomenon of 'false positives' means that individual young people face the prospect of the negative consequences. Unwanted and unneeded intervention might be visited upon them solely due to their membership of a 'high risk' group rather than their own individual 'risk profile' or, moreover, any actual behaviour (Case, 2007). Such labelling confers a negative totalizing status on youths who are targeted through the linking of key categorical descriptions in particular ways (for example, Muslim, terrorist, gangs), a process that has been shown to play a vital part in the criminalization of particular ethnic minority youth (Poynting et al., 2004). In other words, the justification for intervention is based upon processes of categorization and labelling that define young people as deviant (even if expressed as 'at risk' rather than 'criminal' as such). This is essentially a question of social control.

When applied to 'gangs', risk analyses typically take the form of *social profiling*. This involves constructing a matrix of variables and matching individuals to the variables described in the gang matrix. Such processes tend to be descriptive and do little to provide a basis for understanding *why* and *how* specific groups of young people experience problems or find meaning in their lives. Moreover, while to some extent social characteristics and social background provide insight into probabilities of opportunity and life chances (based on historical experience and previous patterns), it is much more problematic to generalize from general trends down to individual experience. We know, for example, that there is a strong correlation between poverty and crime, yet all poor people do not become engaged in criminal activity; nor do all 'criminals' originate from poor backgrounds (White and Wyn, 2008: 159). The same applies to gang membership and gang activities.

Social profiling in the name of risk assessment assumes certain things about 'normality' and the inherent legitimacy of the status quo. In effect, it resorts to stereotypes. It is useful in this regard to compare and contrast two types of social profiling—one based upon actual criminal incidents, the other on predictive factors (see Figure 3).

The first type of profiling acts as a funnel, to sift individuals until a small number of suspects are identified against whom police can then proceed to take action. The second type of profiling, however, is geared to expanding the suspect terrain. As more variables are added to the list of key identifiers, the process tends to widen the scope of surveillance and intervention.

The second form of social profiling identified in Figure 3 is especially problematic from the point of view of gangs intervention. This is because there is

Figure 3. Two types of social profiling

Funnelling:	Net-widening:
Focus:	*Focus:*
Criminality	Gang association
Criminal Act	Group membership
—specific offence	—general behaviour
Process:	*Process:*
Reactive	Pre-emptive
—action after something has occurred	—action before anything has happened
Evidence:	*Evidence:*
Based on crime scene investigation and flowing outwards from there	Based on loose descriptors, stereotypes and local reputation
Movement from individual event/person to group of suspects, then back to particular matching profile	Movement from identification of group as a whole to inclusion of more and more selected individuals as having (at least some) attributes of the target group
Consequence:	*Consequence:*
Narrows the range and number of suspects around specific criminal cases, based on CSI findings	Increases the range of those potentially placed under surveillance and subject to possible intervention

often confusion between identification of a 'gang' and those who engage in 'gang-related behaviour'. This opens the door for extensive *net-widening* vis-a-vis social profiling. For example, in practical terms there is frequently a conflation of gangs and ethnicity. There is also often confusion surrounding the link between gang status and fighting. In this instance, groups of youths who engage in street fights may be perceived to be members of 'gangs.'

Increased surveillance and intervention, based upon association, and reinforced through social profiling, can lead to greater likelihood of the young people adopting a 'gang' identification and thus engagement in violent and/or criminal behaviour. For example, we know that self-identity shapes involvement in gang-related activity: young people tend to behave in accordance with who they say they are. If police and other authority figures intervene in ways that bolster a particular form of identity over other possible identities (ultimately, ethnic youth gang versus 'ordinary' member of the community), then there is a greater likelihood that group violence and anti-social behaviour will follow. In theoretical terms, the insights of labelling perspectives, and indeed of cultural criminology, point to the probable negative consequences of constructing social identities in this manner (White and Haines, 2008). These processes need not be deterministic, one-dimensional or reductionist (in the sense that labelling *must* unequivocally lead to certain types of behaviour); but, overall, they materially contribute to how young people behave, especially in group settings.

As illustrated in the first two sections of this article, group activity, social identity and gang formation are complex and multilayered social processes. Inappropriate intervention can thus generate the very behaviour it is meant to preclude, namely, the formation and intensification of gangs and gang activity.

CONCLUSION

This article has examined how ethnic minority youth form into groups, based on ethnicity and other factors, and how 'gangs' as an object of study and intervention remain highly ambiguous and amorphous. Interventions based upon totalizing discourses of deviance and totalizing statistical categorisations are also profoundly ideological. They entrench rather than challenge the structural nature of oppression and victimization that constitute the essential realities which many young people endure in their daily lives.

All of this is bound to have a major impact on the development of anti-gang strategies. For example, perceptions of criminality on the part of the police are an important ingredient in how community-police relations are constructed at the grassroots level (Collins et al., 2000). Social profiling that is heavily dependent upon racial and ethnic markers certainly can entrench negativity in these relations, particularly if it is linked to a crime control agenda rather than one where the emphasis is on social inclusion, access and equity (Gillies, 2004). Negative forms of social profiling involve police assumptions that some ethnic groups are more likely to commit crime than others, and to target such groups accordingly. Moreover, such profiling tends to be based upon officer interpretations of typical offender appearance and typical racial characterizations. In other words, there is great scope for police intervention to be based upon stereotyped and subjective assessment. Ethnicity, and criminality, is thus in the eye of the beholder.

Discussion of social belonging and social identity allows for insights that show the dynamics of social relationships as they are constructed in the crucible of everyday choices, negotiations and actions. Who we are is, and always has been, an evolving process. The contours of this process are structurally influenced by matters pertaining to class, gender and ethnicity—but the process itself is marked by ambiguity and paradox as much as by broad propensities and continuities.

For gangs and the question of how best to respond to gangs, this means focusing on the social conditions that give rise to gang formation, and developing responses that affect communities, not just individuals. Analyses based upon methodological individualism merely reproduce stereotypes and the notion that individuals choose to be 'bad' by virtue of who they are. Gangs are historical and social creations. They emerge out of definite social relations grounded in specific community processes, including the nature of policing. As acknowledged worldwide (White, 2007b; Hagedorn, 2007), including a recent study by the Royal Canadian Mounted Police in Canada (2007), this demands responses that are systemic and structural as well as tactical and immediate. In specific terms, this translates into policies and practices that enhance employment and educational opportunities, as well as adoption of community policing and restorative justice strategies.

Finally, it needs to be acknowledged that 'gangs' as such may not be the principal problem. Given their fluctuating nature and variable activities, the gang often acts as a forum for social belonging more than a criminal organization per se. Nevertheless, what gang research demonstrates is that youth violence, particularly violence associated with young men in groups, is a dramatic and worrisome phenomenon (White and Mason, 2006). Violence prevention is not the same as gang prevention, however. It is vital, therefore, that we understand the difference between the two, and how and why the difference counts at the level of direct service provision and youth intervention.

REFERENCES

Case, S. (2007) 'Questioning the "Evidence" of Risk that Underpins Evidence-led Youth Justice Interventions,' *Youth Justice: An International Journal*, 7(2): 91–106.

Collins, J., Noble, G., Poynting, S. and Tabar, P. (2000). *Kebabs, Kids, Cops and Crime: Youth, Ethnicity and Crime*. Sydney: Pluto Press.

Cunneen, C. and White, R. (2006) 'Australia: Control, Containment or Empowerment?', in J. Muncie and B. Goldson (eds) *Comparative Youth Justice*. London: SAGE.

Decker, S.H. (1996) 'Collective and Normative Features of Gang Violence,' *Justice Quarterly*, 13(2): 243–64.

Developmental Crime Prevention Consortium (1999) *Pathways to Prevention: Developmental and Early Intervention Approaches to Crime in Australia*. Canberra: National Crime Prevention, Attorney General's Department.

Esbensen, F.-A., Winfree, Jr., L., He, N. and Taylor, T. (2001). Youth Gangs and Definitional Issues: When Is a Gang a Gang, and Why Does It Matter? *Crime and Delinquency*, 47(1), 105–30.

Farrington, D. (1994) 'Early Developmental Prevention of Juvenile Delinquency,' *Criminal Behaviour and Mental Health*, 4(3): 209–27.

Gillies, R. (2004) 'Identifying Ethnicity in Police Data Sets,' Conference Paper, Crime in Australia: International Connections [held at Hilton on the Park, Melbourne]. Canberra: Australian Institute of Criminology.

Goldson, B. and Muncie, J. (eds) (2006) *Youth Crime and Justice*. London: SAGE.

Gordon, R. (2000) 'Criminal Business Organizations, Street Gangs and 'Wanna-be' Groups: A Vancouver Perspective,' *Canadian Journal of Criminology*, January: 39–60.

Hagedorn, J. (ed.) (2007) *Gangs in the Global City: Alternatives to Traditional Criminology*. Urbana and Chicago: University of Illinois Press.

Howell, J.C. (1998) *Youth Gangs: An Overview*, Bulletin. Washington DC: US Department of Justice, Office of Justice Programs, Office of Juvenile Justice and Delinquency Prevention.

Klein, M.W. (2002) 'Street Gangs: A Cross-National Perspective,' in R. Huff (ed.), *Gangs in America*, 3rd Edition. Thousand Oaks, California: SAGE.

Klein, M., Kerner, H-K, Maxon, C. and Weitekamp, E. (eds) (2001) *The Eurogang Paradox: Street Gangs and Youth Groups in the US and Europe*. Dordrecht: Kluwer Academic Publishers.

MacDonald, R. (2006) 'Social Exclusion, Youth Transitions and Criminal Careers: Five Critical Reflections on "Risk,"' *Australian and New Zealand Journal of Criminology*, 39(3): 371–83.

Miller, W.B. (1992) *Crime by Youth Gangs and Groups in the United States*. Washington, DC: US Department of Justice, Office of Justice Programs, Office of Juvenile Justice and Delinquency Prevention.

Muncie, J. and Goldson, B. (eds) (2006) *Comparative Youth Justice*. London: SAGE.

Palmer, D. (1999) 'Talking about the Problems of Young Nyungars,' in R. White (ed.) *Australian Youth Subcultures: On the Margins and In the Mainstream*. Hobart: Australian Clearinghouse for Youth Studies.

Palmer, D. and Collard, L. (1993) 'Aboriginal Young People and Youth Subcultures,' in R. White (ed.) *Youth Subcultures: Theory, History and the Australian Experience*. Hobart: National Clearinghouse for Youth Studies.

Poynting, S., Noble, G., Tabar, P. and Collins, J. (2004) *Bin Laden in the Suburbs: Criminalising the Arab Other*. Sydney: Sydney Institute of Criminology.

Priday, E. (2006) 'New Directions in Juvenile Justice: Risk and Cognitive Behaviourism,' *Current Issues in Criminal Justice*, 17(3): 343–59.

Royal Canadian Mounted Police [RCMP] (2007) *Gang Prevention and Intervention Strategies.* Ottawa: RCMP.

Short, J. and Hughes, L. (eds), *Studying Youth Gangs.* Walnut Creek, CA: AltaMira Press.

Standing, A. (2005) *The Threat of Gangs and Anti-Gangs Policy,* ISS Occasional Paper 116. South Africa: Institute for Security Studies.

van Gemert, F., Peterson, D. and Lien, I-L. (eds) (2008) *Youth Gangs, Migration, and Ethnicity.* Devon: Willan Publishing.

White, R. (2006) 'Youth Gang Research in Australia,' in J. Short and L. Hughes (eds), *Studying Youth Gangs.* Walnut Creek, CA: AltaMira Press.

White, R. (2007a) *Youth Gangs, Violence and Anti-Social Behaviour.* Perth: Australian Research Alliance for Children and Youth. [available on-line at http://www.aracy.org.au/AM/Template .cfm?Section=Evidence_into_Action_Topical_Papers].

White, R. (2007b) *Anti-Gang Strategies and Interventions.* Perth: Australian Research Alliance for Children and Youth [available on-line at http://www.aracy.org.au/AM/Template .cfm?Section=Evidence_into_Action_Topical_Papers].

White, R. (2008) 'Australian Youth Gangs and the Social Dynamics of Ethnicity,' in F. van Gemert, D. Peterson and I-L Lien (eds) *Youth Gangs, Migration, and Ethnicity.* Devon: Willan Publishing.

White, R. and Haines, F. (2008) *Crime and Criminology: An Introduction,* 4th Edition. Melbourne: Oxford University Press.

White, R. and Mason, R. (2006) 'Youth Gangs and Youth Violence: Charting the Key Dimensions,' *Australian and New Zealand Journal of Criminology,* 39(1): 54–70.

White, R. and Wyn, J. (2008) *Youth and Society: Exploring the Social Dynamics of Youth Experience,* 2nd Edition. Melbourne: Oxford University Press.

*****Rob White** is professor of sociology at the School of Sociology and Social Work, University of Tasmania, Australia.

Racial, Ethnic, and Gender Differences in Perceptions of the Police: The Salience of Officer Race Within the Context of Racial Profiling

by Joshua C. Cochran and Patricia Y. Warren*

Criminological research has long explored the salience of race and ethnicity in understanding citizens' evaluations of the police (Black & Reiss, 1970; Brunson, 2007; Hurst, Frank, & Browning, 2000; Weitzer & Tuch, 1999, 2006). This growing body of research has demonstrated that Black and Hispanic citizens hold lower levels of trust and confidence in the police than do Whites and other racial minorities. These perceptions result in part from the disadvantages that racial and ethnic minorities experience across the justice system, along with any gratuitous treatment that they may have experienced during their encounters with police. In recent years, racial profiling has emerged as a major factor shaping minority citizens' evaluations of the police (Warren, Tomaskovic-Devey, Zingraff, Smith, & Mason, 2006; Weitzer & Tuch, 2002). The term *racial profiling* describes the practice of targeting or stopping an individual based primarily on race, rather than on any individualized suspicion (Beckett, Nyrop, & Pfingst, 2006; Engel & Johnson, 2006; Weitzer, 2000a). As a result of these experiences, Black and Hispanic communities have raised questions about police legitimacy as well as the procedural fairness of police organizations more generally (Engel, 2005; Smith & Holmes, 2003; Tyler, 2001).

Although prior studies have demonstrated that racial minorities are more likely to perceive police as racially biased and unfair, there continues to be ongoing questions about the factors that underlie these perceptions. In particular, prior studies have overwhelmingly highlighted the salience of direct and vicarious experiences (e.g., Rosenbaum, Schuck, Costello, Hawkins, & Ring, 2005; Weitzer & Tuch, 2006), neighborhood context (e.g., Brunson, 2007; Brunson & Weitzer, 2009; Sampson & Bartusch, 1998; Schuck, Rosenbaum, & Hawkins, 2008; Stewart, Baumer, Brunson, & Simons, 2009), along with the outcome of the police encounter (e.g., Brown & Frank, 2006; Johnson & Kuhns, 2009; Warren & Tomaskovic-Devey, 2009) when evaluating racial/ethnic differences. However, to date, few studies have explored the relevance of officer race (for exceptions, see Engel, 2005; Gilliard-Matthews, Kowalski, & Lundman, 2008; Lersch & Mieczkowski, 2000). The lack of empirical attention to officer race is anomalous given the push from both policy makers and scholars to diversify U.S. police organizations in efforts to improve citizen-police relations and to dispel notions of racial profiling.

The debate surrounding the relevance of officer race began in the late 70s and early 80s when many police departments adopted diversification strategies to foster trust and improve police-minority community relations (Brown & Frank, 2006; Kuykendall & Burns, 1980; Skolnick & Fyfe, 1993; Smith & Holmes, 2003; Weitzer, 2000b; Zhao, Herbst, & Lovrich, 2001). Despite these efforts, there have been relatively few empirical studies to demonstrate that officer race significantly influences citizens' evaluations of them (see also Engel, 2005; Kaker, 2003). In fact, the National Research Council (Skogan & Frydl, 2004) contends that there is little evidence to suggest that minority officers behave differently than their White counterparts.

Against this backdrop, the purpose of the current study is multifaceted. First, we explore the salience of officer race in understanding citizen perceptions of police behavior. We do so by examining how the combined effects of race, ethnicity, and gender influence evaluations of police encounters across the race and the ethnicity of the officer. By exploring the combined effects of race, ethnicity, and gender, we can capture how racial, ethnic, and gender groups evaluate White and minority officers' behavior differentially. In addition, our analyses move beyond the Black-White divide by also empirically investigating Hispanic ethnicity. Prior studies have generally failed to incorporate Hispanic ethnicity (Brunson & Miller, 2005; Warren, 2010), which ignores the unique experiences that Hispanic citizens have with police and assumes that Hispanic citizens' perceptions will be similar to those expressed by Black citizens. We also emphasize the salience of gender as prior studies have shown that males across racial and ethnic groups are more likely than are females to report negative encounters (Weitzer & Tuch, 2005). Ultimately, by examining these combined effects we can more specifically isolate the groups that are most vulnerable to negative encounters with and evaluations of the police.

Understanding how officer race influences racial variation in perceptions of the police is particularly relevant in contemporary society because police organizations have increasingly come under scrutiny for unfairly targeting minority drivers during traffic and pedestrian stops. It has been widely assumed by policy makers and citizens alike that allegations of racial profiling are mostly associated with the policing practices of White officers and their treatment of racial and ethnic minorities. This in part results from the tenuous historical relationship between police and minority communities coupled with police organizations traditionally limiting their employment to White citizens. Some commentators have suggested that this racial mismatch is a major cause of the ongoing allegations of racial profiling. Despite these claims, there is mixed evidence to suggest that enforcement practices vary across officer race. In addition, researchers know little as to how perceptions of officers vary, if at all, based on the race of an officer.

Using traffic stop data from the 2005 BJS Police-Public Contact Survey, we assess the following two research questions:

Research Question 1: Do evaluations of police encounters vary across officer race?

Research Question 2: Do the combined effects of race, ethnicity, and gender influence evaluations of police behavior differently for White and for minority officers?

In the next section, we provide a brief discussion of prior theory and research relevant to the discussion of race, biases, and perceptions of the police. Following this discussion, we empirically evaluate whether citizens' evaluations of the police vary across officer race.

BACKGROUND

Conflict theory and its subsidiaries (e.g., group position, group threat) have commonly been used as frameworks for understanding the relationship between race, class, and evaluations of the police (Hagan & Albonetti, 1982; Johnson & Kuhns, 2009; Matsueda & Drakulich, 2009; Shedd & Hagan, 2006; Weitzer & Tuch, 2006). Conflict theory and more formalized racial threat hypotheses (e.g. Blalock, 1967; Blumer, 1958; Liska, 1992) propose that perceptions of threat held by societal elites work to invoke reactions through social control, including disparate arrest practices (e.g., Parker, Stults, & Rice, 2005) and greater police force presence in areas where the perceived threat (i.e., minority population size) posed by minority groups is higher (e.g., Stults & Baumer, 2007). While conflict theory arguments speak to macro-level functions of race and ethnic relations, group threat hypotheses have provided a useful framework for scholars attempting to understand individual-level interactions between citizens and the police (Novak & Chamlin, 2008; Weitzer & Tuch, 2006; Weitzer, Tuch, & Skogan, 2008). These perspectives maintain that racial and ethnic differences in perceptions of police exist largely because Whites are more likely to view police actions as legitimate since the amount of crime control exercised against minorities is often viewed as necessary given the criminal threat that they pose to mainstream society. Racial minorities, on the other hand, "may construe their encounters with police less in terms of the immediate circumstances and more in terms of their group's societal position" (Weitzer et al., 2008, pp. 400). In this case, it is plausible that minorities, relative to Whites, are more inclined to view the police as representatives of the state and thus see police misconduct as reprehensible and racially biased (Weitzer et al., 2008; Weitzer & Tuch, 2006). As a result, minority group members express higher levels of distrust and dissatisfaction with the police.

Within the conflict perspective, multiracial explanations have been incorporated because of the growing population of Hispanic citizens as well as their expanding influence on American society (Sampson & Lauritsen, 1997; Solis, Portillos, & Brunson, 2009; Weitzer & Tuch, 2006). This perspective explores the complex ways in which ethnic minorities interact with the criminal justice system (see Hagan, Shedd, & Payne, 2005; Spohn & Holleran, 2000; Steffensmeier & Demuth, 2000, 2001; Weitzer & Tuch, 2006). Broadly, this approach emphasizes a racial hierarchical pattern of citizen trust and dissatisfaction with the police, with Whites at the lower end, Hispanics in the middle, and Blacks expressing the highest levels of police dissatisfaction (Weitzer & Tuch, 2006). For example, Weitzer and Tuch (2006) note that although Hispanic citizens are more likely to report that they are distrustful of police organizations than are Whites, their levels of distrust never rise to those held by Black citizens.

There are also reasons to expect gender to play an important role in predicting citizens' trust and evaluations of the police. Criminologists have consistently emphasized the differential treatment that males experience in comparison to females across the criminal justice system (Spohn & Beichner, 2000). Prior studies have found that minority males are more likely to express dissatisfaction with the police as well as report more discriminatory treatment by police in comparison to White and minority females (Weitzer & Tuch, 2006). This research provides some baseline evidence that future studies should continue to explore how their combined effects, in conjunction with officer race, provide a broader understanding of citizens' evaluations of the police. We therefore, emphasize the importance of assessing the interplay of race/ethnicity and gender in defining citizens' experiences and perceptions of police encounters.

The Interaction of Citizen and Officer Race

In light of these perspectives and prior research, we expect officer race to have an influence on racial, ethnic, and gender differences in perceptions of police behavior, based largely on the idea that individuals organize their perceptions based on their position in society. That is, citizens develop their perceptions of police based not only on perceptions of fairness but also on comparable social positions and circumstances between themselves and the contacting officer (see also Weitzer et al., 2008). For example, minority males and females are more likely to perceive improper behavior by a White officer because of feelings of exclusionary treatment and subordination by White-dominant society. On the other hand, minority citizens might view the actions and behavior of minority officers as favorable and more trustworthy because they feel minority officers will enforce the law more fairly and impartially.

Despite the commonly proposed influence of officer race on citizen perceptions, the effects of officer race on evaluations of the police have rarely been explored, and when they have the results have yielded mixed findings (Brown & Frank, 2006; Engel, 2005; Lersch & Mieczkowski, 2000). For example, some research finds that Black officers interact with Black citizens differently than their White counterparts (Brown & Frank, 2006; Mastrofski, Reisig, & McCluskey, 2002; Sun & Payne, 2004; Sun, Payne, & Wu, 2008). These studies acknowledge the importance of diversifying police forces to improve communication and minority citizen-police relations, as well as to quell accusations of racial bias on the part of officers (Sun, 2003; Weitzer & Tuch, 2006). Sun (2003) writes that increasing the number of Black officers will improve officer-citizen relations because Black officers develop better connections to citizens in disadvantaged areas. Brown and Frank (2006) note, however, that empirical evidence supporting this idea is relatively weak, and results from their study partly support the opposite position. That is, although White officers were more likely to make an arrest, Black officers were significantly more likely to arrest Black citizens in comparison to Whites.

It is generally believed that in areas with a greater minority presence, minority officers are better equipped to handle problems, and promote better relationships with local citizens (Decker & Smith 1980; Skogan, 1979; see also Weitzer et al., 2008; Weitzer & Tuch, 2006). Similarly, the presence of minority officers could help to limit the tensions that White officers may typically invoke among minority citizens. Policing behavior studies have shown that during police-citizen contacts, citizens who display negative behavior, such as disrespectfulness or rudeness, are more likely to receive sanctions or be arrested, than citizens who behave more positively (Mastrofski et al., 2002; Garner, Maxwell, & Heraux, 2002; Reisig, McCluskey, Mastrofski, & Terrill, 2004). Because minority citizens are more likely to perceive the behavior of White officers as inherently biased or illegitimate, they will be more likely to behave poorly during citizen-police contact, which will also increase their rate of receiving tickets and getting arrested. Police departments have a large stake then in not only appearing fair, but being trusted and perceived as a legitimate authority (Sunshine & Tyler 2003).

In prior studies there does appear to be a general belief that police force diversification and differential disbursement of minority officers to certain communities can improve perceptions of the police by partly limiting perceived biases that may be present when minorities come in contact with White officers. That is, a minority officer may be inherently less likely to appear racially biased, or more likely to appear legitimate to a minority citizen, than would a White police officer. It is possible that minority citizens are more likely to perceive racial profiling when stopped by a White officer than they would be if the officer were a minority. And in turn, police force diversification would then be an efficient solution for enhancing police officer legitimacy. However, the counter argument to police force diversification suggests that race and ethnicity of the officer has no effect on the officers' treatment of citizens, and more importantly, citizens perceive any officer that wears the police uniform as untrustworthy and more likely to treat them unfairly (Weitzer, 2000b; Weitzer & Tuch, 2006); which would then raise questions regarding what policies *would* be effective to dispel notions of racially biased policing.

Racial Profiling and Perceptions of the Police

In recent years, researchers have devoted significant attention toward understanding how racial profiling influences citizens perceptions of the police (Reitzel & Piquero, 2006; Warren et al., 2006). Racial profiling has become a "hot topic" for researchers as well as for politicians and by now it is likely that most citizens are at least aware of the common accusations of racial bias pitted against law enforcement. Citizens, particularly minority citizens, who perceive that they have been stopped as a result of racial profiling, are more inclined to express dissatisfaction with the police (Weitzer & Tuch, 2006). The widespread cognizance of racial profiling, in our view, presents an additional challenge for researchers when exploring perceptions of the police, since the awareness that profiling occurs, regardless of whether or not someone feels that they have actually been stopped as a result of racial profiling, may be enough to influence perceptions of police behavior. In other words, minority citizens who hear about racial profiling practices, even if they themselves do not believe they have been racially profiled, may be more likely to view future experiences with the police skeptically (Rosenbaum et al., 2005).

The Current Study

The current study underscores the importance of prior research in examining racial variation in perceptions of the police, and in doing so we pay particular attention to how the interaction of citizen and officer race differentially influences citizens' evaluations of their encounter with police officers. Using self-report data from the BJS Police-Public Contact Survey, we seek to answer the following research questions: (a) Does officer race influence perceptions of police encounters? (b) Do the combined effects of race, ethnicity and gender influence evaluations of police behavior differently for White and for minority officers?

[...]

Discussion and Conclusions

Understanding citizen perceptions of police is an important concern for criminological scholars and policy makers alike (Engel, 2005; Smith et al., 2003; Weitzer & Tuch, 2005). Prior studies have consistently highlighted that racial and ethnic minorities are more likely to question the legitimacy of their encounters with police. However, despite this, few studies have explored the salience of officer race and how it influences citizens' evaluations of police. The lack of consistent empirical attention in part results from limited availability of data sets that include officer race, a problem we avert by using the PPCS data set.

The main focus of the current study was to explore whether and how racial and ethnic variation in perceptions of police behavior varies across officer race. We specifically explored one primary research question: Do the combined effects of race, ethnicity, and gender influence evaluations of police behavior differently for White and for minority officers? Our results provide several important findings. First, we found that Black males and females are more likely to negatively evaluate police behavior when the stop is initiated by a White officer; even after controlling for the reported reason given for the stop. However, this is not the case when the officer is a minority. For minority officer stops, we found no citizen-race or ethnicity effects, and the primary predictor of citizens' perceptions of the legitimacy of the stop was the "reason" given to the citizen by the officer. This finding suggests in part that citizens, particularly minority citizens, "rate" officer legitimately more objectively when they are stopped by minority officers. When minority citizens are stopped by White officers they seemingly viewed officer behavior more skeptically.

The findings presented here reiterate the findings from prior racial profiling and public opinion research which suggest that in general, minority group members, especially Black citizens, have a higher propensity for viewing police behavior and other parts of the criminal justice system as illegitimate. Interestingly, both Hispanic males and females yielded null findings in regard to skepticism of the police, suggesting that rifts between the police and citizens may be primarily focused in African American communities. Racial profiling in the United States has been traditionally geared toward the relationship between Black citizens and the police, and only until recently have Hispanic citizens been linked to biased experiences with and perceptions of the police (Engel, 2005; Weitzer & Tuch, 2006). However, this study's findings suggest that Black citizens are still the most skeptical of police officers' behavior and the most likely to perceive that they have been treated unfairly or perhaps racially profiled—especially when the officer is White.

Generally speaking, the results of this study appear to describe differential predictors of negative perceptions of the police, depending on the race of the officer. This differential effect is also suggestive of the idea that diversification practices of police forces may indeed be one viable option for improving citizens' views of officer legitimacy for some racial groups. Despite this thinking, our results demonstrate that in some cases minority officers may tend not to incite the same type of initial skepticism that minority citizens seem to display when the officer is White.

Related to these findings, it is important to note that in a study by Engel (2005), using an earlier version of the Police-Public Contact Survey, the author found no significant effect of an interaction between officer and citizen race, which would suggest that perhaps minority groups' hold lower perceptions of police irrespective of officer race. We believe the approach taken in this research effort builds on the work by Engel, by not only exploring the direct and interactive effects of officer race but also the combined effects of race, ethnicity, and gender. By assessing these combined effects we demonstrate that officer race may play a more substantial role in the development of citizens' perceptions than previous findings would suggest.

The analyses employed here did not however reveal any significant influences of other relevant factors consistently considered in conflict theory literature; in particular, income and citizen area of residence (apart from the effect of rural residence [...]). These concepts touch on important underlying theoretical ties for understanding how race and gender effects may influence how citizens perceive police officers as well as other aspects of the criminal justice system. It is possible that the measures employed here that attempt to encompass class and neighborhood effects fail to fully capture how characteristics of a citizens' neighborhood of residence and their socioeconomic status influence their views of and attitudes

5. Searches incident to arrest are excluded because if there is sufficient evidence to arrest, the search is considered routine practice.

6. It is important to note that the outcome measure included in the analyses is not mutually exclusive, and therefore there is no excluded reference category. In other words, someone could have been searched as well as received a citation. The comparison group for each of these variables is therefore the opposite outcome, meaning that the comparison group for someone who was searched is someone who was not searched. Other outcomes, such as being handcuffed and/or arrested were originally included in the survey. However the minimal amount of positive responses led to unstable analytical results.

7. Prior research has categorized similar stop characteristics as either procedural/instrumental (e.g., reason for a stop, use of force, searches) or distributive/normative (e.g., citation, warning, arrest) to evaluate the equal importance of procedural and distributive factors in understanding citizen evaluations of the police. For further discussion see Tyler (1990) and Engel (2005).

8. This is admittedly a proxy measure of neighborhood context, an observation similarly utilized by previous studies using an earlier version of the PPCS (see Engel, 2005). However, while this measure does not capture the area in which the police contact occurred, Brunson (2007) notes that the respondents' neighborhood is likely a more important factor than the context under which the traffic stop actually occurred since it is primarily experiences in or around home neighborhoods that define citizens' views of police going into a traffic stop or police contact.

9. It is important to note that, because it is a supplementary questionnaire to the NCVS survey, the police-public contact survey is similarly susceptible to the cluster sample design effect of the NCVS, and researchers must therefore account for clustering effects within the data. In doing so, we utilized the "cluster" option for logistic regression in STATA, but note that other methods for this accountability do exist. Ancillary analyses (not shown here) implementing weighting procedures were conducted and revealed no substantive differences to the results reported here. By using the clustering technique, we report robust standard errors.

10. The positive relationship between age in all three models is unexpected, in part because younger citizens generally have more frequent contacts with police, greater exposure to officer misconduct, and heightened negative attitudes toward the police. However, it is possible that the negativity expressed by younger citizens is in response to various procedural and distributive processes captured here. Or, perhaps older drivers are more inclined to view police officers skeptically, if perhaps police contact is more unexpected in older populations or if older individuals have simply had more experience with perceived injustices.

11. It is notable here that the "Search" variable was not a significant predictor of negative perceptions of the police. This null association may in part be due to the minimal number of minority respondents included in Model 3 [ed. note: not included] who reported being searched by a minority officer.

References

Beckett, K., Nyrop, K., & Pfingst, L. (2006). Race, drugs, and policing: Understanding disparities in drug delivery arrests. *Criminology, 44,* 105–137.

Black, D. J., & Reiss, A. J., Jr. (1970). Police control of juveniles. *American Sociological Review, 35,* 63–77.

Blalock, H. M. (1967). *Toward a theory of minority group relations.* New York, NY: Wiley.

Blumer, H. (1958). Race prejudice as a sense of group position. *Pacific Sociological Review, 1,* 3–7.

Brown, R. A., & Frank, J. (2006). Race and officer decision making: Examining differences in arrest outcomes between Black and White officers. *Justice Quarterly, 23,* 96–126.

Brunson, R. (2007). "Police don't like Black people:" African American young men's accumulated police experiences. *Criminology and Public Policy, 6,* 71–102.

Brunson, R. K., & Weitzer, R. (2009). Police relations with Black and White youths in different urban neighborhoods. *Urban Affairs Review*, 44, 858–884.

Brunson, R. K., & Miller, J. (2005). Young Black Men and Urban Policing in the United States. *British Journal of Criminology*, 46, 613–640.

Campbell, V. (1980). Double marginality of Black policemen: A Reassessment. *Criminology*, 17, 477–484.

Decker, S., & Smith, R. (1980). Police minority recruitment. *Journal of Criminal Justice*, 8, 387–393.
[…]

Engel, R. S., & Johnson, R. (2006). Toward a better understanding of racial and ethnic disparities in search and seizure rates. *Journal of Criminal Justice*, 34, 605–617.

Garner, J. H., Maxwell, C. D., & Heraux, C. G. (2002). Characteristics associated with the prevalence and severity of force used by the police. *Justice Quarterly*, 19, 705–746.

Gilliard-Matthews, S., Kowalski, B. R., & Lundman, R. J. (2008). Officer race and citizen-reported traffic ticket decisions by police in 1999 and 2002. *Police Quarterly*, 11, 202–219.

Graziano, L., Schuck, A., & Martin, C. (2009). Police misconduct, media coverage, and public perceptions of racial profiling: An experiment. *Justice Quarterly*, 27, 52–76.
[…]

Hagan, J., Shedd, C., & Payne, M. R. (2005). Race, ethnicity and youth perceptions of criminal injustice. *American Sociological Review*, 70, 381–407.

Hurst, Y. G., Frank, J., & Browning, S. L. (2000). The attitudes of juveniles towards the police: A comparison of black and white youth. *Policing: An International Journal of Police Strategies and Management*, 23, 37–53.

Johnson, D., & Kuhns, J. (2009). Striking out: Race and support for police use of force. *Justice Quarterly*, 26, 592–623.

Kaker, S. (2003). Race and police officers' perceptions of their job performance: An analysis of the relationship between police officers' race, education level and job performance. *Journal of Police and Criminal Psychology*, 18, 45–56.

Kuykendall, J. L., & Burns, D. E. (1980). The Black police officer: An historical perspective. *Journal of Contemporary Criminal Justice*, 1, 4–12.

Lersch, K. M., & Mieczkowski, T. (2000). An examination of the convergence and divergence of internal and external allegations of misconduct filed against police officers. *Policing*, 23, 54–68.

Liska, A. E. (1992). *Social threat and social control*. Albany: State University of New York Press.

Mastrofski, S. D., Reisig, M. D., & McCluskey, J. D. (2002). Police disrespect toward the public: An encounter-based analysis. *Criminology*, 40, 519–552.

Matsueda, R. L., & Drakulich, K. (2009). Perceptions of criminal injustice, symbolic racism and racial politics. *ANNALS*, 623, 163–178.

Novak, K. J., & M. B. Chamlin. (2008). Racial threat, suspicion, and police behavior: The impact of race and place in traffic enforcement. *Crime & Delinquency*. Advance online publication. doi: 10.1177/0011128708322943

Parker, K. F., Stults, B. J., & Rice, S. K. (2005). Racial threat, concentrated disadvantage and social control: Considering the macro-level sources of variation in arrests. *Criminology*, 43, 1111–1134.

Reisig, M. D., McCluskey, J. D., Mastrofski, S. D., & Terrill, W. (2004). Suspect disrespect toward the police. *Justice Quarterly*, 21, 241–268.

Reisig, M., & Parks, R. (2000). Experience, quality of life, and neighborhood context. Justice Quarterly, 17, 607–629.

Reitzel, J., & Piquero, A. R. (2006). Does it exist? Studying citizens' attitudes of racial profiling. *Police Quarterly*, 9, 161–183.

Rosenbaum, D. P., Schuck, A. M., Costello, S. K., Hawkins, D. F., & Ring, M. K. (2005). Attitudes toward the police: The effect of direct and vicarious experiences. *Police Quarterly*, 3, 343–365.

[...]

Sampson, R. J., & Lauritsen, J. L. (1997). Racial and ethnic disparities in crime and criminal justice in the United States. *Crime and Justice*, 21, 311–374.

Schuck, A. M., Rosenbaum, D. P., & Hawkins, D. F. (2008). The influence of race/ethnicity, social class, and neighborhood context on residents' attitudes toward the police. *Police Quarterly*, 11, 496–519.

Shedd, C., & Hagan, J. (2006). Toward a developmental and comparative conflict theory of race, ethnicity and perceptions of criminal justice. In R. D. Peterson, L. J. Krivo, & J. Hagan (Eds.), *The many colors of crime: Inequalities of race, ethnicity, and crime in America* (pp. 313–333). New York: NYU Press.

Sherman, L. W., Gartin, P. R., & Buerger, M. E. (1989). Hot spots of predatory crime: Routine activities and the criminology of place. *Criminology*, 27, 27–55.

Skogan, W. (1979). Citizen satisfaction with police services. In R. Baker & F. Meyer, (Eds.), *Evaluating alternative law enforcement policies* (pp. 29–42). Lexington, MA: Lexington Books.

Skogan, W. & K. Frydl. (Eds., 2004). *Fairness and Effectiveness in Policing: The Evidence*. National Academies Press: Washington, D.C.

Skolnick, J. H., & Fyfe, J. J. (1993). *Above the law: Police and the excessive use of force*. New York, NY: Free Press.

Smith, B. W., & Holmes, M. D. (2003). Community accountability, minority threat, and police brutality: An examination of civil rights criminal complaints. *Criminology*, 41, 1035–1063.

Smith, W. R., Tomaskovic-Devey, D., Zingraff, M. H., Mason, M., Warren, P. Y., Wright, C. P.,... & Felson, R. C. (2003). *The North Carolina highway traffic study. Final Report to the National Institute of Justice*. Washington, DC: U.S. Department of Justice.

Solis, C., Portillos, E. L., & Brunson, R. K. (2009). Latino youths' experiences with and perceptions of involuntary police encounters. *ANNALS*, 623, 39–51.

Spohn, C., & Beichner, D. (2000). Is preferential treatment of female offenders a thing of the past? A multisite study of gender, race, and imprisonment. *Criminal Justice Policy Review*, 11, 149–184.

Spohn, C. C., & Holleran, D. (2000). The imprisonment penalty paid by young, unemployed Black and Hispanic male offenders. *Criminology*, 38, 281–306.

Steffensmeier, D., & Demuth, S. (2000). Ethnicity and sentencing outcomes in U.S. federal courts: Who is punished more harshly—White, Black, White-Hispanic, or Black-Hispanic defendants? *American Sociological Review*, 65, 705–729.

Steffensmeier, D., & Demuth, S. (2001). Ethnicity and judges' sentencing decisions: Hispanic-Black-White comparisons. *Criminology*, 39, 145–178.

Stewart, E. A., Baumer, E. P., Brunson, R. K., & Simons, R. L. (2009). Neighborhood racial context and perceptions of police-based racial discrimination among black youth. *Criminology*, 47, 847–887.

Stults, B. J., & Baumer, E. P. (2007). Racial context and police force size: Evaluating the empirical validity of the minority threat perspective. *American Journal of Sociology*. 113, 507–546.

Sun, I. Y. (2003). Police officers' attitudes toward their role and work: A comparison of Black and White officers. *American Journal of Criminal Justice*, 28, 89–108.

Sun, I. Y., & Payne, B. K. (2004). Racial differences in resolving conflicts: A comparison between Black and White police officers. *Crime and Delinquency*, 50, 516–541.

Sun, I. Y., Payne, B. K. & Wu, Y. (2008). The impact of situational factors, officer characteristics, and neighborhood context on police behavior: A multilevel analysis. *Journal of Criminal Justice*, 36, 22–32.

Sunshine, J., & Tyler, T. R. (2003). The role of procedural justice and legitimacy in shaping public support for policing. *Law and Society Review, 37,* 513–548.

Tyler, T. R. (1990). *Why people obey the law.* New Haven, CT: Yale University Press.

Tyler, T. R. (2001). Public trust and confidence in legal authorities: What do majority and minority group members want from the law and legal institutions? *Behavioral Sciences and the Law, 19,* 215–235.

Tyler, T. R. (2004). To better serve and protect: Improving police practices. *Annals of the American Academy of Political and Social Sciences, 593,* 84–99.

Warren, P. Y. (2010). The continuing significance of race: An analysis across two levels of policing. *Social Science Quarterly, 91,* 1025–1042.

Warren, P. Y. (2011). Perceptions of police disrespect during vehicle stops: A race-based analysis. *Crime & Delinquency, 57,* 356–376.

Warren, P. Y., & Tomaskovic-Devey, D. (2009). Racial profiling and searches: Did the politics of racial profiling change police behavior? *Criminology and Public Policy, 8,* 343–369.

Warren, P. Y., Tomaskovic-Devey, D., Zingraff, M., Smith, W., & Mason, M. (2006). Driving while Black: Bias processes and racial disparity in police stops. *Criminology, 4,* 709–737.

Weitzer, R. (2000a). Racialized policing: Residents' perceptions in three neighborhoods. *Law & Society Review, 34,* 129–155.

Weitzer, R. (2000b.) White, Black, or blue cops? Race and citizen assessments of police officers. *Journal of Criminal Justice, 28,* 313–324.

Weitzer, R., & Tuch, S. (1999). Race, class, and perceptions of discrimination by the police. *Crime & Delinquency, 45,* 494–507.

Weitzer, R., & S. Tuch. (2002). Perceptions of racial profiling: Race, class, and personal experience. *Criminology, 40,* 435–456.

[…]

Weitzer, R., Tuch, S., & Skogan, W. G. (2008). Police-community relations in a majority-Black city. *Journal of Research in Crime and Delinquency, 45,* 398–428.

Wilkins, V. M., & Williams, B. N. (2008). Black or blue: Racial profiling and representative bureaucracy. *Public Administration Review, 68,* 652–662.

Wilkins, V. M., & Williams, B. N. (2009). Representing blue: Representative bureaucracy and racial profiling in the Latino community. *Administration and Society, 40,* 775–798.

Zhao, J., Herbst, L., & Lovrich, N. (2001). Race, ethnicity and the female COP: Differential patterns of representation. *Journal of Urban Affairs, 23,* 243–257.

*Joshua C. Cochran is a doctoral candidate in the College of Criminology and Criminal Justice at Florida State University. His research interests include race and the criminal justice system, imprisonment and reentry, criminological theory, and comparative criminology.

Patricia Y. Warren is an assistant professor in the College of Criminology and Criminal Justice at Florida State University. Her current research interests include racial profiling, sentencing, racial/ethnic inequality in crime, and social control.

Public Opinion on the Use of Consumer Racial Profiling to Identify Shoplifters: An Exploratory Study

*by Shaun L. Gabbidon and George E. Higgins**

INTRODUCTION

Few scholars would argue that, since the 1990s, racial profiling has emerged as a major emphasis among criminologists. Consequently, the literature is now abundant with scholarship on the nature and extent of profiling. The caveat here, though, is that much of the literature has centered on one aspect of profiling—traffic stops. This almost singular focus on traffic stops has limited the body of scholarship on racial profiling in other contexts such as in airports and retail establishments. Even so, there is emerging research in these other areas. Within the racial profiling scholarship, there has been a body of public opinion scholarship that has investigated how citizens view profiling (Jordan, Gabbidon, & Higgins, 2009; Weitzer & Tuch, 2002, 2005). In general, this literature has sought to determine whether the public is supportive of such policing practices and, if so, what factors are indicative of support (Higgins, Gabbidon, & Vito, 2010; Weitzer & Tuch, 2006). This literature has generally excluded one critical focus—the reasons *why* citizens either support or do not support profiling.

With retailers losing billions of dollars each year to shoplifting (Hollinger & Adams, 2009), numerous measures have been tried in an effort to reduce losses. Most citizens are aware of the use of preventive measures such as CCTV, merchandise alarms, fitting room attendants, and uniform guards. However, in recent years, it has been alleged in litigation that racial/ethnic profiling represents another preventive tactic that has been used by well-known retailers such as Wal-Mart, JCPenney, Dillard's, and Cracker Barrel, among others (Gabbidon, 2003; Harris, 2003). This is despite the fact that research has shown no difference in shoplifting trends by race/ethnicity (Dabney, Hollinger, & Dugan, 2004). Nonetheless, some citizens and retailers alike continue to support such practices.

The present study delved into this unexplored aspect of public opinion on racial profiling. Moreover, this research also represents a divergence from previous literature in that it investigated public opinion on consumer racial profiling (CRP) or the use of race/ethnicity to profile customers as suspected shoplifters in retail settings. To understand this support among citizens, this study investigated whether factors such as perceived effectiveness, ethical concerns, or the belief that CRP is discriminatory influences the perceived existence of the practice and the level of support for the practice. We begin with a review of the scholarly literature on CRP.

LITERATURE REVIEW

Much of the early literature on CRP explored case studies of instances in which retailers were found to be providing poor service to racial/ethnic minorities (Adamson, 2000; Crockett, Grier, & Williams, 2003; Fifield, 2001; Harris, 2003; Henderson, 2001; Lee, 2000; O'Connell, 2001; Williams, Henderson, & Harris, 2001). This literature was largely descriptive or interview-based and did not emphasize the aspect of CRP in which racial/ethnic groups are targeted as suspected thieves. Two exceptions to this early scholarship were the works of Feagin (1991) and Asquith and Bristow (2000). Feagin's interview-based study on the experiences of Black middle-class citizens in public places found that Blacks felt they were targeted for "excessive surveillance." Asquith and Bristow found that students viewed racial/ethnic minorities as the ones most likely to shoplift both before and after they were exposed to an experimental stimulus in the form of a video highlighting actual demographics of shoplifters.

Few additional empirical studies on CRP appeared again until the mid-2000s. During this period, scholars turned to litigation from the state and federal levels as a way to determine the nature of CRP incidents. The legal cases represent litigation pursued by racial/ethnic minorities who felt they had been profiled in a retail setting. These empirical analyses of cases pointed to the fact that sales clerks, as opposed to security personnel, were the ones most likely to be accused of CRP. The litigation also found that many of the false arrests were caused because clerks or security personnel acted on unsubstantiated hunches. Finally, in nearly 60% of the cases, the plaintiffs were victorious (Gabbidon, 2003). Using similar methods, other researchers also found that discrimination (both subtle and overt) in general and CRP in particular was occurring in retail settings (Harris, Henderson, & Williams, 2005; Williams, Harris, & Henderson, 2006).

More recent research has continued to explore the nature and extent of CRP. Gabbidon and Higgins (2007) conducted a victimization survey of 500 randomly selected Philadelphia area residents to find out how frequently they perceived themselves as having been targeted by retailers as suspected shoplifters. Though less than half of the sample reported experiencing CRP (43%), Blacks were 10 times more likely than Whites to report having experienced CRP (Gabbidon & Higgins, 2007). The results also noted that Blacks and Whites who encountered CRP expressed negative emotions as a direct result of the incident (Gabbidon & Higgins, 2008; Higgins & Gabbidon, 2009). A similar victimization study on the CRP experiences of several hundred students at several historically Black universities found nearly identical results to the Philadelphia research (Gabbidon, Craig, Okafo, Marzette, & Peterson, 2008). It is notable that in both studies, those respondents who experienced CRP rarely reported the incident to officials at the store, still made a purchase at the store, and often later returned to the store.

Researchers have conducted experimental research to determine the nature and extent of CRP. Dabney et al. (2004) examined the question, "Who actually steals?" Their research was conducted in an Atlanta drugstore where they were granted permission to study the racial/ethnic trends in shoplifting. To do so, the researchers used trained observers to determine the percentage of each racial/ethnic group that shoplifted. The researchers found no significant differences between the levels of stealing by race/ethnicity. These findings give additional credence to the notion that behavioral cues (looking around for clerks, examining security measures, and tampering with merchandise) are likely to be much more effective in identifying shoplifters. An unexpected finding from the research, though, was that even trained observers of all racial/ethnic groups still held an unconscious bias toward racial/ethnic minorities (Dabney, Dugan, Topalli, & Hollinger, 2006).

Schreer, Smith, and Thomas (2009) recently conducted another experimental study to investigate CRP. Their field experiment focused on overt and subtle retail discrimination. Conducted in high-end retailers in Westchester County, NY, the researchers observed the behavior of 33 White sales clerks toward Black and White customers (trained student participants) in groups and as individual customers. The experiment required the customers to head to the sunglass counter while two trained recorders observed the behavior of the clerks. While the clerks were willing to remove the security sensor tags for all the consumers, the Black customers "[did] arouse more suspicion than White customers...More specifically, after removing the sensor, salespeople stared at Black customers more often than White customers" (Schreer et al., 2009, p. 1437). The researchers also found that individual Blacks as well as groups of Black males or Black females were more closely followed than groups comprised of Whites. These findings provide additional support for the existence of CRP.

Jordan et al. (2009) have also explored public opinion on CRP. Using national Gallup data, they investigated the perceived prevalence and support for CRP. In support of their hypotheses, the research revealed that Blacks were more likely than Whites to believe CRP was widespread and justified. On both fronts, the views of Hispanics were closer to those of Whites. The research also revealed that those with conservative views were more supportive of CRP while those respondents with higher levels of income and education were less likely to support the practice (see also Gabbidon & Higgins, 2009).

The current study builds on the more recent public opinion research on CRP. Though informative, virtually all the large-scale public opinion research on racial profiling is focused on whether or not respondents believe the practice is widespread and whether it is justified (or supported). This study moved beyond prior research by investigating why people support CRP. In particular, this study sought to determine why citizens might believe CRP exists and are supportive of the practice. Specifically, we investigated the explanatory power of three new measures to assess whether views about the ethical nature of CRP, its perception as being discriminatory, and notions about its effectiveness influences views on CRP. The first of these measures pertained to ethics. Here, we wanted to determine if the respondents' felt CRP was unethical whether it would result in less support for using the approach to identify shoplifters. We anticipate that respondents who find CRP unethical will not support it. Second, we created a measure to capture respondents' views as to whether CRP was a discriminatory practice. To a certain extent, this measure examines whether conventional wisdom holds true. Specifically, the most significant concern about racial profiling in general is that it uses discriminatory practices to identify criminals. This measure allows us to empirically explore this question. In general, we anticipate that those respondents who regard CRP as being discriminatory will be less likely to support racial profiling in retail settings.

Finally, in our view, the core reason why someone might support racial profiling is that it is believed to be effective. As such, we created a measure to test our notions about this question. In short, we anticipate that those respondents who perceive CRP to be effective will be more likely to support it.

On the whole, our research examines two multifaceted questions that consider the role of these new measures. First, how does perceived effectiveness, the view that CRP is discriminatory, or that the practice is not ethical, influence whether individuals believe that CRP occurs while controlling for demographics (e.g., age, race, gender, income, and education)? Second, how is perceived support for CRP influenced by the ethical nature of the practice, its perceived effectiveness, and the feeling that it is discriminatory while controlling for demographics (e.g., age, gender, etc.)? The next section outlines the methods used in the research.

METHOD

Data

The data for this research were collected during the annual Penn State Poll conducted by the Center for Survey Research at Penn State Harrisburg. For more than two decades, the Center has conducted an annual poll on issues germane to the Commonwealth of Pennsylvania. The Center also solicits sponsors that, for a few, can include questions on the poll that are of interest to their organization. We responded to the 2009 solicitation and provided funds to include several poll questions related to racial profiling. To conduct the poll, the Center used 30 trained professionals to conduct their interviews using the computer-assisted telephone interviewing (CATI) system. The 2009 poll was conducted between October 5, 2009, and November 4, 2009. The sample drawn for the 2009 Penn State Poll used a random-digit-dialing (RDD) sampling procedure that guaranteed every land-line telephone household in Pennsylvania had an equal chance of being selected. Moreover, a randomized respondent selection technique ensured that every adult within each sample household had an equal probability of being interviewed. Each interview lasted approximately 14 minutes. The survey cooperation rate was 74.1% as calculated using the American Association of Public Opinion Research's Cooperation Rate 3 (COOP3) formula. A margin of error of ±3.4% at the 95% confidence interval is associated with the survey results.

Measures

Dependent measures. For this study, we used 2 items as dependent measures. The first measure is "Do you believe racial profiling occurs in retail stores to identify shoplifters?" The respondents used a dichotomous answer choice (0 = *No* and 1 = *Yes*) to indicate their belief. The second measure is "Do you support racial profiling in retail stores?" Like the belief measure, the respondents used a dichotomous answer choice (0 = *No* and 1 = *Yes*) to indicate their support.

Analysis Plan

The analysis plan takes place in a series of steps. The first step is a presentation of the descriptive statistics that provides some indication of the distribution of the measures. The second step is a presentation of a series of logistic regression analyses. The logistic regression analyses allow us to address our research questions given that both dependent measures are dichotomous. Bachman and Paternoster (2004) argued that using Ordinary Least Squares regression was an improper technique for understanding the correlates of dichotomous dependent measures. Pampel (2000) showed that logistic regression was better in this regard because it is sensitive to the non-normal distribution of the dichotomous measure. An important condition for all forms of regression is multicollinearity. Multicollinearity occurs when more than one independent measure captures the same information resulting in a correlation that is so high that it distorts the proper estimation in a regression analysis (Freund, Wilson, & Sa, 2006). To detect multicollinearity, the authors used the tolerance measure. Field (2003) wrote that tolerances below 0.20 showed multicollinearity. Menard (2002) indicated that tolerances were acceptable to use with logistic regression analysis to detect multicollinearity.

RESULTS

Step 1

Table 1 presents the descriptive statistics for the measures used in this study. The average age of the respondents is between 35 and 44 years old. Black respondents comprised 4% of the sample. The average income of the respondents in the sample is between 40,000 and 59,999. The average educational level of the respondents is some college. Males made up 48% of the sample. More than half of the respondents indicated that they held the belief racial profiling occurs in stores (62%), but only 14% of the respondents indicated that they supported racial profiling in the stores.[1] Close to 80% of the respondents (79%) agreed that racial profiling was not ethical in stores and a similar amount (80%) agreed that racial profiling in stores is a discriminatory practice. The respondents indicated that they did not believe that racial profiling was effective in identifying shoplifters (mean = 2.91). Following Kline's (2004) argument that measures should have skewness below 3 and kurtosis below 10, the measures have normal distributions. In Appendix A, we provide a correlation matrix of the measures to show how they share variance.

Step 2

Table 2 presents the first logistic regression analysis. This logistic regression analysis addresses our first research question: how does perceived effectiveness, the view that CRP is discriminatory, or that the practice is not ethical influence whether individuals believe that CRP occurs while controlling for demographics (e.g., age, race, gender, income, and education)? The analysis revealed that as the respondents' age increases, respondents are less likely to

Table 1. Descriptive Statistics for the Measures

Measure	Mean	SD	Skew	Kurtosis
Age	35–44	1.82	0.15	−0.94
White versus non-White	.90	0.31	−2.60	4.78
Income	40,000–59,999	2.14	0.42	−0.59
Education	3.67	1.56	0.09	−1.31
Male	0.48	0.50	0.08	−2.00
Belief that racial profiling occurs in stores	0.62	0.49	−0.51	−1.75
Support for racial profiling in stores	0.14	0.35	2.07	2.28
Racial profiling in stores is not ethical	0.79	0.41	−1.39	−0.06
Racial profiling in stores is discrimination	0.80	0.40	−1.48	0.18
Racial profiling in stores is effective	2.91	1.72	0.58	−0.60

Note: N = 852

Table 2. Logistic Regression Analysis Belief Racial Profiling Occurs in Stores

Measure	B	SE	Exp(b)	Tolerance
Age	−0.17**	0.06	0.84	0.91
White versus non-White	−0.52	0.35	0.59	0.90
Income	−0.14**	0.05	0.87	0.70
Education	0.08	0.07	1.08	0.75
Male	−0.03	0.19	0.98	0.95
Racial profiling in stores is not ethical	0.10	0.27	1.10	0.74
Racial profiling in stores is discrimination	1.31**	0.26	3.69	0.80
Racial profiling in stores is effective	0.33**	0.07	1.39	0.81

Chi-square = 74.60***
−2 Log likelihood = 692.22
Cox & Snell R^2 = .12
Nagelkerke R^2 = .16

Note: N = 852; **$p < .01$. ***$p < .001$.

Table 3. Logistic Regression Analysis Support for Racial Profiling in Stores

Measure	B	SE	Exp(b)	Tolerance
Age	0.03	0.07	1.03	0.91
White versus non-White	−0.41	0.40	0.66	0.90
Income	−0.04	0.07	0.96	0.72
Education	0.10	0.10	1.10	0.76
Male	−0.05	0.27	0.87	0.94
Racial profiling in stores is not ethical	−1.66**	0.30	0.19	0.73
Racial profiling in stores is discrimination	−0.20	0.31	0.82	0.79
Racial profiling in stores is effective	0.44**	0.08	1.55	0.81

Chi-square = 115.99***
−2 Log likelihood = 397.65
Cox & Snell R^2 = .17
Nagelkerke R^2 = .30

Note: N = 852; **$p < .01$. ***$p < .001$.

believe that racial profiling occurs in stores ($b = -0.17$, Exp(b) = 0.84). Similarly, as the respondents' incomes increases, they are less likely to believe that racial profiling occurs in stores ($b = -0.14$, Exp(b) = 0.87). On the other hand, individuals who believe that racial profiling in stores is a discriminatory practice are 3.69 times more likely to believe that racial profiling occurs in stores ($b = 1.31$, Exp(b) = 3.69). Similarly, individuals who believe that racial profiling is effective in stores at identifying criminal activity are 1.39 times more likely to believe that CRP does occur ($b = 0.33$, Exp(b) = 1.39). The tolerances for each of the measures are above 0.20, suggesting that multicollinearity is not a problem with these measures.[2] Overall, the results from this analysis shows that older and wealthier respondents are less likely to believe that CRP occurs, but the respondents that believe that the practice are discrimination and effective are more likely to believe that CRP occurs.

The results in Table 3 address the second research question. Specifically, the logistic regression analysis addresses our second research question: How is perceived support for CRP influenced by the ethical nature of the practice, its perceived effectiveness, and the feeling that it is discriminatory while controlling for demographics (e.g., age, gender, etc.)? Individuals who believe that racial profiling in stores is unethical are not as likely to support the practice (b = –1.66, Exp(b) = 0.19). Individuals who believe that racial profiling is effective in identifying criminal activity are 1.55 times more likely to support racial profiling in stores (b = 0.44, Exp(b) = 1.55). The tolerances indicate that multicollinearity is not a problem in this analysis.[3]

DISCUSSION

This research investigated public opinion on racial profiling in retail settings. First, it investigated whether respondents felt that CRP occurs in retail establishments. Slightly more than 60% of the sample felt that it did. This figure is identical to previous research on the subject using national poll data from 2004 (Jordan et al., 2009). The results suggest that the views of Pennsylvanians are in line with citizens across the country, who largely believe that the practice is being used by retailers.

The first research question investigated how the ethical nature of the practice, its perceived effectiveness, and the feeling that it is discriminatory influence whether the individual believed that CRP occurred. In contrast to previous public opinion on CRP, older Pennsylvanians were less likely to believe that CRP exists. Older residents are likely less in touch with racial profiling in any context. While researchers have argued that it has been occurring for more than a century (Harris, 2003), some of these older respondents likely lived through a time when they were oblivious to such practices because they had little contact with non-Whites; much older respondents lived through a time when non-Whites could not even enter some retail stores. It is still perplexing how in 2009 they would not have heard of some of the more high-profile CRP incidents. It might be that, even with the occurrence of high-profile incidents, the media does not publicize such incidents as much as they do the incidents that occur on roadways or in airports. Also, the authors speculate that older citizens might also be skeptical of CRP claims leveled against retailers. Those with higher incomes also expressed skepticism that CRP was occurring. This might be the product of the fact that wealthy residents receive the most privileged treatment in retail businesses and cannot perceive that disparaging treatment such as profiling occurs.

Two additional findings relate to the new measures explored in the research. First, the measure related to perceived discrimination showed that those respondents who felt that CRP was discriminatory felt it existed in stores. Given the newness of this measure, the authors can only speculate as to the reason for this finding. It could be that these individuals are likely to have liberal political leanings that tend to perceive that discrimination is a problem in society and, for example, just as they believe employers discriminate in hiring and support equal opportunity programs such as affirmative action (Federico & Sidanius, 2002), they are also more likely to believe that CRP likely occurs (Jordan et al., 2009). Including a question on political orientation in future qualitative responses might have shed additional light on this finding. The finding that respondents who believed that profiling in retail stores was effective would have believed that CRP exists in the first place makes sense. Those respondents who see the practice as being effective would intuitively believe that it was being used.

The second research question investigated how the perceived support for CRP is influenced by the ethical nature of the practice, its perceived effectiveness, and the feeling that it is discriminatory while controlling for common demographics. It was promising to find that only 14% of the respondents supported profiling in retail settings. Nonetheless, it was still instructive to explore the multivariate findings related to support for profiling in retail stores. The only two variables that were significant in the model were two of the new exploratory measures. Those who felt that CRP was not ethical did not support the practice. This might point to the fact that those respondents who believe CRP violates their mores are not likely to support the practice. This generally represents an understudied aspect of public opinion; that is, whether moral beliefs influence views. Though limited, one recent research study did not find church attendance to be significant on views regarding profiling at airports (Gabbidon, Penn, Jordan, & Higgins, 2009); however, the preliminary findings herein might reflect that researchers are excluding a potentially important variable in public opinion—ethical beliefs.

The measure related to the perceived effectiveness of CRP and support for its use in retail stores was significant. Here, it also makes sense that those who believe the practice is effective will also support its use. Notably, even with the inclusion of this measure, there is still a knowledge gap as to why they believe it is effective. Thus, it is likely that they have not done research on the effectiveness of CRP or seen it in practice, yet they believe it works. Here again, more qualitative insights might be required to get a better understanding of their views. Another interesting finding was that race was not significant. Previous CRP research has been clear in that non-Whites are significantly less likely than Whites to support CRP (Jordan et al., 2009) or racial profiling in any context (Higgins, Gabbidon, & Jordan, 2008; Reitzel, Rice, & Piquero, 2004; Weitzer & Tuch, 2006).

This research was limited in several ways. First, it was restricted to the views of citizens in one state. Thus, future researchers might want to pursue regional or national studies on this topic. Second, the sample had a limited number of racial/ethnic minorities. Consequently, the researchers could not run split-sample analyses that have been instructive in past studies (see Reitzel et al., 2004). Third, as noted above, the close-ended questions limited the qualitative responses that would have provided additional nuances to the research findings. Fourth, the data are cross-sectional; thus, we are not able to determine how these perceptions might change over time. Finally, since the research was exploratory, we did use a particular theory to contextualize our results. We anticipate that future researchers will build on our work by engaging in more theoretically grounded work that further tests our measures.

CONCLUSION

This study continued the exploration into public opinion on racial profiling in retail stores. It expanded the previous literature by including measures that revealed whether respondents' views related to ethics, discrimination, and the effectiveness of profiling in retail settings were influential in the perceived existence and support for profiling. The results found support for the utility of these measures. Of particular note were the findings related to support for CRP. Racial/ethnic minorities who have experienced CRP and know that it exists need to be more vocal of their experiences. A prior study found only a small number of those who felt they experienced CRP reported it (Gabbidon et al., 2008). In the absence of taking action and, in warranted cases, suing retailers who engage in these discriminatory practices, the general public will continue to be in the dark regarding the existence of CRP.

To be clear, there is no scholarly evidence that CRP is an effective practice. In fact, the empirical research that has examined shoplifting trends in retail stores found no differences by race/ethnicity (Dabney et al., 2004). Nonetheless, even though a minority of respondents supported the practice and felt it was effective, these same respondents represent everyday people who work at retailers and can become the clerks who profile racial/ethnic minorities (see Gabbidon, 2003; Schreer et al., 2009). Consequently, it is in the interest of researchers who have data that speak to this issue to work through the media to let the existing empirical research tell the story. Similarly, civil rights organizations should lead campaigns that will ensure that CRP becomes a relic of the past.

Appendix A. Bivariate Correlations of the Measures

Measure	1	2	3	4	5	6	7	8	9	10
1. Belief that racial profiling occurs in stores	1.00									
2. Support for racial profiling in stores	0.11*	1.00								
3. Racial profiling in stores is not ethical	0.02	-0.40*	1.00							
4. Racial profiling in stores is discrimination	0.23*	-0.19*	0.42*	1.00						
5. Racial profiling in stores is effective	0.21*	0.35*	-0.37*	-0.18*	1.00					
6. Age	-0.10*	0.10*	-0.12*	-0.11*	0.12*	1.00				
7. White versus Non-White	-0.10*	-0.03	-0.07*	-0.04	-0.10*	0.14*	1.00			
8. Income	-0.08*	-0.10*	0.14*	0.15*	-0.18*	-0.18*	0.18*	1.00		
9. Education	0.00	-0.04	0.07	0.14*	-0.22*	-0.01	0.08*	0.46*	1.00	
10. Male	-0.06	0.03	-0.04	-0.12*	-0.05	0.07	0.09*	0.15*	0.03	1.00

Note: $*p < .05$.

NOTES

1. These results indicate that the measure of whether respondents indicated that they supported racial profiling in stores is non-normal. The non-normality is due to a preponderance of zero responses. This would suggest that censoring might be important in addressing our research questions. In addition, for all of the measures, we analyzed them for missing data. We found a small amount of missing data in the sample, but it was not enough to bias the results. Results of the bias tests may be obtained from the second author on request.

2. One of the reviewers suggested that Tobit regression analysis may be the proper analysis for our data. In the instance of the belief that CRP occurs, we did not find a large number of zero or one responses. Thus, we believed that our logistic regression sufficed in this instance.

3. In this instance, we found a large number of zeros. This indicates a strong "floor" effect in the data. To supplement our logistic regression analysis, we performed Tobit analysis. The results from the Tobit analysis are substantively the same. The substance of our results includes significance level and direction of the effect. We did not include these analyses in our results because the interpretation of the Tobit analysis is not intuitive. For instance, McDonald and Moffitt (1980) argued that proper interpretation of Tobit analysis requires a researcher to develop marginal effects. Marginal effects are different lenses that are data-driven to understand the effect of one measure on another measure. Given that the results were substantively the same, we felt that the odds ratios were easier for presentation and consumption. However, our Tobit analysis is available from the second author on request.

REFERENCES

Adamson, J. (2000). *The Denny's story: How a company in crisis resurrected its good name and reputation.* New York, NY: John Wiley & Sons.

Asquith, J. L., & Bristow, D. N. (2000). To catch a thief: A pedagogical study of retail shoplifting. *Journal of Education for Business, 75,* 271–276.

Bachman, R., & Paternoster, R. (2004). *Statistical analysis for criminology and criminal justice students* (2nd ed.). New York, NY: McGraw Hill.

Crockett, D., Grier, S. A., & Williams, J. A. (2003). Coping with marketplace discrimination: An exploration of the experiences of black men. *Academy of Marketing Science Review, 4,* 4–21.

Dabney, D. A., Dugan, L., Topalli, V., & Hollinger, R. C. (2006). The impact of implicit stereotyping on offender profiling: Unexpected results from an observational study of shoplifting. *Criminal Justice and Behavior, 33,* 646–674.

Dabney, D. A., Hollinger, R. C., & Dugan, L. (2004). Who actually steals? A study of covertly observed shoplifters. *Justice Quarterly, 21,* 693–728.

Feagin, J. R. (1991). The continuing significance of race: Antidiscrimination in public places. *American Sociological Review, 56,* 101–116.

Federico, C. M., & Sidanius, J. (2002). Sophistication and the antecedents of whites' racial policy attitudes: Racism, ideology, and affirmative action in America. *Public Opinion Quarterly, 66,* 145–176.

Field, A. (2003). *Discovering statistics using SPSS for windows.* London, England: SAGE.

Fifield, A. (2001). Shopping while black. *Good Housekeeping, 233,* 129–136.

Freund, R. J., Wilson, W. J., & Sa, P. (2006). *Regression analysis* (2nd ed.). Burlington, MA: Academic Press.

Gabbidon, S. L. (2003). Racial profiling by store clerks and security personnel in retail establishments: An exploration of "Shopping while black." *Journal of Contemporary Criminal Justice, 19,* 345–364.

Gabbidon, S. L., Craig, R., Okafo, N., Marzette, L., & Peterson, S. A. (2008). The prevalence and nature of consumer racial profiling experiences among students at historically black colleges and universities: An exploratory study. *Journal of Criminal Justice, 36*, 354–361.

Gabbidon, S. L., & Higgins, G. E. (2007). Consumer racial profiling and perceived victimization: A phone survey of Philadelphia area residents. *American Journal of Criminal Justice, 32*, 1–11.

Gabbidon, S. L., & Higgins, G. E. (2008). Profiling White Americans: Exploring "Shopping while White." In M. J. Lynch, E. B. Patterson, & K. Childs (Eds.), *Racial divide: Race, ethnicity and criminal justice* (pp. 179–209). Monsey, NY: Criminal Justice Press.

Gabbidon, S. L., & Higgins, G. E. (2009). Contextualizing public opinion on consumer racial profiling: A Marxist approach. *Journal of Ethnicity in Criminal Justice, 7*, 222–235.

Gabbidon, S. L., Penn, E.B., Jordan, K., & Higgins, G. E. (2009). The influence of race/ethnicity on the perceived prevalence and support for racial profiling at airports. *Criminal Justice Policy Review, 20*, 344–358.

Harris, A. G. (2003). Shopping while black: Applying 42 U.S.C. § 1981 to cases of consumer racial profiling. *Boston College Third World Law Journal, 23*, 1–56.

Harris, A. G., Henderson, G. R., & Williams, J. D. (2005). Courting customers: Assessing consumer racial profiling and other marketplace discrimination. *Journal of Public Policy & Marketing, 24*, 163–171.

Henderson, T. P. (2001). Perception that some merchants practice racial profiling generates debate. *Stores, 83*, 26–30, 32.

Higgins, G. E., & Gabbidon, S. L. (2009). Perceptions of consumer racial profiling and negative emotions: An exploratory study. *Criminal Justice and Behavior, 36*, 77–88.

Higgins, G. E., Gabbidon, S. L., & Jordan, K. L. (2008). Examining the generality of citizens' views on racial profiling in diverse situational contexts. *Criminal Justice and Behavior, 35*, 1527–1541.

Higgins, G. E., Gabbidon, S. L., & Vito, G. (2010). Exploring the influence of race relations and public safety concerns on public support for racial profiling during traffic stops. *International Journal of Police Science & Management, 12*, 12–22.

Hollinger, R. C., & Adams, A. (2009). *2008 National retail security survey: Final report*. Gainesville, FL: Security Research Project.

Jordan, K., Gabbidon, S. L., & Higgins, G. E. (2009). Exploring the perceived extent of and citizens' support for consumer racial profiling: Results from a national poll. *Journal of Criminal Justice, 37*, 353–359.

Kline, R. (2004). *Principals and practices of structural equation modeling* (2nd ed.). New York, NY: Guilford.

Lee, J. (2000). The salience of race in everyday life: Black customers' shopping experiences in Black and White neighborhoods. *Work and Occupations, 27*, 353–376.

McDonald, J. F., & Moffitt, R. A. (1980). The uses of Tobit analysis. *The Review of Economics and Statistics, 62*, 18–21.

Menard, S. (2002). *Applied logistic regression analysis* (2nd ed.). Thousand Oaks, CA: SAGE.

O'Connell, T. (2001). Retail racism: Caught red handed. *Security, 38*, 9–10, 12, 14.

Pampel, F. C. (2000). *Logistic regression: A primer. Sage quantitative applications in the social sciences series #132*. Thousand Oaks, CA: SAGE.

Reitzel, J., Rice, S. K., & Piquero, A. R. (2004). Lines and shadows: Perceptions of racial profiling and the Hispanic experience. *Journal of Criminal Justice, 32*, 607–616.

Schreer, G. E., Smith, S., & Thomas, K. (2009). "Shopping while Black:" Examining racial discrimination in a retail setting. *Journal of Applied Social Psychology, 39*, 1432–1444.

Tabachnick, B. G., & Fidell, L. S. (2000). *Using multivariate statistics*. New York, NY: Allyn & Bacon.

Weitzer, R., & Tuch, S. A. (2002). Perceptions of racial profiling: Race, class, and personal experience. *Criminology, 40*, 435–456.

Weitzer, R., & Tuch, S. A. (2005). Racially biased policing: Determinants of citizen perceptions. *Social Forces, 83*, 1009–1030.

Weitzer, R., & Tuch, S. A. (2006). *Race and police in America.* New York, NY: Cambridge University Press.

Williams, J. D., Harris, A. M., & Henderson, G. R. (2006). Equal treatment for equal dollars in Illinois: Assessing consumer racial profiling and other marketplace discrimination. *Law Enforcement Executive Forum, 2006*, 83–104.

Williams, J. D., Henderson, G. R., & Harris, A. M. (2001). Consumer racial profiling: Bigotry goes to market. *The New Crisis, 108*, 22–24.

*Shaun L. Gabbidon is Distinguished Professor of Criminal Justice in the School of Public Affairs at Penn State, Harrisburg. His most recent books include *Race and Crime* (3rd edition; 2012, SAGE) and the co-authored book, *A Theory of African American Offending* (2011; Routledge). He is the coauthor of the recently published book, *A Theory of African American Offending: Race, Racism, and Crime* (Routledge, 2011). He currently serves as the founding editor of the SAGE journal *Race and Justice: An International Journal.*

George E. Higgins is a professor in the Department of Justice Administration at the University of Louisville. His most recent publications appear or are forthcoming in the *Journal of Criminal Justice, Deviant Behavior, Criminal Justice and Behavior, Youth and Society,* and the *American Journal of Criminal Justice.*

Controlling Police Officer Behavior in the Field: Using What We Know to Regulate Police-Initiated Stops and Prevent Racially Biased Policing

*by Michael D. White**

INTRODUCTION

> *"Such fundamental change is critical, because history teaches that if reform is to last, it must change the systems and values to which officers adhere rather than just the officers themselves (Skolnick and Fyfe, 1993: 187)."*

Police-initiated stops of citizens have become an established crime-control tactic in many police departments, often as part of order maintenance and gun suppression strategies. This practice is rooted in the police powers granted through the U.S. Supreme Court ruling in *Terry v. Ohio* (392 U.S. 1, 1968), which allows police to stop and question a person if the officer has *reasonable suspicion* to believe that the person is engaged in or is about to engage in criminal activity. The stop decision must be based on facts that can be articulated, and if there is a reasonable belief that the individual may be armed, the officer is also permitted to conduct a protective over-the-clothes search for weapons. This tactic has become divisive in some jurisdictions. For example, recent studies show that the New York Police Department (NYPD) has been routinely stopping (questioning and searching), on average, more than 500,000 citizens annually since 2006. This practice has served as a major source of tension between the NYPD and minority communities, and has been tied to substantial increases in civil rights claims against police and citizen complaints (Greene, 1999) and two class-action law suits against the NYPD alleging racial profiling.[1] Similar events have transpired in Philadelphia.[2]

The core controversy surrounding police-initiated stops of citizens centers on the constitutionality of the practice—are police stopping citizens based on race or ethnicity, rather than reasonable suspicion that can be articulated? In other words, does the practice amount to racial-ethnic profiling? A second and equally important issue involves the consequences of the crime-control practice for police legitimacy and police-minority community relations (Tyler, 2006). The purpose of this paper is to assess how police departments can control their officers' decision-making with regard to police-initiated stops of citizens. That is, how can departments prevent their officers from engaging in racially biased policing?[3]

This question is examined through a larger discretion control framework, drawing upon what we already know about how police departments can effectively control their officers' behavior—or misbehavior—in the field. As the quote from Skolnick and Fyfe above suggests, these are complex issues that go far beyond simply removing a few bad apples, or adding a few extra hours of training. Clearly, the challenges surrounding this question are daunting. Also clear however, is that the larger discretion control framework offers numerous lessons on effective internal accountability strategies. These lessons are the focus of this paper. Four different organizational areas are described: 1) careful recruitment and selection (screening out [and in] processes); 2) training; 3) administrative policy; and 4) supervision, accountability and commitment from the Chief. With each area, the paper reviews what we know from prior research on other areas of officer behavior, and highlights how these lessons can guide the dialogue over controlling racial bias in police-initiated stops of citizens. The paper concludes with some final thoughts and ongoing challenges for police accountability.

LESSONS LEARNED FROM PRIOR RESEARCH ON ORGANIZATIONAL CONTROL STRATEGIES

Careful Recruitment and Selection of Personnel

More than 40 years ago, the President's Commission on Law Enforcement and the Administration of Justice (1967) recommended proper screening of applicants to identify those who are ill-suited for the policing profession. Thought the traditional approach to recruit selection has been focused on "screening out" those who are mentally (or otherwise) unfit to be a police officer, this important process also involves efforts to identify candidates with sought-after qualities who should be "screened in" during the application process. This dialogue over screening out (and in) job applicants has typically occurred within the context of concerns over corruption and brutality, but the lessons are equally relevant for racially biased policing.

"Screening Out" processes: Both empirical research and practical experience have demonstrated that it is very difficult to identify individuals who are unfit for the police profession (Mollen Commission, 1994). For example, Grant and Grant (1995) concluded that "efforts to improve the quality of police officer performance by screening out those recruits who will not make good police officers have generally been unsuccessful." Grant and Grant (1995: 152) were especially critical of

psychological testing (e.g., MMPI) and clinical interviews, which seek to identify applicants with "poor mental health and undesirable personality traits." Nevertheless, most police leaders would agree on two key points: 1) that there are certain characteristics that should serve as red flags for potential employment; and 2) police departments should conduct extensive background examinations to determine whether applicants possess those characteristics. In fact, numerous misconduct scandals (e.g., in Miami, Washington, DC and Los Angeles) have been linked to "mass hiring," where departments hired hundreds of officers in a short period of time and did not carry out thorough selection processes (Skolnick and Fyfe, 1993; Fyfe and Kane, 2006). Background investigations typically include a criminal history check, credit check, and interviews of family members, neighbors, and former employers. Among other red flags such as prior criminal behavior, drug use, poor performance in prior employment, and questionable morality (e.g., lying on the job application), departments should also be looking for any evidence that a candidate possesses prejudicial attitudes that could lead to discriminatory actions on the job. Background examinations are costly and time-consuming, but recent research continues to highlight their importance for screening out poor applicants (e.g., the old axiom, 'one the best predictors of future behavior is past behavior,' remains true; Kane and White, 2011). In their study of career-ending misconduct in the NYPD, Kane and White (2009: 765) highlighted the importance of "screening out" processes.

> Perhaps the most salient policy implications of the present study relate to departmental screening processes. Because of the low visibility of police work, the unique opportunities for misconduct presented to police officers, and the conflict that often exists between the police and the public in certain communities, it seems clear that police departments should continue to exclude people from policing who have demonstrated records of criminal involvement and employee disciplinary problems. These represent evidence-based policy recommendations for which criminological perspectives developed for the general population (i.e., outside of policing) produced support (e.g., control theories, opportunity theories, and perhaps even routine activities theory).

"Screening In" Processes: The second aspect of recruit selection involves the identification of qualities which "predict" good policing on the street. The interest in identifying those best-suited for police work (rather than those who are ill-suited) gained traction in the 1960s, particularly with the passage of the Civil Rights Act of 1964, amid concerns that prevailing "screening out" processes disproportionately affected minority and female applicants (Grant and Grant, 1995). Kane and White (2009: 765) highlighted this aspect of the application process

as well, noting that their "findings also suggest the importance of screening *in* or identifying potential police officers whose presence in police organizations may have the effect of making them better behaved."[4]

Though efforts at identifying predictors of good policing have had limited success (see Grant and Grant, 1995), relevant personal attributes would certainly include good judgment, an even temperament, respect and appreciation for diversity, creativity and problem-solving skills, ability to think on one's feet and handle pressure, and leadership skills. The skill-set for good policing can be traced back to the very earliest writings on the profession by Sir Robert Peel, who stated that recruits should be intelligent, in good physical condition, of good moral character and in possession of an even temperament (Miller, 1977). These qualities have been a mainstay in discussions of good policing since that time: from the President's Commission on Law Enforcement and the Administration of Justice (1967), the classic works of Bittner (1967) and Muir (1977), to Goldstein's (1979, 1990) work on problem-oriented policing and the recent work of the National Research Council (Skogan and Frydl, 2004). However, few have captured the complexity of these qualities better than Muir (1977) in his book, *Police: Streetcorner Politicians*. Borrowing from Weber's model of the professional politician, Muir (1977: 50) argued that the *professional policeman* possesses two important qualities: the officer is morally reconciled with the use of coercive force (called "passion"), and the officer understands the dignity and tragedy of the human condition (called "perspective," or empathy).[5] Within this framework, Muir (1977) also described three types of nonprofessional policeman: *enforcers* (those with passion but no perspective); *reciprocators* (those with perspective but no passion); and *avoiders* (those who lacked both passion and perspective).

In his book, Muir (1977) introduces three police officers who work on skid row: two who lacked the qualities to be professional policeman (Jim Longstreet and Bee Haywood), and one who was a professional (Mike Marshall). Muir uses their stories to highlight the consequences of poor policing, and these characterizations are especially relevant for consideration of the importance of recruit selection for reducing the prevalence of racially biased policing. The first officer, Jim Longstreet, was an *avoider* who lacked both passion and perspective. Muir (1977: 65, 67) observed that Longstreet worked hard to avoid "difficulty" and "hot situations." Unfortunately, this avoidance/neglect strategy had dire consequences for the community, as those "who stood to profit from the policeman's absence—the strong-arm, the bully, the vicious" took control of Longstreet's beat. The second officer, Bee Haywood, thrived on using physical violence. He was an *enforcer* who had passion but no perspective. Muir (1977) noted that officers like Haywood experienced a number of negative consequences from their brutal actions. First, the use of violence by police inevitably escalated police-citizen encounters, as residents soon learned what to expect and responded in kind (Muir, 1977). Second, residents learned to avoid the violence-prone officers and gave them little in the way of useful information. As a result, Haywood—and others like him—became completely disconnected from the goings-on in the neighborhood (Muir, 1977).

The third officer, Mike Marshall, had both passion and perspective. Unlike Longstreet and Haywood, Marshall had developed both eloquence and empathy in the way he carried out his work; and in doing so, Marshall "neutralized the fear, distrust and antagonism" that characterized the beats worked by Longstreet and Haywood. The consequences of Marshall's efforts for both himself and his beat were profound.

> Marshall's development of skid row had transformed the dispossessed of that community into 'good citizens,' into people who had something to lose and therefore something to protect—a line of credit, a decent friendship, a good public servant, whatever it was that Marshall had come to represent through 'a life spent in doing good before their eyes.'

> One consequence of this professional response was that the community tended to develop confidence in the beat patrolman. It became more open, had a greater sense of security, and enjoyed a number of little productive happinesses. For the officer himself, one result was that he developed a feeling of safety, a more informed understanding of his beat, and considerable moral gratification from doing the job well. (Muir, 1977: 79–80)

Relevance for Racially Biased Policing: Though the research by Muir is more than 30 years old, I believe the principles of good policing that he describes are still relevant today. Importantly, these principles—empathy, moral acceptance of coercive authority, protection of the vulnerable, and problem solving—reflect what Bittner (1967) and Muir (1977) called good craftsmanship. These qualities are also central tenets of community and problem-oriented policing, the prevailing philosophies of good policing (or good craft) today. Quite simply, officers who possess these skills will be less likely to engage in racially biased behavior, and departments should aggressively seek them out in their recruitment and selection processes.

Training

Careful recruitment and selection must be followed with effective training in the police academy, as well as later through field and in-service training. At the academy, the goal of training is to provide officers with the basic skills and knowledge necessary to become a police officer. Cadets must receive a clear message at this early stage that racially biased policing is inappropriate, illegal and that it will not be tolerated. Following graduation from the academy, officers are typically assigned to a veteran officer for a period of field training (the FTO program). The FTO experience is intended to bridge the gap between the classroom environment of the academy and the "real world" of policing on the street. This is a formative stage of a police officer's career, and it is critically important for field training officers to impart the message that racially biased practices are not consistent with the principles of good policing. Fyfe (1995: 164) highlighted the importance of the FTO role:

> When sergeants or older officers give young cops those fabled instructions to 'forget what they told you in the police academy, kid, you'll learn how to do it on the street,' formal training is instantly and irreparably devalued. Worse, when officers actually see firsthand that the behavioral strictures in which they were schooled are routinely ignored in practice, formal training is neutralized and the definitions of appropriate behavior are instead made in the secrecy of officers' locker rooms.

The final form of training, called "in-service" where officers periodically receiving additional training while on the job, can be used to "refresh" officers on ethical issues, such as avoiding discriminatory decision-making, and to re-send the message that the department leadership denounces racial bias and expects the same from its officers.

In his review of how police training can be structured to reduce violence between police and citizens, Fyfe (1995) presented a number of key recommendations that are equally relevant for how training can reduce racially biased policing. These recommendations and how each applies to racially biased policing are described below.

1. Effective training in violence prevention and reduction must be realistic.

For police-citizen violence:

> "Training for any endeavor should simulate as closely as possible the actual working conditions for which trainees are being prepared ...
> Although it cannot be eliminated, the artificiality of police training can be minimized. Perhaps the best way to do this is in role-play scenarios

in facilities that duplicate as closely as possible the conditions officers encounter in the field, both indoors and outdoors (Fyfe, 1995: 167)."

For racially biased policing:

Many scholars have argued for police training that moves away from the traditional pedagogical, lecture-based curriculum. For example, Bayley and Bittner (1984: 55) stated that learning can be "accelerated and made more systematic" by relevant training that brings the reality of police work into the academy. The question is how best to accomplish this. Andragogy has emerged as an effective adult learning technique in a variety of fields (Brookfield, 1986; Caffarella, 1993; Merriam and Caffarella, 1999), and several scholars have suggested that the approach could serve to increase the relevancy of police academy training (Birzer, 2003). Andragogy highlights self-directed learning with the instructor playing a facilitating role, with students participating in "self-directed group discussions and active debate," while the instructors "...manage the classroom by allowing participants to share their experiences and knowledge...integrate new knowledge, and...provide strategies that will allow transfer of learning back to the job (Birzer, 2003: 34–35)."[6] Instead of listening to dry lectures and war stories, recruits learn through critical discussion and interaction with other recruits and instructional staff. When this form of instruction is matched with the scenario-based role-plays described by Fyfe, police instructors can develop valued, informative curricula that eliminate the traditional artificiality of training; more sufficiently prepares recruits for the street; and most importantly, clearly conveys the message that racially biased policing will not be tolerated.

2. Violence reduction training must be carefully tailored to the officers; and community's experiences and needs.

For police-citizen violence:

> "Every community also possesses unique characteristics that create specific challenges for officers, and these must be taken into account in training...One of the best ways to assure that training closely fits the actual needs of the community and the police is to base it on the real experience of the community and the police. Noteworthy police encounters with citizens—both those that have come to unhappy endings and those in which potential disaster was averted—should be documented and reviewed thoroughly for their training implications (Fyfe, 1995: 171)."

For racially biased policing:

Related to Fyfe's point, for years there have been calls for police to be racially and ethnically representative of the communities they serve (e.g., Commission on Accreditation for Law Enforcement Agencies [CALEA; 2009] standards). There are a number of reasons why diversity in police departments is emphasized, most notably the perceived link between under-representation and long-term tense conflict between police and minority communities (Skolnick and Fyfe, 1993). Moreover, many believe that increasing the diversity of the police force so that it reflects the community demographic trends will enhance police legitimacy, which will ultimately increase community cooperation and police effectiveness (e.g., Skogan & Frydl, 2004). Logically, a representative police department is more likely to understand the culture and views of the community, and is more likely to be tolerant of those views. Importantly, this tolerance and understanding must be imparted early on to recruits during academy training (Haberfeld, 2002).

As an illustration, the Glendale (AZ) Police Department created a training curriculum to address the new state immigration law (SB1070), and they tailored the law to meet the mission of their department and the experiences of their community. This is perhaps best highlighted by the opening statements in the training:

- It is the mission of the GPD to protect the lives and the property of the people we serve.
- We serve everyone in this community regardless of their immigration status.
- We have worked very hard to build a trusting relationship with our community.
- We are effective as a law enforcement agency because we do have the community's trust.
- It is important that we work to maintain this trust, which is the foundation of our community policing efforts.
- It is, however, equally important that we enforce the law. This duty is part of the oath that we took when we became police officers (Glendale Police Department, 2010).

These statements highlight the critical importance of community trust and convey the clear message that Glendale police officers, though required to enforce state law (including the new immigration law), must honor the primary mission of the department. The tailored approach developed by Glendale is very different from other law enforcement agencies that have taken on immigration enforcement as a primary responsibility (e.g., Maricopa County Sheriff's Office).[7]

3. Violence-reduction training must be continuous.

For police-citizen violence:

> "Some of the most critical police violence prevention and reduction skills are needed so rarely that they are likely to atrophy into uselessness unless they are the subjects of frequent refresher training... Thus, as in medicine and other emergency professions, constant in-service training is necessary to keep officers' most critical, but rarely employed skills at a useful level (Fyfe, 1995: 173)."

For racially biased policing:

Fyfe's recommendation for continuous training is important for racially biased policing, but his rationale is less applicable. Though use of force is rare and his concerns over skill atrophy are on the mark, the applicable skill set for avoiding racially biased behavior is employed by police on a daily basis—with each police/citizen encounter. As a result, the need for continuous training on issues related to race/ethnicity, cultural diversity and tolerance, and legal issues is even more critical. Besides the day-to-day use of these skills, there are number of additional reasons why this is important, such as changes in the law which impact police practice (e.g., SB1070 in Arizona). Also, the racial and ethnic makeup of a community can change very quickly, and failure on the part of the police department to recognize these changes can lead to significant conflict between police and those new population groups (e.g., Cuban immigration to Miami and the Liberty City riot in 1980; Los Angeles leading up to the riots in the early 1990s; Fyfe, 1995). In simple terms, departments must remain aware of changes in their constituency, and they must insure through proper training that their officers are prepared to handle those changes. Palmiotto (2003: 15) highlighted the importance of this point, noting that: "Continuing police training throughout a police officer's career enable the officer to function more efficiently and safely, and is considered important in curtailing civil liability actions against an officer and his department."

4. Appraise the effects of violence-reduction training by concentrating on officers' conduct rather than incident outcomes.

For police-citizen violence:

> "Like assessments of surgeons' efforts, judgments about the propriety of officers' conduct and the adequacy of training should be based on what

the officer *did*, rather than on the outcome of what they did. To do otherwise is to overlook inappropriate conduct until it results in disaster... (Fyfe, 1995: 174)."

For racially biased policing:

Scholars such as Bayley (1986) and Binder and Scharf (1980) have maintained that police-citizen encounters involve multiple decision points, with decisions made at earlier stages clearly affecting decisions made later in the encounter.[8] At each phase of the encounter, the police officer and the citizen make decisions and respond to the decisions of the other participant—much like a chess match. The importance of this perspective is that it highlights Fyfe's point above about process or conduct. How did the officer behave at each stage of the encounter? How could the officer have acted differently to achieve a more just outcome? With regard to deadly force incidents, Fyfe (1986) described police departments' tendency to focus on the final frame of a decision—what he called the split-second syndrome—while neglecting the earlier and just as important decisions that an officer made that resulted in him/her being in a position where force was necessary. To judge the appropriateness of police behavior based solely on the outcome—whether that outcome is a use of force, or a search that led to confiscation of a small amount of marijuana—is shortsighted; in effect, allowing the ends to justify the means. As Fyfe (1995: 174) suggests, this final-frame perspective is too limiting and will "overlook inappropriate conduct." The implications of this split-second syndrome for police-initiated stops of citizens are profound, as questions surrounding the lawfulness of a stop become irrelevant based on the results of the subsequent search.

Summary Statements on Training: The overall goal of training is to provide officers with the skills and knowledge necessary to perform their duties effectively, lawfully and humanely, and the principles outlined above by Fyfe (1995) offer an excellent roadmap for imparting those skills.[9] In plain terms, officers who are properly trained are less likely than poorly trained officers to engage in racially biased policing. We can return to Fyfe's (1995: 163–164) discussion of the impact of training on violence—combined with Muir's professional policeman from the discussion above—to illustrate this point (again substituting in racially biased stops of citizens).

The development of successful boxers, diplomats, combat soldiers, and trial lawyers demonstrates that maintaining one's temper under stressful and confrontational conditions is a skill that can be taught. At the broadest level, police training designed to do so may involve providing students with what Muir (1977) called *understanding*—a nonjudgmental sense that people's behavior, no matter how bizarre or provocative, may usually be explained factors that go beyond the dichotomy of good and evil... Even if genuine *understanding*, as defined by Muir, cannot be imparted to individuals who bring extremely narrow views to policing, officers can be made to know in training that they simply will not be permitted to act out their prejudices through violent, or even discourteous conduct.[10]

Administrative Policy

Over the last 30 years, administrative rulemaking has emerged as the dominant form of discretion control in American policing. Administrative guidance in the form of policies, rules and procedures communicates to the rank and file officers what the department expects, what is considered acceptable, and what will not be condoned (Kappeler et al., 1998). Both CALEA and the American Bar Association (ABA) recommend written rules and policies as an effective manner in which to structure police decision-making. Importantly, prior police research has demonstrated that administrative rulemaking can effectively control police officer behavior in a number of misconduct and racial bias-prone areas. For example, research has consistently demonstrated that administrative policies—when enforced—can substantially curtail the rate of police shootings (Fyfe, 1988; Gain, 1971; Geller and Scott, 1992). Alternatively, administrative permissiveness can also lead to *higher* rates of police shootings (Fyfe, 1979). White (2001), for example, found that the number of police shootings in Philadelphia increased significantly after a restrictive administrative policy was abolished in 1974. Walker (1992: 32) concluded that:

> ... administrative rules have successfully limited police shooting discretion, with positive results in terms of social policy. Fewer people are being shot and killed, racial disparities in shootings have been reduced, and police officers are in no greater danger because of these restrictions.

Similarly positive results have been documented with high-speed pursuits, use of police dogs and responses to domestic violence incidents (White, 2007). For example, Alpert (1997) found that the number of pursuits, accidents and injuries all dropped significantly in Miami following the adoption of a restrictive pursuit policy.

The adoption of clearly articulated policies governing police stops of citizens, with specific prohibitions of racial profiling, is absolutely crucial for controlling unlawful police behavior. Research that highlights the ability of departments to manage their officers' behavior across a wide range of police actions (see above) serves as a foundation for administrative rulemaking as an effective strategy for preventing racially biased policing. As an illustration, the Glendale (AZ) Police Department developed clear administrative rules regarding immigration enforcement following the passage of SB1070, including an *Immigration Enforcement Field Card* [...].[11] The field card provides officers with guidance on a range of important issues, including relevant factors for determining reasonable suspicion and whether an immigration investigation is "practicable," valid forms of identification, and procedures for immigration questioning and arrest. When administrative policy is clearly articulated and disseminated to officers in the field—as Glendale PD has done with this Field Card—the potential for racially biased policing is greatly reduced.

Supervision, Accountability and Commitment from the Top of the Organization

The Police Department Leadership

Yet, department policies and rules, by themselves, are not enough to control racially biased policing.[12] It is absolutely critical that the policies be supported and enforced by the organizational leadership. If the informal norms of the department support racially biased policing, and those who engage in it go unpunished, administrative policies become meaningless. The informal norms of the department are greatly determined by the leadership of the organization. Chiefs of police that demand accountability, that punish officers for their transgressions, and that hold supervisors accountable for their subordinates' misbehavior will send a clear message to their line officers regarding what will (and will not) be tolerated. Darryl Gates in Los Angeles, Frank Rizzo in Philadelphia and Harold Breier in Milwaukee demonstrate how attitudes of the chief can send a message to line staff that abusive and racially biased conduct is acceptable (Skolnick and Fyfe, 1993). Alternatively, police chiefs can change the informal norms of a department, as Pat Murphy did for the NYPD following the Serpico scandal. "Murphy used his three and a half years in office to create an environment that loudly and clearly condemned abusive police conduct, those who engaged in it, and—equally important—those who tolerate it (Skolnick and Fyfe, 1993: 179–80)." Twenty years later, the Mollen Commission (1994: 112) concluded in their investigation of misconduct in the NYPD that "commitment to integrity cannot be an abstract value...It must be reflected not only in the words, but in the deeds of the Police Commissioner."

The words and deeds of the chief are equally important for preventing racially biased policing and setting lawful standards for officers' behavior during stops of citizens. I return again to the illegal immigration debate in Arizona. Following passage of SB1070, several police chiefs publicly challenged the new law. Then-Chief Jack Harris of the Phoenix Police Department stated in his declaration before the United States District Court for the District of Arizona:

> Deterring, investigating and solving serious and violent crimes are the department's top priorities, and it would be impossible for us to do our job without the collaboration and support of community members, including those who may be in the country unlawfully (http://www .scribd.com/doc/33979389/Declaration-of-Jack-Harris-on-SB-1070).

George Gascon, former Chief of the Mesa Police Department similarly noted that the law:

> will put officers in the impossible position of trying to enforce the law without racially profiling... Most professional law enforcement leaders around [the] country are fairly united in their concerns about the impact that making immigration enforcement the primary function of local policing would have on resources, our ability to fight crime and our ability to work with various communities that may have significant representation of immigrants whether here with or without authority (http:// www.azcentral.com/news/articles/2010/04/21/20100421policereax-ON .html#ixzz1Q8MtXhVF)

Statements such as these from the chief send a clear message to officers regarding what is expected of them on the street. Accountability begins and ends in the Chief's office.

Supervision

Supervision of police officers is a critical department task that serves as a foundational element in the agency's effort to control officer field behavior. Weisburd and colleagues (2000) reported that nearly 90 percent of police officers surveyed agreed that effective supervision prevents misconduct such as racially biased policing. Fyfe (1995: 164) noted that:

> *Everything* that supervisors do or tolerate, every interpretation of broad departmental philosophy, every application of specific rules and policies is a training lesson that has at least as much impact on officers' performance as what they may have learned in their rookie days.

There are many good discussions of how to insure effective supervision (see, for example, Kappeler et al. 1998; Skolnick and Fyfe, 1993; White, 2007), and key principles include proper span of control (8–10 officers per sergeant), proper training (good supervision can and should be taught), and holding supervisors accountable for the behavior of their subordinates. The International Association of Chiefs of Police (IACP, 1989: 53) stated that "many officers face temptations everyday . . . management has the capacity and control to reinforce high integrity, detect corruption, and limit opportunities for wrong doing." These words apply to racially biased policing as well as they do for other forms of police misconduct. Simply put, if officers believe they will be caught and punished for their racially biased actions, they will be less likely to engage in those activities (Klockars et al., 2000).

Concluding Remarks

This paper applies a larger discretion control framework to examine the question of how police departments can prevent their officers from engaging in racially biased behavior during police-initiated stops of citizens. This framework allows us to draw on what we already know about controlling police officer misbehavior, and offers important lessons for insuring the lawfulness of officer actions during Terry stops. These lessons are:

- Careful recruitment and selection includes both "screening out" and "screening in" processes. Muir's (1977) professional policeman, Mike Marshall, offers an excellent starting point for hiring officers who will both avoid racially biased behavior and bring a sense of empathy and compassion to policing.
- Fyfe's (1995) recommendations for violence reduction training offer a solid foundation for training to prevent racially biased policing. This can be achieved with training that is:
  - Realistic (adult learning and role plays) and continuous;
  - Tailored to the department and the community (e.g., Glendale PD's response to SB1070) ;
  - Focused on the means (or process), not just the ends (i.e., avoiding the split second syndrome).
- Administrative rules that are clear and routinely enforced will effectively control officer behavior on the street.
- Accountability begins in the Chief's office and flows down through the organization to the first-level supervision of line officers.

Ongoing Challenges

These lessons are clear and straightforward, with obvious implications for policy and practice. Just as important, they are supported by empirical research. However, police departments do not function in a vacuum, and as a result, there are a number of challenges or pressures—both internal and external—that serve as barriers for moving forward. With regard to external pressures, both the political and economic environments will shape this ongoing discussion of organizational responses to racially biased policing. For example, the current economic recession has severely limited police departments' ability to hire new officers and retain the ones they currently employ. While there is evidence to indicate that the recession has increased and changed the profile of applicants seeking to enter police work (e.g., former real estate agents and bankers) budgetary constraints have prevented departments from taking advantage of the surging interest of people with diverse background who may fit Muir's vision of a professional police officer.

The issue of racial bias in policing is highly politically charged, and nowhere is this clearer than in Arizona. The immigration debate surrounding SB1070 has been divisive and has generated an inconsistent response among law enforcement agencies (with some supporting the law, and others opposed to it). In fact, SB1070 served as a major point of dissension between Phoenix Police Chief Jack Harris and the Phoenix Law Enforcement Association (PLEA, the primary union for rank-and-file officers). Moreover, Bornstein (2005) highlighted the impact of increased scrutiny on Arabic and Muslim residents (especially in New York City), suggesting that many of the concerns associated with racial profiling of African Americans are now increasingly evident in a new form of terrorist profiling. Bornstein (2005) noted an important distinction between the two forms of profiling, however. While there is near universal agreement that profiling of African Americans (and Hispanics) is wrong and should be outlawed, there is much less consensus on the inappropriateness of profiling Arabic and Muslim residents. It goes without saying that this political context has important implications for policing.

There are internal challenges facing police departments as well. Departments have a long history of resisting both change and efforts at regulation (especially external efforts). Guyot (1975) coined the term "bending granite" to describe police resistance to change (see also Reuss-Ianni, 1983), and Skolnick and Fyfe (1993: 176) noted that "even the best-respected police administrators have failed as reformers." The battle between Phoenix Police Chief Harris and PLEA underscores this point (notably, Harris resigned in May 2011, in large part due to his battles with the union). And once reform has been achieved, there are major obstacles to sustaining that change, especially during an economic climate defined by employee turnover and attrition (at all levels of the organization), and concomitant expectations to do more with less. It is extremely difficult for a police department in these circumstances to maintain a strategic vision and avoid slipping into crisis management mode. Last, departments are faced with increasing pressure to be transparent about their operations. Transparency flies in the face of the traditional, professional model of policing but it is crucial to building trust, especially with minority communities that have long histories of tense, antagonistic relationships with police. The challenge for police is to engage in open and frank dialogue, to provide access to their data, and to embrace perceived legitimacy as an important measure of their overall performance. When this occurs, true reform will be achieved.

NOTES

1. The first, *Daniels, et al. v. the City of New York*, was filed in 1999 by the Center for Constitutional Rights (CCR) and settled in 2003. Despite this settlement, the CCR filed a second suit in 2008, *Floyd, et al. v. The City of New York*, alleging that the NYPD had violated the earlier settlement and was continuing to "engage in racial profiling and suspicion-less stops of law-abiding New York City residents... (Jones-Brown et al., 2010: 20)."

2. The Philadelphia Police Department (PPD) stopped more than 250,000 citizens in 2009, and in November 2010 the ACLU of Pennsylvania filed a lawsuit in Federal Court alleging that the PPD was engaged in widespread racial profiling.

3. I use the term "racially biased policing" instead of racial profiling because it is more general and encompasses a wider range of officer street behavior.

4. Protective factors against misconduct that emerged in their study include college education, older age at appointment, married at appointment, and a recommendation to hire from the department's background investigator (Kane and White, 2009).

5. Muir's emphasis on coercion reflected a growing recognition of the centrality of force to the police role. Bittner (1970: 40), for example, stated that the capacity to threaten or use physical force is a core function of the police:

   "Whatever the substance of the task at hand, whether it involves protection against an undesired imposition, caring for those who cannot care for themselves, attempting to solve a crime, helping to save a life, abating a nuisance, or settling an explosive dispute, police intervention means above all making use of the capacity and authority to overpower resistance."

6. Proponents of the andragogical approach for police training argue that it: 1) draws on trainees' past experiences; 2) treats trainees as adults; 3) adapts to the needs of participants; and 4) fosters critical thinking and creativity (Birzer and Tannehill, 2001).

7. SB1070 was signed into law by Arizona Governor Jan Brewer on April 23, 2010 and was set to go into effect July 29, 2010. Seven different law suits were filed challenging the law, including one by the U.S. Department of Justice. In July 2010, Federal District Court Judge Susan Bolton issued an injunction prohibiting four major components of the law from going into effect. The major thrust of her injunction was that immigration is the responsibility of the federal government, not individual states. On April 11, 2011 the 9th Circuit Court of Appeals upheld Bolton's injunction. Arizona has since petitioned the U.S. Supreme Court to overturn the ruling (http://www.azcentral.com/news/election/azelections/articles/2011/04/11/20110411arizona-immigration-law-appeals-court-stay.html).

8. Binder and Scharf (1980) characterized five important decision phases in police/citizen encounters: anticipation, entry and initial confrontation, dialogue and information exchange, final frame decision, and aftermath.

9. Fyfe (1995: 171) described several other principles that are relevant for violence reduction training, but not for racially biased policing. These include: *Violence-reduction training must not make matters worse by creating a sense of paranoia among officers* (dealing with the traditional over-emphasis on danger); *Violence-reduction training must address the role of police officers during their non-working hours* (e.g., off-duty conduct).

10. Notably, Fyfe (1989) put these principles in practice as part of the Metro-Dade Police/Citizen Violence Reduction Project, which culminated in the development of a five-day role-play training program. Results from the project indicate substantial reductions in use of force, officer injuries and citizen complaints after the training program was implemented. See also Klinger (2010).

11. Of course, much of the training and policy associated with SB1070 is on hold while litigation questioning its constitutionality is being decided by the Federal Courts.

12. See Skolnick and Fyfe (1993) and White (2007) for a discussion of the limitations of administrative rulemaking.

REFERENCES

Bayley, D.H. (1986). The tactical choices of police patrol officers. *Journal of Criminal Justice,* 14, 329–348.

Bayley, D.H. & Bittner, E. (1984). Learning the skills of policing. *Law and Contemporary Problems,* 47, 35–59.

Binder, A. & Scharf, P. (1980). The violent police-citizen encounter. *Annals of the American Academy of Political and Social Science,* 452, 111–121.

Birzer, M.L. (2003). The theory of andragogy applied to police training. *Policing: An International Journal of Police Strategies and Management,* 26 (1), 29–42.

Birzer, M.L. & Tannehill, R. (2001). A more effective training approach for contemporary policing. *Police Quarterly,* 4(2), 233–252.

Bittner, E. (1967). The police on skid row: A study of peace keeping. *American Sociological Review,* 32, 699–715.

Bittner, E. (1970). *The functions of the police in modern society.* Rockville, MD: National Institute of Mental Health.

Brookfield, S. (1986). *Understanding and facilitating adult learning.* San Francisco: Jossey-Bass.

Caffarella, R.S. (1993). Self-directed learning. In S. Merriam (ed.) *An update on adult learning theory, new directions for adult and continuing education.* San Francisco: Jossey-Bass.

Commission on Accreditation for Law Enforcement Agencies. (2009) *Standards for law enforcement agencies.* Retrieved on June 24, 2011 from http://www.calea.org

Fyfe, J.J. (1979). Administrative interventions on police shooting discretion: An empirical examination. *Journal of Criminal Justice,* 7, 309–324.

Fyfe, J.J. (1986). The split-second syndrome and other determinants of police violence. In *Violent Transactions.* (eds.) Campbell, A & Gibbs, J.J. Oxford: Basil Blackwell.

Fyfe, J.J. (1988). Police use of deadly force: Research and reform. *Justice Quarterly,* 5, 165–205.

Fyfe, J.J. (1989). Police/citizen violence reduction project. *FBI Law Enforcement Bulletin,* 58, 18–25.

Fyfe, J.J. (1995). Training to reduce police-civilian violence. In Geller, W.A. & Toch, H. (eds.) *And justice for all: Understanding and controlling police abuse of force.* Washington, DC: Police Executive Research Forum.

Fyfe, J.J. & Kane, R.J. (2006). *Bad cops: A study of career-ending misconduct among New York City police officers. Final Report.* Grant No. 96-IJ-CX-0053. Washington, DC: National Institute of Justice.

Gain, C. (1971). *Discharge of firearms policy: Effecting justice through administrative regulation.* Unpublished memorandum, December 23.

Geller, W. & Scott, M.S. (1992). *Deadly force: What we know.* Washington, DC: Police Executive Research Forum.

Grant, J.D. & Grant, J. (1995). Officer selection and the prevention of abuse of force. In Geller, W.A. & Toch, H. (eds.) *And justice for all: Understanding and controlling police abuse of force.* Washington, DC: Police Executive Research Forum.

Glendale (AZ) Police Department. (2010). *SB1070 instructor points.* Glendale, AZ: Author.

Goldstein, H. (1979). Improving policing: A problem-oriented approach. *Crime and Delinquency,* 25 (2), 235–258.

Goldstein, H. (1990). *Problem-oriented policing.* New York: McGraw Hill.

Greene, J. A. (1999). Zero tolerance: A case study of police policies and practices in New York City. *Crime & Delinquency,* 45, 171–187.

Guyot, D. (1979). Bending granite: Attempts to change the rank structure of American police departments. *Journal of Police Science and Administration,* 7, 253–284.

Haberfeld, M.R. (2002). *Critical issues in training.* Upper Saddle River, NJ: Prentice-Hall. http://www.scribd.com/doc/33979389/Declaration-of-Jack-Harris-on-SB-1070). Retrieved on June 24, 2011.

http://www.azcentral.com/news/articles/2010/04/21/20100421policereax-ON.html#ixzz1Q8MtXhVF. Retrieved on June 24, 2011.

International Association of Chiefs of Police (1989). *Building integrity and reducing drug corruption in police departments.* Arlington, VA: IACP.

Jones-Brown et al., D., Gill, J., & Trone, J. (2010). *Stop, question, & frisk policing practices in New York City: A primer.* Retrieved from John Jay College of Criminal Justice website: http://www.jjay.cuny.edu/web_images/PRIMER_electronic_version.pdf.

Kane, R.J. & White, M.D. (2011). *Jammed up: An examination of career-ending police misconduct.* New York University Press (NYU). In Press.

Kane, R.J. & White, M.D. (2009). Bad cops: A study of career-ending misconduct among New York City police officers. *Criminology and Public Policy,* 8 (4), 737–769.

Kappeler, V.E., Sluder, R.D., & Alpert, G.P. (1998). *Forces of deviance: Understanding the dark side of policing.* Prospect Heights, IL: Waveland Press.

Klinger, D. (2010). Can police training affect the use of force on the streets? The Metro-Dade violence reduction field experiment. In McCoy, C. (Ed.), *Holding Police Accountable.* Washington, DC: Urban Institute Press.

Klockars, C., Ivkovich, S., Harver, W., & Haberfeld, M. (2000). *The measurement of police integrity.* Washington, DC: National Institute of Justice.

Merriam, S.B. & Caffarella, R.S. (1999). *Learning in adulthood.* (2nd ed). San Francisco: Jossey-Bass.

Miller, W.R. (1977). *Cops and Bobbies: Police authority in London and New York City, 1830–1870.* Chicago: University of Chicago Press.

Mollen Commission. (1994). *Anatomy of failure, a path for success: The report of the commission to investigate allegations of police corruption and the anti-corruption procedures of the New York City Police Department.* New York: City of New York.

Muir, W.K., Jr. (1977). *Police: Streetcorner politicians.* Chicago: University of Chicago Press.

Palmiotto, M.J. (2003). An overview of police training through the decades: Current issues and problems. In Palmiotto, M.J. (ed.) *Police and training issues.* Upper Saddle River, NJ: Prentice-Hall.

President's Commission on Law Enforcement and Administration of Justice. (1967). *Task force report: The police.* Washington DC: US Government Printing Office.

Reuss-Ianni, E. (1983). *Two cultures of policing.* New Brunswick, NJ: Transaction Books.

Skogan, W. & Frydl, K. (Eds.). (2004). *Fairness and effectiveness in policing: The evidence.* Committee to Review Research on Police Policy and Practices. Washington, DC: The National Academies Press.

Skolnick, J.H. & Fyfe, J.J. (1993). *Above the law: Police and the excessive use of force.* New York: Free Press.

Tyler, T.R. (2006). *Why people obey the law.* Princeton, NJ: Princeton University Press.

Walker, S. (1992). *Taming the system: The control of discretion in criminal justice, 1950–1990.* New York: Oxford University Press.

Weisburd, D., Greenspan, R., with Hamilton, E.E., Williams, H., & Bryant, K.A. (2000). *Police attitudes toward abuse of authority: Findings from a national study.* Washington, DC: U.S. Government Printing Office.

White, M.D. (2001) Controlling police decisions to use deadly force: Reexamining the importance of administrative policy. *Crime and Delinquency,* 47 (1), 131–151.

White, M.D. (2007). *Current issues and controversies in policing.* Boston: Allyn and Bacon/Pearson.

*Michael D. White** is an associate professor at the School of Criminology and Criminal Justice and associate director of the Center for Violence Prevention and Community Safety at Arizona State University.

White, Michael D. "Controlling Police Officer Behavior in the Field: Using What We Know to Regulate Police-Initiated Stops and Prevent Racially Biased Policing." Roundtable at John Jay College of Criminal Justice (August 10–11, 2011).

Used by Permission.

The Dynamics of Public Opinion on Ethnic Profiling After 9/11: Results from a Survey Experiment

by Deborah J. Schildkraut*

In recent years, the American Civil Liberties Union (ACLU) and Amnesty International have issued reports decrying the use of ethnic profiling by law enforcement agencies in the United States in their efforts to combat terrorism. The ACLU report tells the story of Muhammad Siddiqui, a Houston architect who was contacted by FBI agents who said they wanted to ask him questions. Siddiqui told the agents, "I'd be happy to talk to you, but I'd like to have my attorney present," a request that frustrated the agents, with one telling him that getting a lawyer would only make him look guilty and another pulling his coat aside to reveal his gun (ACLU, 2004). Justice Department policy prohibits racial or ethnic profiling in federal law enforcement, but activities related to the border and national security are exempt. A recent Justice Department study of Arab Americans concluded that many of them fear being a victim of profiling by law enforcement more than they fear being the victim of a hate crime (Elliott, 2006).

Since 9/11, in addition to wondering if they would give up some of their own liberties, Americans have debated whether certain people, namely, Muslims and people of Middle Eastern or Arab descent, should give up more of their liberties than the rest of us. Polls have shown that many Americans are indeed willing to curtail the civil liberties of Arab Americans and Middle Eastern immigrants. In one survey conducted shortly after 9/11, 66% of Americans said it would be acceptable for law enforcement officials to stop and search anyone who looked Middle Eastern in order to prevent another attack, and in another, 31% said that they would support putting Arab Americans in camps until their innocence could be determined (Schildkraut, 2002).

Although no policy as extreme as internment developed after 9/11, support for profiling has been high enough to warrant further investigation. Investigation is warranted for other reasons as well. First, the issue of domestic counterterrorism policy is part of a broader class of salient and contentious "boundary related" policies generating debate and activism in the United States today, so called because they invoke both the territorial and conceptual boundaries of the nation. Other salient boundary related policies include immigration and language policy. In terms of territorial boundaries, these policies deal with the question of who is allowed in and who is not, and counterterrorism policy in particular addresses the very security of the nation's physical space. In terms of conceptual boundaries, these policies call on us to consider factors that determine whether a person is "truly" American and, as such, deserving of the full range of rights and opportunities that come with membership in the American political community. Normative views about the boundaries of membership should therefore be key ingredients shaping how people evaluate such policies. Indeed, activists on both sides of the immigration debate often frame their efforts as representing what it means to be American. On the pro-immigration side, immigrants and their supporters at rallies have been praised as showing native-born Americans what active citizenship, a defining element of American identity, is all about. On the anti-immigration side, groups such as the Ku Klux Klan (KKK) and the Council of Concerned Citizens have seen their membership surge and spread to parts of the country that have traditionally had low levels of White supremacy activism. Leaders of these groups point to their desire to preserve America's European heritage as their motivation.[1] Ideas about the meaning of American identity are thus fueling activism. Studying systematically the role of these ideas in shaping opinions is the central goal of this article.

Second, Supreme Court rulings on Japanese internment as well as subsequent rulings on ethnic profiling near the U.S. border with Mexico suggest that profiling in the name of national security would likely be deemed constitutional should legal challenges arise (Braber, 2002; Harris, 2003). Third, non-White Americans who think that they or their group have suffered discrimination can become alienated and withdraw from the very political process that has the potential to protect them (Schildkraut, 2005b). Finally, elected officials and other prominent commentators have publicly advocated profiling. In August 2006, Representative Pete King (R-NY), recent chair of the House Committee on Homeland Security, urged airport screeners to use ethnic and religious profiling at airports (Palmer, 2006).

To date, however, few studies have examined public opinion about profiling of any kind, including the more traditional form of profiling targeting African American drivers. This study builds on these investigations using a national telephone survey with split-sample manipulations in question wording. These wording experiments allow me to compare support for counterterrorism profiling with support for profiling Black motorists. It also allows me to investigate whether the status of the profilee as a U.S. citizen of Arab or Middle Eastern appearance or as an immigrant alters support for allowing law enforcement authorities to use high-discretion methods for preventing terrorist activity. In both analyses, I draw on public opinion scholarship that shows how competing ideas about the meaning of American identity can be strong influences over opinions on boundary related policies (Citrin, Reingold, & Green, 1990; Schildkraut, 2005a). I pay particular attention to liberalism's emphasis on the rights of citizenship and ethnocultural-ism's emphasis on the ascriptive boundaries of American identity. I find that sup-port for profiling Arabs and Arab Americans is higher than support for profiling Black motorists, that people are more supportive of profiling immigrants than they are of profiling U.S. citizens of Arab descent, and that how people define what it means to be American is a powerful predictor of such support, in some cases overshadowing "the usual suspects," including race, partisanship, education, and fearing another terrorist attack. The perspective promoted by groups like the KKK—that being American means being a White European Christian—is the most powerful predictor of support. A liberal understanding of being American can offset some, but not all, of that support.

DEFINING ETHNIC PROFILING

Ethnic profiling is when law enforcement authorities use racial or ethnic charac-teristics to determine which people to subject to heightened scrutiny in order to prevent crimes from occurring. Heightened scrutiny can range from interrogation to searches of one's person or property to arrests or even removal from the com-munity, as in the case of Japanese internment during World War II. Profiling does not refer to the use of ethnic characteristics to catch a particular suspect once a crime has been committed and when the suspect has been described by witnesses. The phrase *racial profiling* entered popular discourse in the 1990s with increased media attention devoted to charges that Black motorists were disproportion-ately pulled over, with traffic violations serving as a pretext for police officers to search for drugs or weapons. The conventional wisdom was that such profiling constituted efficient policing because Blacks were considered to be more likely to commit drug and weapons crimes than Whites. Subsequent investigations have failed to confirm the conventional wisdom (Harris, 2003). In this study, *traditional profiling* refers to this kind of profiling. In contrast, *9/11 profiling* refers to prac-tices that involve subjecting people who look Middle Eastern, Arab, or Muslim to discretionary law enforcement attention as a way to *prevent* terrorist activity.

PUBLIC OPINION ABOUT PROFILING

Traditional Profiling

Polls consistently show that a majority of Americans disapprove of traditional profiling. In March 2005, Princeton Survey Research Associates found that 75%

of Americans say they disapprove of the practice.[2] This figure is in line with other recent surveys (Weitzer & Tuch, 2002). Despite the media and legislative attention that traditional profiling has received in recent years, few studies examine public opinion about its use. Indeed, a literature search returned only two studies, both by Weitzer and Tuch (2002, 2005). They note that overall support for profiling is low for both Blacks and Whites but that the race of the respondent was one of the strongest predictors of support. Other factors generating support included living in a high crime neighborhood and being personally afraid of crime. Black respondents with more education were less likely to approve of profiling than Black respondents with lower levels of education, and having personal experience with racial profiling also decreased approval.

PROFILING AFTER ATTACK: PEARL HARBOR AND 9/11 PROFILING

As with traditional profiling, few studies look at views on 9/11 profiling. But first, it is instructive to examine what is known about public reactions to Japanese internment after Pearl Harbor, our most well-known case of profiling after a foreign attack. Although the survey industry was in its infancy in the 1940s, studies suggest that there was little sustained outrage at the time, with even Black and Jewish antidiscrimination organizations largely silent on the matter. Their silence has been attributed to a combination of factors, including a desire to seem patriotic and loyal, a preoccupation with defeating Germany, and prevailing anti-Japanese stereotypes (Greenberg, 1995). Analysis of editorials in *The New York Times* and the *Los Angeles Times* in 1942 likewise reveals an acceptance of internment (Schildkraut, 2002). A 1942 survey by the National Opinion Research Center found that 93% of Americans felt that the government was doing the right thing with internment. Fifty-nine percent still approved when asked about moving American citizens of Japanese descent. A 1942 Gallup poll found that 49% of Americans thought the internees should not be allowed to return to the coast when the war ended. Of those, 55% thought they should be sent to Japan, 11% thought they should stay in camps, and 8% thought they should be "destroyed" (Berinsky, n.d.). It is thus clear that the attack at Pearl Harbor was met with majoritarian support of internment. Yet, we know little about the individual-level factors that led to such views because the original data sets are not available.

After the attacks on 9/11, the topic of internment reentered popular discourse. As noted earlier, roughly one third of Americans expressed support for placing Arab Americans in camps until their innocence could be determined. Although support for internment is not as high as it was in 1942, it is still at a nontrivial level. And support for milder forms of profiling, including random searches of people who look Middle Eastern, have been considerably higher. Existing studies of such support show some important similarities with studies of traditional profiling as well as some differences. For instance, just as being afraid of crime generates support for traditional profiling, being afraid of another attack on the United States ("sociotropic threat") and being afraid that one or one's family will be victims of an attack ("personal threat") have each been shown to generate support for 9/11 profiling. Likewise, people with lower levels of education have higher levels of support for profiling (Huddy, Feldman, Taber, & Lahav, 2005; Kim, 2004; Schildkraut, 2002). Unlike studies of traditional profiling, however, the race of the respondent has not proven to be a significant determinant of support for 9/11 profiling. And whereas studies of traditional profiling do not examine political attitudes, studies of 9/11 profiling find that Republicans and conservatives are often more supportive than Democrats and liberals.

Despite these insights, there is still much to learn about public opinion about profiling. First, existing studies look at only "mild" forms of 9/11 profiling, such as allowing searches or vaguely worded "greater surveillance." No study looks at the one third of people who support measures as extreme as internment. Second, no study looks at whether support for profiling is tempered when the profilee is described as an American citizen or whether respondents would treat all people who look Arab or Muslim the same regardless of whether they are U.S. citizens or immigrants. Third, no study compares attitudes about traditional profiling with attitudes about 9/11 profiling. Do people see these as essentially the same kind of "efficient" policy, or are they situated in fundamentally different frameworks?

Finally, there is an important set of independent variables that has been absent from studies of profiling, namely, the ways in which people define what being American means. Yet, when talking about policies that involve the boundaries of the nation, the norms and values people use to constitute their vision of what makes being American unique can be a powerful influence over how they interpret the specific policy debates and whether their attitudes become translated into activism. How people define being American has been shown to be a powerful influence over attitudes on other boundary related policies such as immigration, language policy, and social welfare programs (Citrin et al., 1990; Schildkraut, 2005a; Theiss-Morse, 2006). In the case of a foreign attack, the territorial and conceptual boundaries of the nation are clearly salient. Many people believe that what the United States stands for was attacked on 9/11 just as much as U.S. territory was. But Americans have wide-ranging views of what it is, exactly, that the United States stands for. To understand what motivates attitudes and behaviors in response to 9/11, we thus need to include measures of what people think being American means. When we see which elements of American identity are brought to bear on these debates, we learn more about what people think such debates are even about, and we learn about the type of America that people seek to preserve through their preferred policy solution.

Although scholarship has identified multiple sets of norms that popularly constitute American identity (Schildkraut, 2005a; Smith, 1997), two are particularly relevant here: liberalism and ethnoculturalism. Liberalism stresses universal rights, calls for minimal government intervention in private life, and promotes economic and political freedoms along with equality of opportunity. Most Americans consider liberal norms to be an essential element of American identity (Citrin, Haas, Muste, & Reingold, 1994; McClosky & Zaller, 1984). Liberalism emphasizes the rights of people to be free from arbitrary government intervention and provides a normative prescription to provide civil liberties even in cases where the majority would prefer restrictions. As such, people who use liberalism to define American identity might be less likely than others to support profiling.

Ethnoculturalism, on the other hand, is an ascriptive tradition that sets rigid boundaries on group membership. In its extreme, it maintains that Americans are White, English-speaking Protestants of northern European ancestry (Smith, 1997). Over time, this tradition has become discredited, although many people still say that to be a true American, a person should be Christian and be born in the United States (Citrin et al., 1990; Schildkraut, 2005a). Ethnoculturalism promotes exclusion from the national community based on ascriptive characteristics, which could lead to a greater willingness to deny the rights and liberties that come with membership to people who do not possess such characteristics. Thus, people who use ethnoculturalism to define American identity might be more likely than others to support profiling.

The remainder of this analysis seeks to advance the study of public opinion on profiling by testing three hypotheses: first, that support for 9/11 profiling is higher than support for traditional profiling and that support for 9/11 profiling is higher when the profilee is an immigrant than when the profilee is a U.S. citizen; second, that liberalism and ethnoculturalism are as influential over support for profiling, if not more so, as more tangible factors such as sociotropic threat, with liberalism leading to opposition and ethnoculturalism leading to support; and third, that the factors that dictate support are similar across all types of profiling, indicating more similarities across these realms of high-discretion tactics than differences.

DATA AND KEY MEASURES

To test these hypotheses, I used the 21st Century Americanism Survey (21-CAS), a national random-digit-dial (RDD) telephone survey conducted in 2004 with oversamples of Blacks, Latinos, and Asians.[3] It has 2,800 [sic] respondents: 1,633 White, non-Hispanic; 300 Black; 441 Latino; and 299 Asian.[4] The 21-CAS contains two split-sample question wording manipulations that can test the hypotheses described above. In the first manipulation, half of the respondents (randomly determined) were asked if they approve or disapprove of traditional profiling, whereas the other half were asked if they approve or disapprove of stopping and searching people who look Arab or Muslim to see if they may have ties to terrorism. In the second manipulation, half of the respondents (randomly determined) were asked if they would support or oppose interning Arab Americans should there be another attack on the United States, whereas the other half were asked if they would support or oppose interning Arab immigrants. The split-sample methodology was used to avoid bias toward consistency in respondents' answers. Had all respondents been asked all questions, a person objecting to traditional profiling might then feel the need to be consistent and object to 9/11 profiling even if he or she really feels that 9/11 profiling is acceptable. Because the question wording is randomly assigned, any statistically significant differences between aggregate responses to the two versions can reasonably be assumed to be due to the question wording itself and not to any other factor.[5]

SPLIT-SAMPLE RESULTS

For the first split-sample manipulation, half of the sample was asked, "It has been reported that some police officers stop motorists of certain racial or ethnic groups because the officers believe that these groups are more likely than others to commit certain types of crime. This practice is known as racial profiling. Do you approve or disapprove of the use of racial profiling by police?"[6] Twenty-three percent approve and 77% disapprove.[7] The other half was asked, "Since September 11th, some law enforcement agencies have stopped and searched people who are Arab or of Middle Eastern descent to see if they may be involved in potential terrorist activities. Do you approve or disapprove of this kind of profiling?"[8] Here, 66% approve and 34% disapprove. The increase in approval of 9/11 profiling compared with traditional profiling is an impressive 43 percentage points ($p < .000$).

In the second split-sample manipulation, half of the sample was asked, "If there were another terrorist attack in the U.S. with Arab or Middle Eastern suspects, would you support or oppose allowing the government to hold Arabs who are U.S. citizens in camps until it can be determined whether they have links to terrorist organizations?"[9] Of those who were asked this question, 29.5% support internment and 70.5% oppose. The other half was asked the same question but with "Arab immigrants" replacing "Arabs who are U.S. citizens." Here, 34% support internment and 66% oppose, a small but statistically significant increase in approval of 4.5 percentage points ($p < .006$).[10].

These results confirm the first hypothesis. Support for 9/11 profiling is considerably higher than support for traditional profiling. People are even more likely to approve of placing people who fit the 9/11 profile into camps than they are to approve of pulling over minority motorists. There are two other points to note here. First, of the four questions, the only one in which a majority of respondents approves is the case of searching people who look Middle Eastern. In the remaining questions, most respondents oppose the profiling in question. Second, although a majority opposes placing people in camps, the percentage of people supporting it a full 3 years after the 9/11 attacks is high, accounting for roughly one third of the respondents in both conditions.

WHY PEOPLE SUPPORT OR OPPOSE PROFILING

In the aggregate, the type of profiling and the type of profilee in question can affect levels of support for profiling. But what about at the individual level? To investigate the remaining hypotheses, individual-level analysis is necessary. In this section, I first describe the independent variables under investigation. Next, I examine bivariate relationships between those variables and support for profiling, and then I conduct more rigorous probit analyses.

Based on the findings of earlier studies, I examine the role of the respondent's race, level of education, and partisan identification, with the expectation that Whites, people with lower levels of education, and Republicans will be more supportive of profiling (see the appendix for question wording not described in text). I also examine whether people who feel they personally have been a victim of discrimination or that their ethnic group is discriminated against ("panethnic discrimination") are less supportive of profiling than people who do not perceive discrimination. In all but the traditional profiling models, I test whether personal threat and/or sociotropic threat increase support for profiling. Likewise, in all but the traditional profiling models, I test whether one's level of pride in being American influences support (Davis & Silver, 2004; Greenberg, 1995).

Finally, I include measures that account for the extent to which respondents define the content of American identity in liberal and/or ethnocultural terms. Respondents were asked, "I'm going to read a list of things that some people say are important in making someone a true American. The first one is _____. Would you say that it should be very important, somewhat important, somewhat unimportant, or very unimportant in making someone a true American?" To measure liberalism's emphasis on political freedoms, people were asked if "letting other people say what they want no matter how much you disagree with them" is an important aspect of being American, where 0 = *very unimportant* and 1 = *very important*. Sixty-six percent of respondents said "very important" and 22% said "somewhat important." To measure ethnoculturalism's exclusivity, respondents were asked to rate the importance of being born in America, being a Christian, having European ancestors, and being White. Answers were combined to form a 0–1 ethnoculturalism scale, where 0 means that all items were very unimportant and 1 means that all items were very important (α = 0.72, M = 0.30, SD = 0.26, average inter-item correlation = 0.40).[11]

Table 1 shows bivariate relationships between these independent variables and support for the four types of profiling, with significant differences between split-sample manipulations noted.[12] The results show that most people across each category within each independent variable (reading across the rows) feel differently when asked about motorists than when asked about profiling Arabs and Muslims. In all cases, the higher level of support for 9/11 profiling is statistically significant, with a majority supporting it and a majority opposing traditional profiling. In contrast, people within each independent variable often feel similarly when asked about interning citizens versus interning immigrants. The differences are insignificant in 17 of the 28 comparisons and significant in 11. In all significant cases, support is higher for interning immigrants. In general, however, the aggregate differences across the types of profiling and profilee hold up regardless of the individual-level characteristics under investigation.

However, some strong differences in the level of support for profiling exist within the independent variables. Looking down each column, most independent variables seem to influence attitudes toward profiling in the three 9/11-related questions. With education, for instance, 55% of people with a high school diploma or less approve of interning Arab immigrants compared with only 17% of people with a graduate education. Likewise, only 18.0% of people who do not fear being a victim of a terrorist attack approve of interning Arab Americans compared with 48.5% of people who harbor such fears. With regard to ideas about the meaning of American identity, ethnoculturalism looks to be a more powerful influence over attitudes than liberalism, although both seem to shape opinions in the expected direction. In contrast to the 9/11-related columns, most differences in the column for traditional profiling are more modest.

To test the remaining hypotheses more thoroughly, a more rigorous test is needed. Table 2, therefore, shows the results of four probit analyses, one for

Table 1. Bivariate Relationships: Percentage Who Approve or Support

	Profiling of motorists (Form 1)	Profiling of Arabs (Form 2)	Intern-ment of Arab Americans (Form 1)	Intern-ment of Arab Immi-grants (Form 2)	N (Form 1/ Form 2)
White	26.44	70.31**	27.01	30.30	779/741
Black	6.52	53.02**	35.59	43.66	138/149
Asian	21.12	50.43**	26.92	31.93	161/115
Latino	20.28	66.34**	39.90	49.45**	217/202
High school or less	22.88	71.39**	52.09	55.00	329/339
Some college	21.00	67.69**	32.22	36.32	419/390
College graduate	26.09	64.02**	18.50	27.57**	253/239
Some grad/grad degree	23.23	56.04**	15.56	17.09	310/273
Democrat (including leaners)	13.88	52.36**	23.45	28.47**	598/573
Independent	13.85	65.06**	39.06	29.41	65/83
Republican (including leaners)	35.54	82.17**	33.63	42.90**	453/387
Victim racial discrimination (scale)					
Low	22.96	66.10**	29.04	33.08**	1150/1059
Medium	25.00	57.02**	37.63	45.61	104/114
High	15.87	69.57**	37.50	50.00	63/69
Panethnic group discrimination (scale)					
Low	22.01	64.12**	23.95	27.26	668/641
Medium	23.72	69.72**	34.95	41.57*	392/360
High	23.35	62.66**	39.57	46.98	257/241
Doesn't fear being victim of terrorism	—	58.72	18.00	26.72**	470/470
Fears being victim of terrorism	—	77.62	48.50	55.61	275/210

Doesn't fear nation being attacked	—	46.98	21.43	27.51	238/232
Fears nation being attacked		77.17	39.32	47.34**	395/346
Proud to be American					
Disagree strongly/ somewhat	—	30.56	7.32	18.92	40/36
Agree strongly/ somewhat	—	66.95	29.58	33.55	1153/1077
Political liberalism					
Very/somewhat unimportant	27.95	68.93**	45.58	38.92	161/177
Very/somewhat important	21.81	64.51**	27.83	34.28**	1105/1034
Low ethnoculturalism	21.07	60.79**	17.04	21.99**	859/806
Medium ethnoculturalism	24.42	74.06**	51.07	57.65*	356/320
High ethnoculturalism	30.39	74.14**	73.20	70.09	102/116

Source: 21st Century Americanism Survey (2004).[13]
Note: Unweighted results; DK/NA dropped.
*p < .10. **p < .05.

each dependent variable. All nondummy variables were coded to range from 0 to 1. The results partially confirm the second and third hypotheses. The second hypothesis was that liberalism and ethnoculturalism would be strong predictors of opinions, possibly even overshadowing traditional variables. Liberalism and ethnoculturalism are indeed strong predictors in some models, but not in all of them, with liberal ideas about being American generating opposition to 9/11 profiling and to interning Arab Americans, and ethnocultural ideas about being American generating support for all three types of 9/11 profiling. Whether these conceptions of American identity are more influential than other predictors is addressed below. It is notable that neither conception of American identity is a significant predictor of attitudes toward traditional profiling, suggesting that 9/11 profiling invokes the conceptual boundaries of the United States in a way that traditional profiling does not.

Table 2. Support for Profiling and Internment, Probit

Independent Variable	Profiling motorists	Profiling Arabs	Internment of Arab Americans	Internment of Arab Immigrants
Black	−0.90***	−0.52***	−0.29	0.12
	(0.23)	(0.16)	(0.19)	(0.16)
Asian	−0.19	−0.61***	0.15	−0.05
	(0.19)	(0.24)	(0.22)	(0.26)
Latino	−0.19	−0.34**	−0.17	0.08
	(0.16)	(0.17)	(0.18)	(0.17)
Education	0.08	−0.24	−0.73***	−0.64***
	(0.17)	(0.17)	(0.19)	(0.17)
Partisan identification	0.78***	0.95***	0.45***	0.62***
(higher value = GOP)	(0.12)	(0.13)	(0.14)	(0.13)
Perceives individual level	−0.16	0.18	−0.15***	0.09**
discrimination	(0.23)	(0.20)	(0.24)	(0.20)
Perceives group level	0.34**	0.26	0.61***	0.43**
discrimination	(0.17)	(0.18)	(0.19)	(0.18)
Liberal definition of	−0.26	−0.29*	−0.51***	0.06
American identity	(0.17)	(0.16)	(0.58)	(0.17)
Ethnocultural definition of	0.24	0.52**	2.22***	1.57***
American identity	(0.20)	(0.21)	(0.23)	(0.20)
Fears being victim of attack	—	0.13	0.52***	0.43***
		(0.16)	(0.17)	(0.16)
Fears U.S. will be attacked	—	0.42***	0.28	−0.02
		(0.16)	(0.19)	(0.16)
Proud to be American	—	1.02***	0.99**	0.39
		(0.29)	(0.47)	(0.34)
Constant	−1.05	−0.96	−2.24	−1.66
Chi-square	89.38	181.24	293.98	219.77
N	1038	960	951	952

Source: 21st Century Americanism Survey (2004).
Note: All nondummy variables coded 0 to 1. Weighted data. Standard errors in parentheses.
*$p < .10$. **$p < .05$. ***$p < .01$.

This last point brings us to the third hypothesis, that the factors that dictate support for profiling would be similar across all types of profiling. This hypothesis is confirmed for only three variables: Black respondents are less supportive of traditional and 9/11 profiling than White respondents (but race does not matter for internment), Republicans are more supportive of all kinds of profiling than Democrats, and a greater sense of group-level, or panethnic, discrimination also leads to more support. The positive coefficient on panethnic discrimination at first seems curious. But, it is important to remember that most of the respondents in the survey are White Americans, and the way in which White perceptions of mistreatment influence attitudes is poorly understood (Wong & Cho, 2005). Moreover, the average level of perceived panethnic discrimination was much lower for Whites (0.29 on a 0–1 scale) than for other groups (0.74 for Blacks, 0.47 for Asians, and 0.57 for Latinos). When each model was run separately for Whites, Blacks, Latinos, and Asians (results not shown), the measure of group-level discrimination was significant only for Whites. In all other models, this variable failed to achieve significance, although it was negative in nearly every case. For Whites, then, feeling that Whites have been mistreated in the United States leads to a greater willingness to curtail the civil liberties of both minority motorists and Middle Easterners, whereas for all other groups, perceptions of group-level mistreatment are insignificant.[14]

I return now to the question of whether liberal and ethnocultural conceptions of American national identity matter more than other significant predictors. It is difficult to assess this question simply by comparing the size of probit coefficients. Instead, it is necessary to examine the results in terms of predicted probabilities. Tables 3 and 4 show the predicted probability that a respondent would approve of each type of profiling as the independent variable in question (across each row) changes from its minimum to its maximum value (from 0 to 1).[15] The results indicate which variables produce the most change and which variables lead to a change in the predicted outcome (i.e., changing from likely to approve to likely to disapprove).

With regard to the hypothesis that liberal and ethnocultural Americanism will matter as much, if not more, than other significant predictors, the predicted probabilities show mixed results. Table 3 underscores that neither conception of American identity influences attitudes toward traditional profiling. Both conceptions of American identity are significant predictors of support for allowing searches of people who look Arab or Muslim, although both are weaker in magnitude compared with partisanship and patriotism. Partisanship yields a 30 percentage point jump in support when the average respondent goes from being a Democrat (57%) to being a Republican (87%), whereas patriotism yields an

Table 3. Predicted Probability of Approving of Profiling

Independent Variable	Profiling motorists			Profiling Arabs		
	0	1	Change	0	1	Change
White to Black	0.25	0.06	−0.19**	0.73	0.54	−0.19**
Education	0.23	0.26	0.03	0.77	0.69	−0.08
Democrat to Republican	0.15	0.39	0.24**	0.57	0.87	0.30**
Liberal definition of American identity	0.32	0.23	−0.09	0.80	0.71	−0.09*
Ethnocultural definition of American identity	0.23	0.30	0.07	0.67	0.83	0.16**
Fears being victim of attack	—	—	—	0.78	0.75	−0.03
Fears U.S. will be attacked	—	—	—	0.64	0.79	0.15**
Proud to be American	—	—	—	0.37	0.75	0.38**

Source: 21st Century Americanism Survey (2004).
Note: Cell entries = probability of approving when independent variable equals 0 or 1.
*$p < .10$. **$p < .05$.

impressive increase in support of 38 percentage points when the average respondent goes from not being proud to be American (37%) to being proud (75%). Strong Republicans have the highest level of support for 9/11 profiling, shown in Table 3, whereas patriotism is the only variable that changes a person's predicted response from disapprove to approve. The corresponding changes in probability for ethnoculturalism and liberalism, in contrast, are 16 and 9 percentage points, respectively, comparable to sociotropic threat.

Table 4, on the other hand, shows that how a person defines the meaning of American identity can be a very powerful influence over support for internment. People who define American identity ethnoculturally are much more likely to approve of internment than are people who reject ethnoculturalism. Indeed, ethnoculturalism is the most powerful variable in both internment models, and it is the only one that changes a person's predicted response from oppose to support. People who score a 0 on the ethnoculturalism scale have an 8% chance of supporting the internment of Arab Americans, whereas people who score a 1 have a 79% chance. Likewise, people who score a 0 on ethnoculturalism have a 15% chance of supporting the internment of Arab immigrants, whereas people who

Table 4. Predicted Probability of Approving of Internment

Independent Variable	Internment of Arab Americans			Internment of Arab Immigrants		
	0	1	Change	0	1	Change
White to Black	0.22	0.15	−0.07	0.28	0.33	0.05
Education	0.36	0.14	−0.22**	0.42	0.20	−0.22**
Democrat to Republican	0.17	0.30	0.13**	0.20	0.41	0.21**
Liberal definition of American identity	0.37	0.20	−0.17**	0.27	0.29	0.02
Ethnocultural definition of American identity	0.08	0.79	0.71**	0.15	0.71	0.56**
Fears being victim of attack	0.17	0.33	0.16**	0.24	0.39	0.15**
Fears U.S. will be attacked	0.18	0.26	0.08	0.29	0.28	−0.01
Proud to be American	0.06	0.24	0.18**	0.19	0.30	0.11

Source: 21st Century Americanism Survey (2004).
Note: Cell entries = probability of approving when independent variable equals 0 or 1.
**$p < .05$.

score a 1 have a 71% chance. This influence far surpasses that of patriotism and partisanship. Roughly 8.4% of the sample scores in the top third of the ethnoculturalism scale, which means that this substantial level of support for internment applies to a small but nontrivial portion of the U.S. population.

Political liberalism is also an important determinant of support for internment, but only when the target group consists of U.S. citizens of Arab descent. People who say that political freedom is an unimportant component of American identity are 17 percentage points more likely than people who say political freedom is an important component of American identity to support interning Arab Americans. This effect is greater than the magnitude of partisanship, less than the magnitude of education, and roughly the same as personal threat. When the target group is changed to immigrants, political liberalism loses its significance. This finding underscores that people distinguish between citizens and immigrants when it comes to granting the full range of rights that come with being a member of the political community. Seeing America as uniquely defined by its respect for political freedoms such as speech rights decreases support for internment, but only when the potential detainees are legally American.

Finally, a brief word is in order about the race of the respondent and the role of sociotropic and personal threat, because both have received much attention in existing literature. In line with earlier studies, Black respondents are less supportive of traditional profiling than Whites, whereas the race of the respondent returns inconsistent results with 9/11 profiling. Black, Asian, and Latino respondents are less likely than White respondents to support allowing searches of people who look Middle Eastern, but the race of the respondent is insignificant in both internment models. And as in previous studies, both sociotropic and personal threat increase support for profiling, but they do so inconsistently. Sociotropic threat increases support only for searches, whereas personal threat increases support for both kinds of internment.

CONCLUSION

This analysis advances the study of public opinion on profiling in several respects. First, it devotes attention to the sizeable portion of Americans who say they would support removing people from the community and placing them into camps to prevent a terrorist attack. Given how far the United States has come in the past several decades in the march toward racial equality, that one third of Americans would support internment demands scrutiny. I find that lower levels of education, being a Republican, fearing being a victim of an attack, being proud to be an American, and having an ethnocultural definition of American identity all make such support more likely, whereas having a liberal definition of American identity makes such support less likely. Of these factors, ethnoculturalism has the greatest effect.

Second, this study finds that support for profiling is tempered when the profilee is expressly described as an American citizen instead of as an immigrant. However, the individual-level factors that influence opinions in both cases are generally the same. The only notable exceptions are a liberal view of American identity and patriotism, which both influence attitudes toward interning citizens, but not immigrants.

Third, this study compares attitudes about traditional profiling with attitudes about 9/11 profiling. People are much more approving of 9/11 profiling than of traditional profiling. Some factors, such as being a Republican and White, generate support for both kinds of profiling, whereas other factors, such as education and how people define American identity, influence only 9/11 profiling. People think that 9/11 profiling is about preserving one's sense of what America stands for whereas traditional profiling is not.

This last point gets to the final contribution of this study, which is that it demonstrates the powerful role that abstract and entrenched ideas about national identity can have over salient and contentious policy debates relative to more immediate, tangible, and fluctuating concerns about national and personal security. Public opinion about what being American means changes slowly, if at all. Yet, its influence over profiling attitudes remains strong, even years after the 9/11 attacks. On 9/11 profiling, defining America in ascriptive terms is the main factor leading people to be willing to resort to measures as extreme as internment. Framing opposition to 9/11 profiling in terms of America's liberal tradition has the potential to temper the power of ethnoculturalism, in particular with regard to interning Arab Americans. Such framing could also diminish support for milder and more common forms of profiling, such as those detailed by the ACLU and Amnesty International. On internment, however, the frame of liberal Americanism will only temper support when the profilees are fellow Americans. When the profilees are immigrants, America's liberal tradition does not seem to be able to stand in the way of ethnoculturalism's substantial effect. Despite this finding, policy makers and activists concerned about extreme profiling would be wise to do what they can to make this conception of American identity salient when they engage in this policy debate, given how central liberalism is defining what people think it means to be American.

APPENDIX
QUESTION WORDING AND CODING

Level of Education

What is the highest grade of school or year of college you have completed? (recoded to run from 0 to 1)

1 = less than high school diploma; 2 = high school graduate; 3 = trade/vocational school; 4 = some college; 5 = BA or BS; 6 = some graduate school; 7 = graduate level degree

Partisan Identification

Generally speaking, do you consider yourself a Republican, an independent, a Democrat, or something else? (if R or D) Would you call yourself a strong Republican/Democrat or a not very strong Republican/Democrat? (if something else) Do you think of yourself as closer to the Republican or Democratic party? (recoded to run from 0 to 1)

1 = strong Democrat; 2 = Democrat; 3 = leans Democrat; 4 = Independent; 5 = leans Republican; 6 = Republican; 7 = strong Republican

Panethnic Discrimination Scale

In general, do you think discrimination against [Whites/Blacks/Latinos/Asians] is a major problem, a minor problem, or not a problem in schools?

What about in the workplace?

What about in preventing [Whites/Blacks/Latinos/Asians] in general from succeeding in America?

Answers were combined to form a 0 to 1 scale ($a = 0.84$), where 0 means that all three were not a problem, and 1 means that all three were a major problem.

Victim of Discrimination Scale

Do you think you have ever been denied a job or promotion because of your racial or ethnic background?

Do you think you generally receive worse service than other people at restaurants or stores because of your racial or ethnic background?

Do you think your racial or ethnic background has made it difficult for you to succeed in America?

Answers were combined to form a 0 to 1 scale ($a = 0.64$), where 0 means that the respondent said "no" to all three, and 1 means that the respondent said "yes" to all three.

Personal Threat

How worried are you that you or a close relative or friend might be the victim of a terrorist attack in the United States—are you very worried, somewhat worried, or not worried at all? (recoded to run from 0 to 1, where 1 = very worried)

1 = very worried; 2 = somewhat worried; 3 = not worried at all

Sociotropic Threat

How worried are you about the possibility that there will be more major terrorist attacks in the United States in the near future—are you very worried, somewhat worried, or not worried at all? (recoded to run from 0 to 1, where 1 = strongly agree)

1 = very worried; 2 = somewhat worried; 3 = not worried at all

Proud to be American

Please tell me if you strongly agree, somewhat agree, somewhat disagree, or strongly disagree: I am proud to be an American. (recoded to run from 0 to 1)

1 = strongly agree; 2 = somewhat agree; 3 = somewhat disagree; 4 = strongly disagree

Notes

1. Information on recent White supremacist activity was found at the Anti-Defamation League Web site (http://www.adl.org/PresRele/Extremism_72/4973_72.htm, retrieved March 20, 2007) and at the National Public Radio Web site (http://www.npr.org/templates/story/story.php?storyId=7725295, retrieved March 20, 2007).

2. Survey results available at the Polling the Nations Web site (http://poll.orspub.com, retrieved November 29, 2006).

3. Data collection was conducted from July 12 to October 8, 2004, by the Social and Economic Sciences Research Center at Washington State University and was funded by the Russell Sage Foundation. Any U.S. resident older than 18 years and living in a household with a telephone was eligible for selection in the sample. Counties with higher percentages of Black, Latino, and Asian residents were targeted more heavily with random-digit dialing for the oversamples. The cooperation rate, the ratio of interviews to interviews plus refusals, was 31.2%. A Spanish version of the survey was available and was used by 137 respondents. The average interview length was 26 minutes.

4. The remaining respondents identified as either mixed race or Native American or answered the race question in a way that could not be incorporated into this breakdown (e.g., "human").

5. Respondents were randomly assigned to Form 1 or Form 2, where Form 1 asked about profiling motorists and interning citizens and Form 2 asked about 9/11 profiling and interning immigrants.

6. This question wording was adopted from a poll conducted shortly after 9/11 by the Kaiser Family Foundation, the Kennedy School of Government at Harvard University, and National Public Radio. The original survey is available at http://kff.org/kaiserpolls/loader.cfm?url=/commonspot/security/getfile cfm&PageID=13879.

7. Unless noted otherwise, all percentages represent weighed results, using weights provided by the Social and Economic Sciences Research Center.

8. This question wording was adopted from the poll conducted by the Kaiser Family Foundation, the Kennedy School of Government at Harvard University, and National Public Radio.

9. This question wording was adopted from a *Time*/CNN poll taken shortly after 9/11, available at http://poll.orspub.com.

10. All percentages exclude respondents who said "don't know." The percentages offering that response were as follows: traditional profiling (61%), 9/11 profiling (6.7%), interning U.S. citizens (9.0%), and interning Arab immigrants (8.9%).

11. For a discussion of why liberalism is measured with one item whereas ethnoculturalism is measured with a four-variable scale, see Schildkraut (2007).

12. Independent variables with more than four categories are collapsed in Table 1 but are restored to their full precision in subsequent probit analyses.

13. 21-CAS data are available from the author upon request.

14. The 21st Century Americanism Survey does not ask respondents about their personal or sociotropic fear of crime, precluding a test of whether sociotropic and/or personal threat generate support for both traditional and 9/11 profiling.

15. Predicted probabilities are calculated while holding all other variables constant at their means.

REFERENCES

American Civil Liberties Union. (2004). *Sanctioned bias: Racial profiling since 9/11*. New York: American Civil Liberties Union.

Berinsky, A. (n.d.). *America at war: Public opinion during wartime, from World War II to Iraq*. Unpublished manuscript.

Braber, L. (2002). Korematsu's ghost: A post-September 11th analysis of race and national security. *Villanova Law Review*, 47(2), 451–490.

Citrin, J., Haas, E. B., Muste, C., & Reingold, B. (1994). Is American nationalism changing? Implications for foreign policy. *International Studies Quarterly*, 38(1), 1.

Citrin, J., Reingold, B., & Green, D. P. (1990). American identity and the politics of ethnic change. *Journal of Politics*, 52(4), 1124.

Davis, D., & Silver, B. (2004). Civil liberties vs. security: Public opinion in the context of the terrorist attacks on America. *American Journal of Political Science*, 48(1), 28–46.

Elliott, A. (2006, June 12). After 9/11, Arab-Americans fear police acts, study finds. *The New York Times*, p. 15.

Greenberg, C. (1995). Black and Jewish responses to Japanese internment. *Journal of American Ethnic History*, 14(2), 3–37.

Harris, D. A. (2003). *Profiles in injustice: Why racial profiling cannot work*. New York: New Press.

Huddy, L., Feldman, S., Taber, C., & Lahav, G. (2005). Threat, anxiety, and support of antiterrorism policies. *American Journal of Political Science*, 49(3), 593–608.

Kim, P. H. (2004). Conditional morality? Attitudes of religious individuals toward racial profiling. *American Behavioral Scientist*, 47(7), 879–895.

McClosky, H., & Zaller, J. (1984). *The American ethos: Public attitudes toward capitalism and democracy*. Cambridge, MA: Harvard University Press.

Palmer, J. J. (2006, August 17). King eyes ethnic profiling. *Newsday*, p. 4.

Schildkraut, D. J. (2002). The more things change... American identity and mass and elite responses to 9/11. *Political Psychology*, 23(3), 511–535.

Schildkraut, D. J. (2005a). *Press one for English: Language policy, public opinion, and American identity*. Princeton, NJ: Princeton University Press.

Schildkraut, D. J. (2005b). The rise and fall of political engagement among Latinos: The role of identity and perceptions of discrimination. *Political Behavior*, 27(3), 285–312.

Schildkraut, D. J. (2007). Defining American identity in the 21st century: How much "there" is there? *Journal of Politics*, 69(3), 597–615.

Smith, R. M. (1997). *Civic ideals: Conflicting visions of citizenship in U.S. history*. New Haven, CT: Yale University Press.

Theiss-Morse, E. (2006). *The obligations of national identity: Charity, welfare, and the boundaries of the national group*. Paper presented at the annual meeting of the Midwest Political Science Association, Chicago, IL.

Weitzer, R., & Tuch, S. (2002). Perceptions of racial profiling: Race, class, and personal experience. *Criminology*, 40(2), 435–456.

Weitzer, R., & Tuch, S. A. (2005). Racially biased policing: Determinants of citizen perceptions. *Social Forces*, 83(3), 1009–1030.

Wong, C., & Cho, G. E. (2005). Two-headed coins or Kandinskys: White racial identification. *Political Psychology*, 26(5), 699–720.

*Deborah J. Schildkraut is an associate professor of political science at Tufts University. Her research has been published in the *Journal of Politics, Political Behavior,* and *Political Psychology.* She is the author of *Press "One" for English: Language Policy, Public Opinion, and American Identity* (Princeton University Press, 2005).

Racial Profiling and Terrorism

by Stephen J. Ellmann*

THE ISSUE: DOES TERRORISM CHANGE THE RIGHTS AND WRONGS OF PROFILING?

September 11 has forced us to look again at who we are. We have re-encountered our own society, as we came to grips with the deaths of thousands only a few blocks from our law school. We have re-encountered the world, its intractable conflicts and the rage and ruthlessness those conflicts sometimes generate. We have sought to reaffirm, as lawyers, the highest traditions of the bar, in public service and human connection. It is the special responsibility of academics, however, to ask as well whether any of the ideas to which we have long been committed now must be reassessed because the world is different than we thought. In doing this, we must beware of panic and over-reaction, particularly now that the most immediate crisis is past. But at the same time we should not shrink from this task; what may seem to outsiders to be a "defense mechanism" may in fact be "self-defense."[1] In this spirit, I address here the question of whether there are any circumstances in which racial profiling, or profiling on other similar grounds, is justifiable as a response to terrorism.

We know that it must not be a crime to be found "driving while black." We know that it is wrong for a town investigating a violent crime allegedly committed by a young black man to seek to question every black male student at the local college, and many or most black residents of the local town.[2] We know that people of every race should be free to walk in every neighborhood of the country without being quizzed by the police about their reasons for being there—even if all the residents of the neighborhood are of another race.[3]

We know, in short, that racial profiling—that is, deploying the apparatus of law enforcement from brief interrogations on the street to searches, seizures and arrests—on the basis of generalizations about race is, ordinarily, a violation of fundamental principles of the equal protection of the laws.[4] The same would be true of taking such steps simply on the basis of religion, though for some decades the idea that anyone would want to "profile" on the basis of religion would have seemed quite odd in the United States. Profiling among United States citizens on the basis of their national origin is essentially a form of profiling on the basis of race or ethnicity, and equally unacceptable.[5] So too, profiling on the sole basis of gender must, in general, be unconstitutional.[6] And the same must be true of profiling based on some or all of these factors combined.[7]

Constitutional law on discrimination suggests that this prohibition on racial profiling (or profiling on other comparably unacceptable grounds) must be quite strict.[8] It is important to recognize, as well, that this prohibition does not rest on an assumption that there is never any basis in fact for the profiler's stereotypes. Consider two cases from somewhat different equal protection contexts. In *Craig v. Boren* the Supreme Court first established the rule of intermediate scrutiny for gender discrimination.[9] Statistics presented in that case arguably demonstrated that young men were much more likely to get arrested for drunk driving than young women were—though neither men nor women were tremendously likely to get arrested for this reason.[10] On that basis, the state of Colorado had permitted women to buy near-beer (3.2%-alcohol beer) at a younger age than men could. This was a silly statute, but the Court's reasoning is still important; it considered the idea of legislating to disfavor men based on these sociological generalizations "inevitably in tension with the normative philosophy that underlies the Equal Protection Clause."[11] In somewhat the same way, the Supreme Court in *J.E.B. v. Alabama ex rel. T.B.* said that lawyers could not exercise peremptory challenges against jurors on the basis of gender;[12] Justice O'Connor wrote in a separate opinion that this had to be the rule for the government (though not, in her view, for private litigants) even if in fact—as surely is so—a juror's sex can sometimes make a difference to how she or he sees the case.[13] Stereotypes sometimes have some truth to them; what stereotypes do not have, under our law, is a legitimate bearing on the question of how government should treat an individual person, whatever groups he or she belongs to. Too many innocent people are harmed by stereotyping, and too much damage is done to the ideal of equal justice under the law, for it to be acceptable as a tool of domestic law enforcement, even if it turns out to be of some statistical value.[14]

All of which leads to the very unpleasant question of whether terrorism calls for exceptions to this rule. My focus is not on military operations[15] or foreign surveillance[16] or even the enforcement of immigration and customs laws at our borders,[17] though in each of these contexts profiling is, or may well be, underway. Important as those contexts are, I concentrate here on domestic law enforcement. Domestic law enforcement is the setting in which a national debate about racial profiling has already taken place, and I want to explore whether the consensus that racial profiling is wrong in our neighborhoods and on our highways holds true when the target is terrorism rather than ordinary crime.[18]

[...]

PROFILING AS A RESPONSE TO TERRORIST EMERGENCIES

[...]

We cannot employ maximum effort on every person, but we could employ maximum effort on people selected in nondiscriminatory ways. This is, in fact, what airlines now routinely announce they are doing. Everyone is scrutinized more than they would have been before 9/11, but a few people on each flight are, it is said, randomly selected for additional scrutiny. Early in 2002, my daughter, who was 6 years old at the time and travelling with her mother, was selected this way. Her backpack was opened and searched, and she was subjected to a metal detector wand and patdown search of her body.

This is proof that it is possible to avoid discrimination in security measures, but it is not proof that it is wise to do so. It may be that we live in a world where someone is prepared to use his 6-year-old daughter in a terrorist plot; if we're not in that world yet, it may be that we would soon enter it if terrorist adults realized that 6-year-old girls were getting a free pass. Random searches, and universal searches, both make sense because we are far from sure what our adversaries will look like. But it isn't conceivable that 6-year-old girls pose the same threat to airline security—or, to go back to my example, to the security of New York buildings—as grown men do. So if 6-year-olds are actually as likely to be randomly searched as grown men are, then some substantial amount of law enforcement effort is being largely wasted, as far as preventing terrorist attacks is concerned.[34]

If we cannot rely on a combination of screening everyone to the limited extent feasible while more intensively screening a few people selected on a random basis, then we need a non-random basis for choosing some of the people whom we will scrutinize more thoroughly. (Some use of random searching still seems wise, however, to try to dissuade, or catch, those who might seek to slip through the net by falling outside the categories subject to deliberate search.[35]) Essentially there are only three alternatives. First, we can select people for additional screening based solely on race, religion and similar factors. Second, we can select based solely on individual behavioral factors, such as nervousness or (at an airport) lack of a round-trip ticket, while altogether excluding race, religion and similar factors. Or, third, we can consider all of these factors together.

The first alternative, of screening solely on the basis of race and comparable factors, is both discriminatory and foolish. Arabs and Muslims—to name the two most obvious targets for such reactions today—are part of the American mainstream. Many are citizens. The vast majority, citizens or noncitizens, are altogether innocent of any connection with terrorism. Meanwhile, some people who are not Arabs—John Walker Lindh and Jose Padilla come immediately to mind as proven, or alleged, instances—have apparently joined our enemies in Al Qaeda,[36] and what apparently is an Al Qaeda instruction manual tells members to adopt a Western lifestyle that might make them unidentifiable as Muslims.[37] And this is to say nothing of the second worst terrorist in United States history, Timothy McVeigh—a white man with no links to Islam.[38] To screen solely on the basis of discriminatory factors would offensively intrude on the lives of vast numbers of innocent people, while certainly missing some very guilty ones.

The second alternative is to scrutinize people based solely on individual behavioral factors. The factors to be taken into account would depend on the context, but presumably they would be of two types—objective and subjective. At an airport, objective factors might include the lack of a round-trip ticket, or the lack of luggage; subjective considerations might include nervousness or failure to respond readily to initial, universally applied security procedures. If we can proceed this way, achieving protection without discrimination, we should. But there are important reasons to be skeptical of the promise of this approach.

[...]

It is important to recognize, therefore, that one aspect of the answer to the question of whether racial profiling should be a response to terrorism is simply that it *will* be—whether this is authorized or not. To say that there will be some discrimination even under nondiscriminatory rules does not, of course, mean that the rules should authorize discrimination. If discrimination is not an ineradicable aspect of human behavior, then a determined effort to suppress it, reflected in rules that give it no place, should be more successful than an approach that indulges or welcomes it. [...]

[...]

These varying data clearly suggest the unsurprising possibility that racial profiling is more productive in some circumstances than in others. We might expect that profiling would be most productive when it is most nuanced—that is, when it is genuinely combined with other factors, rather than being used as a crude, and usually inaccurate, proxy for criminality all by itself. [...]

Is it impossible, then, to take race or religion sensibly, rather than abusively, into account? Certainly not. No one suggests that a police officer who obtains a detailed description of a suspect—say, that the suspect is 5'10", heavy-set, wearing a blue T-shirt and tan pants, and white—should ignore the racial portion of the description.[78] In these circumstances, race is obviously relevant and obviously should be considered; however prone we are to racial stereotyping, we would be mad to ignore race here. In this and countless other similar circumstances, we must attempt to consider race without it blinding us to other relevant information; much of the time, presumably, we succeed—or, at any rate, we do not fail so egregiously as to make it plausible to try to delete race from our thoughts here.[79]

[...]

The answer, I think, is that there isn't just one answer to this question. Racial profiling may make a real contribution to protecting us from terrorism, but it also is profoundly costly, to its immediate targets and ultimately the entire society. Moreover, we cannot measure precisely either its costs or benefits; we can only attempt to gauge what makes most sense in the dangerous circumstances in which we live. The correct resolution of this dilemma, I suggest, is neither prohibition nor wholesale acceptance, but rather a recognition that profiling can in some circumstances be an appropriate, though never welcome, tool of protection against terrorism. Starting from the premise that ordinarily profiling is unacceptable, we must seek to define the limited exceptions to this rule, by assessing the peril faced, the alternatives for facing it, and the impact of profiling in those circumstances, both for good and ill.

[...]

The upshot of these observations is significant, but incomplete. The answer to the question, "Is racial, religious or gender profiling constitutional as a response to terrorism?" is "yes, sometimes." To say yes at all is painful, yet I believe necessary. To determine the correct definition of "sometimes" will remain a matter for skeptical and complex assessment in light of the many relevant circumstances that will bear on and shape the programs we may undertake. We have stepped out on to a slippery slope; we must now do all we can not to slide down it.

NOTES

1. Danger in some ways worsens our judgment, but in one way it certainly can have the opposite effect: it concentrates our minds on *risk*, and so can make us better at deciding what risk requires than we would be if we entertained the same question in less anxious times. This essay attempts to look at the risks we face, and what steps those risks do and do not justify.

2. *But see* Brown v. Oneonta, 221 F.3d 329, 333–34 (2d Cir. 1999), *cert. denied*, 122 S.Ct. 44 (2001).

3. *Cf.* Kolender v. Lawson, 461 U.S. 352, 353 (1983) (striking down, as unconstitutionally vague, a statute "requir[ing] persons who loiter or wander on the streets to provide a 'credible and reliable' identification and to account for their presence"); Brown v. Texas, 443 U.S. 47, 53 (1979) (holding unconstitutional a Texas statute permitting police "to detain [a person] and require him to identify himself" when "the officers lacked any reasonable suspicion to believe [he] was engaged or had engaged in criminal conduct"). According to Samuel R. Gross and Debra Livingston, "[m]ost courts... have held that... being racially 'out of place' does not create a reasonable suspicion of criminal activity." Samuel R. Gross & Debra Livingston, *Racial Profiling Under Attack*, 102 COLUM. L. REV. 1413, 1432–33 (2002).

4. Implicit in this definition is a distinction between law enforcement actions based on generalizations about race—propositions that particular racial groups are more or less likely to commit crimes—and other law enforcement steps based on information about particular suspects' identifying descriptions. *See* Gross & Livingston, *supra* note 3, at 1415. To act on the basis of a particular suspect's description as belonging to a given race is certainly to take race into account, but it is not to take *generalizations* about race into account.

This distinction, however, is more elusive than might at first appear. Suppose a suspect description consists of nothing more than race and gender (e.g., "Asian male"). Such a description on its face identifies a demographic group rather than an individual, unless the context makes its meaning much more specific (for example, if the suspect is identified as "the only white guy in the room"). If police then initiate indiscriminate stops and searches of members of that demographic group, I would characterize their action as racial (and, here, gender) profiling, based on an implicit generalization that any member of the demographic group in question is likely enough to have committed the crime to be a proper subject of scrutiny. (On this point of classification, I differ with Gross & Livingston, who would not call such action profiling; they would consider it "disturbing," however, *see id.* at 1435–36, and they emphasize that "it is a mistake to focus excessively on labels." *Id.* at 1416.)

As in other constitutional contexts, the test of violation of the general rule against profiling should not be whether race (or similar factors) were the only considerations triggering the law enforcement action, but whether these factors were a "but for" cause of the government's acts. *See* Mt. Healthy City School Dist. v. Doyle, 429 U.S. 274, 285–87 (1977) (adopting "but for" test in First Amendment context). For a case seemingly requiring that race be the "sole motive," *See* United States v. Avery, 137 F.3d 343 (6th Cir. 1997). *Avery*, however, has been circumscribed by Farm Labor Organizing Committee v. Ohio State Highway Patrol, 308 F.3d 523, 538 (6th Cir. 2002) , which characterized the "'sole motive' requirement ... [as] an anomaly in equal protection law ... [which] should not be applied outside the narrow factual context of purely consensual encounters." Although "but for" causation should be sufficient, it must be recognized that if law enforcement officers act largely on the basis of individualized considerations, then—even if racial generalizations do play a "but for" part—their conduct is less like profiling and more like the use of suspect descriptions. Clearly police conduct falls on a spectrum rather than being, unmistakably, either profiling or not profiling; my focus in this essay, however, is on those steps that are largely guided by generalizations rather than individualized inquiry.

5. Profiling on the basis of alienage, however, is another matter. While discrimination on the basis of alienage by states and localities has been subjected to strict scrutiny, Sugarman v. Dougall, 413 U.S. 634, 642 (1973), the federal government has much more leeway in this field, *see* Mathews v. Diaz, 426 U.S. 67, 77–87 (1976). *See infra* note 17.

6. This is so despite the fact that men commit far more crimes than women. William J. Stuntz, *Local Policing After the Terror*, 111 YALE L.J. 2137, 2178 (2002). The insistence on gender-free judgment built into the "exceedingly persuasive justification" test must generally preclude profiling all men as criminals based on the crimes some men commit. *See* United States v. Virginia, 518 U.S. 515 (1996), and *see infra* text accompanying notes 9–13.

7. Profiling on the basis of age presumably can pass constitutional muster more easily, since under current doctrine age discrimination is subject only to rational relationship scrutiny. Kimel v. Florida Bd. of Regents, 528 U.S. 62, 83–84 (2000).

8. In this essay I will often refer simply to racial profiling, which surely is the most egregious of these forms of discrimination. These references, however, are meant as shorthand for profiling on the grounds of race or other, similarly unacceptable, factors.

9. Craig v. Boren, 429 U.S. 190 (1976).

10. *Id.* at 201.

11. *Id.* at 204.

12. J.E.B. v. Alabama *ex rel.* T.B., 511 U.S. 127 (1994).

13. *Id.* at 148–50 (O'Connor, J., concurring).

14. Whether it is of any statistical value in domestic contexts is a contested matter, which I discuss below. *See infra* notes 67–78.

15. Justice Jackson wrote in his dissent in *Korematsu* that "[i]t would be impracticable and dangerous idealism to expect or insist that each specific military command in an area of probable operations will conform to conventional tests of constitutionality. When an area is so beset that it must be put under military control at all, the paramount consideration is that its measures be successful, rather than legal." Korematsu v. United States, 323 U.S. 214, 244 (1944) (Jackson, J., dissenting). Soldiers must make life-and-death decisions in an instant, and some of these must involve profiling. The classic World War II stories of troops identifying German spies by testing their knowledge of the Brooklyn Dodgers offer one illustration. The racial epithets of that and other wars demonstrate that even on the battlefield, such stereotyping can reflect mere prejudice.

16. Here, as in the context of immigration law, *see infra* note 17, I do not mean to examine, or assume the validity of, all possible forms of profiling. Some such steps, however, seem plainly appropriate. Consider the following, probably not hypothetical, example:

    *The government conducts surveillance of electronic communications. It programs the computers that screen the contents of these communications to pay special attention to all messages sent in Arabic, Pashtun and other languages known to be used by Al Qaeda.

    In actuality, it appears that prior to September 11 we were in effect following the opposite policy: because our intelligence agencies had so few speakers of languages that potential terrorists might be speaking, we were paying *less* attention to messages in these languages than sheer random selection would have generated. *See* Joy Kreeft Peyton & Donald A. Ranard, *We Can't Squander Language Skills, at* http://www.international.ucla.edu/lrp/news/joypeyton.html (last visited Aug. 1, 2002) ("Our foreign language deficiency is particularly acute in the uncommonly taught languages of Asia, Africa and the Middle East.") Now, presumably, we are doing everything we can to correct this mistake, and to single out messages in these languages for attention. Since the speakers of these languages are, disproportionately, members of particular ethnic groups and citizens of particular nations, it is quite plausible to describe this new attentiveness as a discriminatory security measure. But it is hard to imagine how we can improve our electronic surveillance if we do not increase the attention we pay to messages in these languages—and so the "necessity" for this step seems clear. At the same time, and for the same reason, it is implausible to see this step as profoundly stigmatizing to, say, Pashtuns. Members of this ethnic group have been central to the Taliban, and the Taliban has been allied with al Qaeda; to state these propositions is not to stigmatize but simply to report, just as it would not have been stigmatizing to report in World War II that we were at war with Japan. To deal with one's enemies one must be able to understand them, and paying attention to messages in Pashtun is not an assertion that all Pashtun are enemies but only that some have been and likely still are. Moreover, even though it is not illogical to describe a focus on Pashtun-language messages as a form of national-origin or ethnic discrimination, there is no indication that the underlying motivation for that discrimination is invidious stereotyping—rather than practical response to real threats. Finally, and somewhat paradoxically, the stigmatizing effect of this program is lessened because it is not public. It is paradoxical to find discrimination less troubling because it is covert, since often the worst discrimination is the hidden, but deliberate, mistreatment. But here the reason for hiding the discrimination is not in order to get away with discrimination, but rather to maintain secrecy about security measures in order to maintain their efficacy. When secrecy has a legitimate justification, as here, the conduct kept secret can be less constitutionally troublesome than more public discrimination by the government of us all.

17. In the context of immigration law, "Congress regularly makes rules that would be unacceptable if applied to citizens." Mathews v. Diaz, 426 U.S. 67, 80 (1976). Notably, distinctions are regularly made on the basis of the non-citizen's country of origin. To take a quite innocuous example, citizens of some countries can enter the United States without a visa; citizens of most nations, however, must get a visa before they travel here. Council on Foreign Relations, *Terrorism: Q & A—Immigration* ("Citizens of some Western countries and other countries with

histories of respecting U.S. immigration policies can travel to the United States without first obtaining visas.") *available at* http://www.terrorismanswers.com/security/ins_print.html (last visited Sept. 3, 2002).

There are, of course, a number of anti-terrorism steps that might be taken, or are already underway, at our borders. One recent proposal is to impose "fingerprinting, photographing, and registration requirements" on citizens of countries from which we see a special danger of terrorism. *See* U.S. Department of Justice, *National Security Entry-Exit Registration System*, June 5, 2002, at 2, *available at* http://www.usdoj.gov/ag/speeches/2002/natlsecentryexittrackingsys .htm (last visited Sept. 3, 2002) ("This initiative will require fingerprinting, photographing, and registration requirements on [sic] the following: (1) All nationals of Iran, Iraq, Libya, Sudan and Syria (2) Certain nationals of other countries whom the State Department and the INS determine to be an elevated national security risk (3) Aliens identified by INS inspectors at point of entry upon specific criteria to be established by the Department of Justice."); Seattle Post-Intelligencer News Services, *Ashcroft Proposes New Guidelines for Foreigners in U.S.: Visitors Would Be Required to Register with Government* (June 6, 2002), *available at* http://seattlepi .nwsource.com/national/73466_visa06.shtml (last visited Aug. 2, 2002) ("Other government officials said men 18 to 35 years of age from about 20 largely Muslim and Middle Eastern nations, including key allies such as Saudi Arabia and Egypt, would make up the bulk of those" covered). This program applies "[e]ven if a man does not live in one of those countries," if "he or a close relative was born in one of them," and it has reportedly caused "interminable" delays and a backlog of 100,000 applications. "[V]ery few visas have been issued to men in this category." Raymond Bonner, *Immigration: New Policy Delays Visas For Specified Muslim Men*, N.Y. Times, Sept. 10, 2002, at A12. Another is the planned Interagency Panel on Advancing Science and Security, which will limit student visas based on, among other things, the sensitivity of the information the student plans to study and whether the applicant is a citizen of a nation "determined as suspicious or dangerous." *See* University of Pennsylvania Almanac, *Government Affairs Update* (May 28, 2002), *available at* www.upenn.edu/almanac/v48/n35/GA-Update.html (last visited Sept. 3, 2002). Yet another idea might be to profile goods imported from particular countries; from the vast number of cargo "containers" now arriving every day, most of which we do not have the resources to search, we might target those from particular countries. *See* Bill Keller, *Nuclear Nightmare*, N.Y. Times, May 26, 2002, § 6, at 22 ("Two thousand containers enter America every hour. . . . Fewer than 2 percent are cracked open for inspection, and the great majority never pass through an X-ray machine.").

Broad as the federal "plenary power" over immigration is, Fiallo v. Bell, 430 U.S. 787, 792 (1976), I do not assume that all forms of profiling at the border would be constitutional under current doctrine (or that that doctrine is necessarily sound), or that these steps would be effective or wise. *Cf.* David Cole, *Enemy Aliens*, 54 Stan. L. Rev. 953 (2002) (criticizing our tendency to sacrifice noncitizens' rights in the name of security). For an example of what appears to be misuse of this power, *see* Dan Chapman, *War on Terrorism: Yemeni Passenger Claims Racial Profiling at Hartsfield; GSU Student Detained Under New U.S. Policy*, Atlanta Journal-Const., June 14, 2002, at 12A. This article reports a Yemeni student's contention that she was detained for an hour, searched and questioned. According to the article, "Immigration and customs officers . . . are simply following a directive from Washington, issued last Friday [June 7, 2002], which compels them to more readily question Yemenis and search their baggage. . . . U.S. officials confirmed this week that an apartment in New York that once was occupied by Yemeni nationals contained bomb-making equipment." If this account is correct, it describes particularly crude and questionable profiling, even in the context of the broad powers the government wields at its borders. A chilling concurrent development has been the passage of legislation limiting the extent to which law enforcement officials can be sued for abuse of such authority. *See* Trade Act of 2002, H.R. 3009, § 341 (a); American Civil Liberties Union, *Trade Bill Lets Customs Service Use Racial Profiling; Makes it Next to Impossible to Sue Agents Who Abuse Traveling Public* (Aug. 1, 2002), *available at* http://www.aclu.org/news/2002/ n080102b.html (last visited Sept. 12, 2002) (criticizing provision of Andean Trade Preference Expansion Act, passed by both Houses of Congress in July–August 2002).

18. Samuel Gross and Debra Livingston begin their recent essay on profiling and terrorism with the observation that "We had just reached a consensus on racial profiling. By September 10,

2001, virtually everyone, from Jesse Jackson to Al Gore to George W. Bush to John Ashcroft, agreed that racial profiling was very bad." Gross & Livingston, *supra* note 3, at 1413.

[...]

34. There are many reports of airport searches equally unlikely to result in catching potential terrorists. *See, e.g.,* Edward Wong, *Airport Has a No-Nonsense Approach to Security,* N.Y. TIMES, July 7, 2002, at 15 (reporting a passenger's statement that "security workers in Phoenix had run a wand over her 2-year-old son, Devin, and asked her to take off his shoes." Devin, Wong writes, "looked about as dangerous as a newborn kitten."); *Simmons Addresses Muslims,* THE BULLETIN'S FRONTRUNNER, June 24, 2002 (quoting NEW LONDON DAY, June 24, 2002) (Congressman Robert Simmons said he flies back and forth between Connecticut and Washington, D.C., almost every week, often on a one-way ticket purchased just hours before. He gets searched, he said, probably more often than anyone else, except for other congressmen and senators"); Stuart Taylor, *The Skies Won't Be Safe Until We Use Commonsense Profiling,* THE NAT'L J., *available at* http://www.theatlantic.com/politics/nj/taylor2002-03-19.htm (Mar. 19, 2002) ("randomly chosen grandmothers, members of Congress, former CIA directors, and decorated military officers" frisked at airports); Joe Sharkey, *A Onetime Top Executive Says Airline Security Has Often Been Secondary to Not Ruffling Customers,* N.Y. TIMES, Jan. 23, 2002, at 8 (search of former Vice President Quayle; strip-search of Congressman John Dingell). Anna Quindlen has criticized random searches of women, arguing that "[g]ender is clearly key, despite the sudden spate of three suicide bombings in Israel by women.... Who knows who could be sliding by while security personnel are checking my lipstick for Plasticine?" Anna Quindlen, *Armed With Only a Neutral Lipstick,* NEWSWEEK, Mar. 18, 2002, at 72. *Cf.* Gross & Livingston, *supra* note 3, at 1425 ("After September 11, nobody could seriously complain about the FBI paying more attention to reports of suspicious behavior by Saudi men than to similar reports about Hungarian women."); Stuntz, *supra* note 6, at 2179 (similar comparison of airport security attention to "travelers with Danish visas and travelers with Yemeni visas").

See also Rob Asghar, *A Show of Grace for Safety's Sake; Airline Passengers Need to Tolerate a Benign Profiling,* L.A. TIMES, July 6, 2002, Part 2, at 23 (Asghar, "a youngish South Asian male traveling alone," criticizing the fact that he was *not* searched during air travel, urges: "stop strip-searching the little old white lady and take another gander at me the next time I come walking through LAX"). While Asghar's view is certainly not shared by all Muslims or Arabs in the United States, shortly after the September 11 attacks 61% of Arab-Americans polled in the Detroit area (home to "the nation's most visible community of Arab immigrants and descendants, estimated at 200,000—350,000") said that "profiling, or extra scrutiny of people with Middle Eastern features or accents" was "justified." Dennis Niemiec & Shawn Windsor, *Arab Americans Expect Scrutiny, Feel Sting of Bias,* DETROIT FREE PRESS, Oct. 1, 2001, *available at* http://www.freep.com/news/nw/terror2001/poll1_20011001.htm (last visited Aug. 9, 2002). Another poll of Arab-Americans in May 2002 found that 48% of those polled believed that it is "justified" for "law enforcement officials to engage in extra questioning and inspections of people with Middle Eastern accents or features," while 43% disagreed. Seven months earlier, the same polling agency had found slightly greater approval rates (54% calling profiling justified, while 36% considered it unjustified). Zogby International, *The Views of Arab Americans Toward Their Ethnicity Since September 11* (May 31, 2002) (on file with the author) [hereinafter cited as Zogby International, *The Views of Arab Americans*]. The Arab-American community is no more monolithic than any other, however, and it is notable that 61.0% of Muslim Arab-Americans polled in May 2002 felt that profiling was unjustified.

35. A profile is not useless simply because it may be evaded, provided that evasion is not easy (for example, because recruiting terrorists who do not fit the profile is also not easy) and provided that the profile does not beguile us into ignoring the possibility of its evasion.

36. Lindh, who recently pled guilty to two of the charges against him, is a white American, "raised in affluent Marin County, Calif.," who "discovered Islam as a teenager and immersed himself in it," and then "joined forces with Taliban troops" in Afghanistan. *A Surprise Ending to Lindh's Strange Story,* AUSTIN AM. STATESMAN, July 16, 2002, at A10. Jose Padilla, also known as Abdullah al-Muhajir, has been accused of plotting to use a nuclear "dirty bomb" against the United States, and is now being held as an "enemy combatant." He has been reported to be a "former

Chicago gang member." *See* Benjamin Weiser, *U.S. Defends Decision to Move Suspect in 'Dirty Bomb' Case*, N.Y. TIMES, July 19, 2002, at A15.

37. The manual, according to the Department of Justice, "was located by the Manchester (England) Metropolitan Police during a search of an *al Qaeda* member's home. The manual was found in a computer file described as 'the military series' related to the 'Declaration of Jihad.' The manual was translated into English and was introduced...at the embassy bombing trial in New York." *The Al Qaeda Manual, available at* http://www.usdoj.gov/ag/trainingmanual.htm [hereinafter cited as "Al Qaeda Manual"]. Among the instructions in the "Fourth Lesson" on "Apartments—Hiding Places" are cautions against "[a]voiding seclusion and isolation from the population" and in favor of "rent[ing] these apartments using false names, appropriate cover, and non-Moslem appearance."

38. The FBI also has suspected that the person responsible for the anthrax letters is "a skilled scientist, acting alone, who works or worked in one of a handful of labs involved in the U.S. biowarfare program." Eric Rich, *Anthrax Mystery Turns Scholars Into Sleuths*, HARTFORD COURANT, Feb. 6, 2002, at A1. Recently a great deal of very public law enforcement attention has focused on a single scientist, a white American man, who apparently fits the profile of a potential anthrax terrorist. It is by no means clear that this individual is guilty of anything, however, and the *New York Times* has commented that the FBI, "and the nation, should be careful about fitting someone to the profile and assuming he is guilty before he is charged, tried and convicted." *See* Editorial, *The Anthrax Investigation*, N.Y. TIMES, Aug. 14, 2002, at A22. Needless to say, these events are a reminder that even very narrowly focused profiles can be inaccurate. The widespread assumption by profilers of serial killers that the snipers who terrorized the area around Washington, D.C. in the fall of 2002 were white appears to be another proof of this proposition. *See* Steven A. Holmes, *An Assumption Undone: Many Voice Surprise Arrested Men Are Black*, N.Y. TIMES, Oct. 25, 2002, at A26.

[...]

78. Harris, for example, agrees that "[i]t does make sense to use racial or ethnic characteristics in enforcement, but only in one context: *cases in which race or ethnic characteristics describe actual suspects.*" HARRIS, *supra* note 39, at 152.

79. R. Richard Banks argues forcefully that race is misused in suspect descriptions, but he does not urge its removal. Banks, *supra* note 27, at 1102–04, 1109–11, 1123–24. Banks concludes that "[t]here is no policy choice that would avoid the imposition of racial inequality. Any choice is a choice among inequalities. That is the tragedy of race. The possibility of truly avoiding state imposition of racial inequality is foreclosed by the pervasive role of race in American society." *Id.* at 1123–24.

*Stephen J. Ellmann is associate dean for faculty development and professor of law at New York Law School.

Ellmann, Stephen J. "Racial Profiling and Terrorism" *New York Law School Law Review* 46 (2003): 675–730, 2002–2003. This text has been shortened. Passages left out are indicated by [...].

Used by Permission.

Profiling in the Age of Total Information Awareness

by Nancy Murray*

Abstract: In recent years, a secretive domestic surveillance apparatus has been created in the US in the name of counter-terrorism. Based on the notion of 'predictive policing', it aims to gather such detailed information about individuals—'total information awareness'—that it is able to anticipate crimes before they are committed. Linked to the return of racial profiling in the name of the 'war on terror' and implemented by local Joint-Terrorism Task Forces, operating effectively with federal powers and little accountability, this new surveillance apparatus is especially focused on Muslims, immigrants and prisoners.

> *'The past is never dead. It's not even past.'*
>
> William Faulkner, *Requiem for a Nun*

When, on 28 October 2009, the FBI gunned down Imam Luqman Ameen Abdullah, the 53-year-old head of a Detroit mosque who was born Christopher Thomas, the ghosts of Black Power and COINTELPRO were given a twenty-first century makeover. The level of violence used against Abdullah had a pedigree steeped in bloody racial history: Luqman Ameen Abdullah, who worked with destitute ex-cons in a hollowed out neighbourhood, died in an exchange of gunfire which, it was said, he initiated.

'I'm comfortable with what our agents did,' stated the Special Agent in Charge of the FBI office in Detroit. 'They did what they had to do to protect themselves.'[1] For ninety days, the government sat on an autopsy that revealed that the imam had been hit by twenty-one bullets, including several in the groin and one in the back, and was found with his wrists handcuffed behind him.

The past was vividly present in inflated claims about the danger presented by Abdullah's Masjid Al-Haqq, based on the assertions of paid informants, and the government's announcement that the imam had been part of a group [of] African-American converts to Islam known as Ummah which, in the words of an FBI press release, 'seeks to establish a separate Sharia-law governed state within the United States. The Ummah is ruled by Jamil Abdullah Al-Amin, formerly known as H. Rapp [sic] Brown, who is serving a state sentence in USP Florence, CO, ADMAX, for the murder of two [sic] police officers in Georgia.'[2]

As chair of the Student Non-Violent Coordinating Committee (SNCC) and then minister of justice of the Black Panther Party, H. Rap Brown was one of the Black leaders singled out by COINTELPRO, the FBI's 'counter-intelligence program' whose mandate was 'to expose, disrupt, misdirect, or otherwise neutralize the activities of black nationalist, hate-type organizations and groupings'.[3] Doggedly pursued by the FBI, he was eventually convicted of armed robbery in 1973. While in prison awaiting trial, he converted to Islam and adopted the name Jamil Abdullah Al-Amin. After his release in 1976, he ran a community grocery store in Atlanta and served as an imam to a congregation that did outreach to former prisoners. But he was not off the government's radar screen.

In August 1995, Al-Amin was arrested in Atlanta by a small army of FBI, local police and agents from the Bureau of Alcohol, Tobacco and Firearms, a forerunner of the 'Joint Terrorism Task Force' model of policing that was to spread across the country after 9/11. He was accused of assault. His alleged victim claimed he had never named Al-Amin as his attacker although he was pressured to do so. This incident set off a chain reaction of improbable events that led to Al-Amin's incarceration for murder in the isolating depths of the supermax prison in Florence, Colorado, from which he is said by the FBI to 'rule' the Ummah (Arabic for 'community') that had included Imam Abdullah as one of its members.[4]

In a piece he wrote about his former SNCC colleague shortly before Al-Amin went on trial for murder in 2002, University of Massachusetts professor Ekwueme Michael Thelwell quoted Al-Amin's brother, Ed Brown, the director of a Voter Education Project:

> Y'know...something happens. Say the first attempt to bomb the Trade Center, right? They feed their infallible profile into their computer. Muslim...radical...violent...anti-American, whatever, who knows. Anyway, boom, out spits the names, H. Rap Brown, prominent among them. Next thing the Feds come storming into the community and haul Jamil in. This actually happened. Of course, it's stupid. And every time they have to let him go. But how do you stop it? A goddamn nightmare, they never quit.[5]

It is now no longer necessary for something to happen for the Feds to 'come storming into the community'. Over the past five years, a secretive domestic surveillance apparatus has been erected with virtually no public discussion to combat not just 'terrorism' but crime—or, more accurately, 'pre crime'. So-called intelligence-led or 'predictive policing' focuses not on collecting evidence about actual wrongdoing but on the broad collection of information about everyday activities with the intention of detecting (and preventing) future behaviour. Racial profiling, which had been significantly discredited by the late 1990s, has been given a new legitimacy as it performs its old 'war on drugs' role of packing the prisons while now also serving as a critical tool in the 'war on terrorism'. The enormous multi-agency bureaucratic system that is being created in the shadows to protect 'national security' needs to be justified and fed, and Muslims, non-citizens and current and former prisoners—especially converts like Imam Abdullah—are perceived to be low hanging fruit.

TOTAL INFORMATION AWARENESS

> '[O]ur goal is total information awareness . . .'
>
> John Poindexter, Speech to defense technology conference,
> 2 August 2002

Navy Admiral John Poindexter, who was to serve as Ronald Reagan's national security adviser and be convicted of numerous felonies for his role in the Iran-Contra affair,[6] was brought to the White House in 1981 'to bring the place into the technology age'.[7] A few years before, in the mid 1970s, Americans had learned about the extent of government spying on activity that was supposed to be protected by the First Amendment and the range of 'dirty tricks' carried out by the FBI and other federal agencies to destroy political and social movements that challenged the status quo.

The unmasking of COINTELPRO coincided with other revelations. The secretive National Security Agency (NSA), through its Operation Shamrock, had for thirty years been collecting the international telegrams to and from Americans, amassing as many as 150,000 messages a month. The CIA, through its Operation CHAOS, had compiled the names of 300,000 persons to be monitored in a computerised index. Its Office of Security had amassed some 900,000 'security files', including files on seventy-five sitting members of Congress.[8] The CIA also routinely opened mail and infiltrated anti-war groups.

The reform put in place by Congress—the 1978 Foreign Intelligence Surveillance Act (FISA)[9]—added a secret court to the surveillance process. But, during decades that saw the jarring economic dislocation brought about by globalisation, the upward redistribution of wealth and the sharply growing inequalities of US society, no serious constraints were put on the use of swiftly evolving computer technology for the purposes of monitoring and social control. As Tony Bunyan has noted, the origins of the 'surveillance society' can be traced to the 1980s, when capitalist globalisation, enabled by advances in information technology, was achieving lift-off.[10]

In 1980, a year before Poindexter's arrival at the White House, Bertram Gross, a political scientist who had served in both the Roosevelt and Truman administrations, published his prescient *Friendly Fascism: the new face of power in America*. In the chapter titled 'Managing information and minds', he set out 'three requirements' that must be met to compile 'womb-to-tomb dossiers' on individuals: 'the recording of all information received', 'the pooling of all available information' by computerising all machine readable data and the 'capability to sift or synthesize available new data'.[11] He points out that significant advances had already been made on all three fronts.

John Poindexter and his colleagues would take that job to completion and attempt to go much further. Once he put the Iran-Contra affair behind him, Poindexter developed ties with the research arm of the Department of Defense, the Defense Advanced Research Projects Agency (DARPA), which had developed the internet in the 1960s. Immediately after 9/11, Poindexter became director of DARPA's Information Awareness Office, where he was given the funds to develop a programme that he promoted as 'a Manhattan Project on countering terrorism'.

In November 2002, the *New York Times* revealed the existence of 'Total Information Awareness' (TIA), whose logo was an Orwellian all-seeing eye in a pyramid.[12] TIA would, the *Times* reported, search all electronic data in commercial and government databases with powerful computers to hunt for hidden patterns indicating terrorist activities. Intelligence and law enforcement officials would be given 'instant access to information from Internet mail and calling records to credit card and banking transactions and travel documents, without a search warrant'. TIA would not just enable the government to develop 'cradle to grave dossiers' on known individuals. It would also (in theory) have the ability to detect terrorists and their plots by subjecting massive troves of electronic information to data mining techniques.

After TIA was publicly unmasked, it faced withering criticism all along the political spectrum. In the words of the right-wing libertarian Cato Institute, this 'power to generate a comprehensive data profile on any US citizen' involved 'the specter of the East German secret police and communist Cuba's block watch system'.[13]

Popular opposition forced Congress to strike TIA from the Department of Defense Appropriations Act for the 2004 financial year. But in a secret, classified annex, Congress preserved funding for TIA's component technologies that were transferred to other government agencies, primarily to the National Security Agency.[14] As the NSA searches for 'suspicious patterns' through TIA, it is also researching the 'mass harvesting of the information that people post about themselves on social networks' and figuring out how to do 'automated intelligence profiling' with this information.[15] In addition, it is working with the FBI to cast a wide net of associations through 'social-networks analysis'.[16] The FBI has meanwhile issued hundreds of thousands of 'national security letters' which are accompanied by a gag order to collect vast amounts of personal information from internet service providers, phone companies and financial institutions and has amassed some 1.5 billion records in its National Security Branch Center for DARPA-style data mining.[17] It is also reportedly building STAR (System To Assess Risks) that would assign scores to individuals based on the information about them in government and commercial databases.[18]

When these programmes have surfaced in the media, they have failed to generate the outrage that forced TIA underground. As the years have passed, both the public and the press have been increasingly conditioned to accept just about any measure draped in the verbal garb of 'national security'. The conclusion of an exhaustive National Research Council study that hunting terrorists through data mining will not work and will lead to 'ordinary, law abiding citizens and businesses' being wrongly treated as suspects was largely ignored by the media and barely registered in the national consciousness.[19] Hyped up incidents like the Christmas 2009 'underwear bomber' plot are manipulated by Fox News and right-wing politicians to forestall any thoughtful public discussion about where the burgeoning homeland security industry is taking the country. Lucrative Department of Homeland Security contracts are being won by Raytheon, Lockheed Martin, Boeing and other major defence contractors, whether or not they can deliver the goods.[20] Corporations with strong ties to Israel, such as Security Solutions International, provide 'counter terrorism' training in the use of new technologies and 'homeland security training in Israel' to businesses and government agencies and simultaneously impart their Islamophobic ideology.

Few Americans are aware of the fundamental transformation that has taken place over the past five years in both law enforcement and intelligence gathering. Jurisdictional boundaries separating federal, state and local authorities and permissible activities have been eroded and a new domestic surveillance network has been built to implement the collection, data mining, analysis and dissemination of information. Its hubs are the seventy-two regional and state 'fusion centres' that have been established all over the country to 'fuse' and analyse information from a broad array of federal, state and local law enforcement agencies, as well as private entities and 'tips' from the public. The organisational structures of fusion centres entangle federal and state law in a manner that confuses lines of authority and enables the new hubs to sidestep state or federal laws when it seems convenient to do so and to evade many public records requests and attempts to hold them accountable.[21]

Customary lines of authority and accountability are further blurred by 'Joint Terrorism Task Forces' (JTTFs) which are now based in more than one hundred cities nationwide and draw participants from six hundred state and local agencies and thirty federal operations. In JTTFs, local and state police are deputised by the FBI and given clearance to conduct 'field investigations of actual or potential terrorism threats'.[22] Often they work side by side with agents from the Defense Department and the Bureau of Immigration and Customs Enforcement (ICE). When local and state police work with JTTFs, they are no longer under the supervision of and accountable to their state and community jurisdictions but instead become federal domestic intelligence agents beyond meaningful state and local control.

As police departments spend more and more resources on 'intelligence' work, and are no longer entirely 'local', their emphasis shifts away from building relationships through the kind of 'community policing' that has long been held up as the best way to overcome anti-police attitudes in communities of colour. No longer are police focused on investigating crimes that have already occurred, using the traditional criminal justice standard of 'reasonable suspicion' in targeting suspects. The federal Suspicious Activity Reporting (SAR) initiative plans to enlist some 800,000 local and state police in the filing of 'suspicious activity reports' (SARs) on even the most common everyday behaviours and the depositing of information in a near real-time 'Information Sharing Environment' (ISE) where it can be accessed by agencies around the country.[23] The SARs will be assessed at the nation's seventy-two fusion centres, which will funnel data to the FBI's National Security Branch Center for TIA analysis.

What are 'suspicious behaviours'? Since 9/11, police have followed up on 'tips' they have received from a public prone to rely on racial and religious profiling. In Massachusetts, for instance, police pursued reports about 'a Middle Eastern looking man who came to buy a used car and ended up not buying the car and two Middle Eastern looking men who were seen driving a Ryder truck on the expressway'.[24] The SAR initiative may well serve as yet another 'platform for prejudice' that invites racial profiling.[25] From what we know of its pilot stage, it also invites the potential criminalisation of a range of innocent behaviours and First Amendment-protected activity. The Los Angeles Police Department, a participant in the pilot SAR project, has defined as 'suspicious' using binoculars in public, taking measurements, taking pictures or video footage, taking notes and espousing 'extremist views'.[26] Under the federal government's definition, a 'suspicious activity report' is 'official documentation of observed behaviour that may be indicative of intelligence gathering or preoperational planning related to terrorism, criminal or other illicit intention'.[27]

The SAR initiative gives little weight to such fundamentals of the US criminal justice system as 'reasonable suspicion' and the 'presumption of innocence'. And how easy it is to slide from 'terrorism' to *any* 'illicit intention' and make suspicious activity reporting a way of sharing information about 'crimes' *before* they happen. Since results would eventually be needed to justify the ongoing flow of federal funds, most fusion centres immediately expanded their mission from detecting terrorist plots in the making—how many terrorists, after all, were really out there?—to an elastic 'all crimes' and 'all threats' approach to 'homeland security'. This has enabled them to contract for the development of new software and obtain access to and widely share information from databases focused not just on actual crime but on *potential* criminal activity.

The tools they are using include the COPLINK Solution Suite, designed 'to consolidate, identify and share information to solve crimes faster' and to uncover 'hidden relationships and associations'[28] and COPLINK ACT (Activity Correlation Technology), which allows an agency 'to automatically monitor for suspicious and potentially dangerous activity patterns'.[29] In addition to COPLINK, the Massachusetts Commonwealth Fusion Center (CFC) is using CrimeNtel, which 'creates a repository that links individuals with associates, locations, and vehicles to assist officers and analysts in connecting the dots'.[30] Like other fusion centres, it uses the Autotrack search engine which provides access to billions of records about individuals. The CFC can access more than thirty other databases, including VGTOF (Violent Gang and Terrorist Organization File), which, according to the Department of Justice website, provides law enforcement with identifying information about 'violent criminal gangs' and 'terrorist organizations' and their members. Leaks have revealed that VGTOF includes eight separate categories of 'extremist', among them 'Black extremist', 'environmental extremist' and 'anarchist'.

The New York Police Department (NYPD), which now has a global 'anti-terror' presence and has led the charge against 'homegrown terrorism' since the publication of its 2007 report, *Radicalization in the West: the homegrown threat*, is paying special attention to its communities of colour. It has created a 'stop and frisk' database for information collected from the two million people it has subjected to street searches over the last five years. The New York Civil Liberties Union has reports that, in 2009 alone, the NYPD conducted 575,304 'stop and frisk' searches, 88 per cent of which revealed no criminal activity. More than half of those targeted in 2009 were African American and 31 per cent were Latino.

So secretive is the emerging intelligence network that there is no way of conducting quality control and finding out exactly what information is being gathered, mined and disseminated. Leaks of information that have occurred from fusion centres in Maryland, Virginia, Texas, Missouri and other states suggest that the mindset of COINTELPRO has been enhanced with twenty-first century technology to enable alerts about reputed 'terrorist threats' to be widely shared among scores of different agencies in near real-time. Revealed in the leaked material is the widespread infiltration and monitoring of anti-war groups, environmental groups, anti-death penalty groups, Muslim groups, and 'Black Extremists', to mention a few.[31] The information that has been collected and shared is riddled with inaccuracies—but how can it be corrected given its broad dispersal through cyberspace?

The 2009 *Virginia Terrorism Threat Assessment Report*, marked 'law enforcement sensitive', makes it clear that the past lives on in the targeting of suspects. Echoing the FBI's old civil rights movement phobia, it classifies historically Black colleges as 'radicalization nodes' and 'a potential avenue of entry for terrorist operatives', while the Nation of Islam—a prime target of COINTELPRO—is listed among thirty-three groups regarded as 'potential terrorist threats'. It asserts that special attention must be paid to any place with a diverse population, especially if people who live there come originally from the Middle East, Southeast Asia or the Horn of Africa: 'While the vast majority of these individuals are law-abiding, this ethnic diversity also affords terrorist operatives the opportunity to assimilate without arousing suspicion'. Another potential danger area is the 'state prison system' which is seen as 'an attractive venue for recruitment and radicalization relating to terror organizations'.[32]

H. Rap Brown may not be an inmate in Virginia but other converts to Islam are, while as many as 350,000 Muslims were estimated in 2001 to be in prisons nation-wide.[33] Having created the largest prison system in the world through the use of racial profiling, the US appears to be banking on new technologies of digital profiling and mass domestic surveillance by multiple agencies as well as COINTELPRO-like infiltration and 'dirty tricks' to deal with what one influential study referred to as 'an enormous challenge—every radicalized prisoner becomes a potential terrorist recruit'.[34]

[...]

The Hunt for the 'Enemy Within'

[...]

Prisoners

Beyond the jurisdiction of ICE in the prison archipelago, it is certain Muslim prisoners who are most likely to 'disappear'—most recently into two new federal 'Communications Management Units' where they are isolated from other prisoners and the outside world. According to a lawsuit filed by the Center for Constitutional Rights, it is Muslims and prisoners with unpopular political beliefs who, despite clean disciplinary records, are being held in these experimental isolation settings in Terre Haute, Indiana, and Marion, Illinois, which were secretly opened in 2006–7.

Unlike foreign-born Muslims who could be deported after serving a prison sentence and naturalised citizens who could be deported after being stripped of their citizenship,[55] native-born American converts—mostly African American—are here to stay and have to be controlled in other ways. The concern that prisons offered fertile ground for 'radical Muslims' to make converts dates back to the days of COINTELPRO and the demonisation of Malcolm X and his Nation of Islam followers. As court rulings beginning in the late 1960s forced prison authorities to protect the rights of inmates to practise their religion, Islam made rapid strides within prison walls until, by some estimates, it was embraced by between 15 and 20 per cent of the increasingly African-American prison population, with the number growing at the rate of up to 40,000 each year.[56]

Almost immediately following the 9/11 attacks, Muslim prisoners were singled out as potential if not actual al-Qaida recruits by David Pipes, columnist and director of the Middle East Forum, and pro-Israel groups and media outlets that would fuel the growth of Islamophobia in the years ahead. They were joined by Christian evangelists like Dr Bob Morey, founder of Faith Defenders, who launched 'Project Take Back' to recolonise prison territory staked out for Allah.

The FBI, working through the National Joint Terrorism Task Force, soon developed the 'Correctional Intelligence Initiative' to interface with the Bureau of Prisons as well as state, local and privatised prisons in order to facilitate the 'coordination of terrorism matters between the Joint Terrorism Task Forces (JTTF) and all correctional agencies through the exchange of intelligence information between the participating agencies... These partnerships have allowed the FBI to detect, deter, and disrupt efforts by terrorist or extremist groups to radicalize or recruit among inmate populations.'[57] According to John M. Vanyur, assistant director of the Correctional Program at the Bureau of Prisons, inmates determined to have terrorist ties 'are clearly identified and tracked' in information systems and placed in the most restrictive conditions.[58] When prisoners are released, they will continue to be tracked. The Association of State Correctional Administrators' 'Re-Entry Information Sharing Initiative' is designed to meet the needs of law enforcement partners seeking 'detailed information pertaining to identity, behavior and associations' of the 650,000 offenders released each year from state and federal prisons.[59]

Much has been made of the potential connection between terrorism and gangs, and the danger of allowing politically radicalised African American inmates to be instructed in Islam by Saudi-financed Wahhabi imams: 'Muslim chaplains have established an Islamic radical regime over Muslim convicts in the American prisons; imagine each prison Islamic community as a little Saudi kingdom behind prison walls.'[60] The reality appeared somewhat different to the study group that produced *Out of the Shadows: getting ahead of prisoner radicalization*. It cited as a main problem the lack of well-trained Muslim chaplains because of the daunting vetting process, which left religious services to be conducted by poorly-educated inmates and volunteers who get access to 'radical materials', including interpretations of the Qur'an that appear to advocate violence, and develop a form of 'jailhouse Islam' that 'incorporates violent prison culture into religious practice'.

Where was the proof of the connection between prison conversions and terrorist recruitment? Pipes and his colleagues had little concrete evidence to point to. They cited the cases of the former Chicago gang member Jose Padilla, who in fact converted to Islam after being released from prison. Padilla, a US citizen who was labelled the 'dirty bomber' by Attorney General Ashcroft, was declared to be an 'enemy combatant' and spent three and a half years in intense solitary confinement on a naval brig without being charged with a crime or allowed access to a lawyer. When the government finally brought criminal charges against him to forestall a Supreme Court consideration of his case, there was no mention of the 'dirty bomb' allegations.

Two other examples are cited to make the prison conversion-terrorist link. First, there was the group Jam'iyyat ul-Islam as-Saheeh or JIS, founded in 1997 by an African American inmate in California's Folsom Prison, Kevin Lamar James. James reportedly compared the plight of oppressed prisoners to the situation of oppressed Muslims around the world. The FBI claimed that beginning in May 2005, four JIS members robbed eleven gas stations to fund attacks they were planning to carry out on US military installations, the Israeli consulate and Jewish synagogues. James was charged with directing a terrorist operation from behind the walls of a maximum security prison and sentenced to a further sixteen years.

A New York synagogue and Jewish centre and the fuel pipes supplying Kennedy International Airport were the alleged targets of a May 2009 'homegrown terrorist' plot. It involved four destitute ex-cons in impoverished Newburgh, New York, one of whom suffered from paranoid schizophrenia. They were given cash, food, rent money, drugs, cell phones, a camera and disabled explosive devices including a Stinger missile by an FBI informant who had been convicted of identity fraud and was hoping for a reduced sentence. The plot commanded considerable media and political attention when it was 'disrupted'. The fact that the African American men were not practising Muslims was largely ignored. A judge later denied the request of the lawyers for James Cromitie, the reputed plot leader, that the charges be thrown out on the grounds that the informant had offered him $250,000 to recruit others to carry out a plot the informant himself had devised. Cromitie was allegedly overruled when he suggested the bombs should go off at night so that no one would get hurt.[61]

Five months later, Imam Luqman Abdullah, a former prisoner whose Detroit mosque had been monitored by three paid FBI informants since 2007 and who had been reported to have made anti-American utterances, was gunned down by the FBI's Joint Terrorism Task Force when it went to arrest him for the illegal possession and sale of firearms and conspiracy to sell stolen goods. On 29 October 2009, some twenty imams from Detroit met with the FBI Special Agent and accused the FBI of seeking to entrap Abdullah and then killing him in cold blood.[62]

The prison conversion/'homegrown terrorism' nexus rested on this scant record. A report released in January 2010, *Anti-Terror Lessons of Muslim-Americans*, suggests that the evidence for major 'homegrown terrorism' threats not involving prison conversions might be just as thin, given the way Muslim Americans are policing their own communities. It cites some compelling statistics to make the case that the focus on Muslims and violence is overblown: since 9/11, a total of 139 American Muslims have been arrested or convicted of terrorism charges involving violence. During that same period, 136,000 murders have been committed in the United States.[63]

Terror has served as the handmaid of racism since chattel slavery was institutionalised in the American colonies. It was the Klan's weapon of choice after the Civil War. In the twentieth century, it served up public spectacles to White citizens, as lynchings were staged in thousands of towns and rural communities, and Congress tried in vain to pass an anti-lynching bill.

The heavy weight of US history was bound to intrude on the Obama presidency. The president has been widely portrayed as a 'Muslim' and 'African' whose citizenship is in doubt by people who say they want 'their country back'. And so there was no real surprise when, in March 2010, a group of self-proclaimed White supremacist 'Christian warriors' were arrested for allegedly planning mass killings of police to spark an anti-government uprising. They were found in possession of dozens of guns, swords, machetes, bomb-making material and crack cocaine, the 'ghetto' drug responsible for filling prisons with African Americans.

What is striking, but again, not surprising, is the response to the action taken by a White man named Joseph Stack, who, on 18 February 2010, expressed his hatred of taxes and 'Big Brother IRS Man' (the phrase he used in a suicide note) by crashing a plane into an Austin, Texas, office complex housing the IRS, CIA and FBI. Stack was initially praised as a patriot by many commentators, who viewed his action as a strike against big government which, under President Obama, had become 'socialist' or even 'communist'. It took a Congressional resolution rejecting 'any statement or act that deliberately fans the flames of hatred or expresses sympathy for those who would attack public servants serving our nation' to affix the label of 'terrorism' onto Stack's deed.

Looking Ahead

'The level of anger and fear is like nothing I can compare in my
lifetime.'

Noam Chomsky, 'Remembering fascism: learning from the past,'
Madison, Wisconsin, 8 April 2010

For Chomsky, Joseph Stack's manifesto and suicide reveal 'the sense of acute betrayal on the part of working people who believed they had fulfilled their duty to society in a moral compact with business and government, only to discover that they had been only instruments for profit and power, truisms from which they had been carefully protected by doctrinal institutions.'[64]

Thirty years ago, Bertram Gross foresaw the coming of 'more concentrated, unscrupulous, repressive, and militaristic control by a Big Business-Big Government partnership that—to preserve the privileges of the ultra-rich, the corporate overseers, and the brass in the military and civilian order—squelches the rights and liberties of other people both at home and abroad. That is friendly fascism.'[65]

Gross was writing before the freeing of corporations to girdle the globe and before the maturation of a full-blown kleptocracy that enabled the twenty-five largest hedge fund managers to pocket a collective $25 billion in 2009, even as millions of jobs were being permanently lost in a country with a sorely attenuated welfare safety net. True to his predictions, electoral democracy has appeared ever more dysfunctional and the two party system, awash with corporate funds, is proving incapable of and unwilling to meet the needs of the people.

In terms of how 'homeland security' and America's wars are pursued, there has been very little difference between the Bush and Obama administrations. Apart from a welcome repudiation of torture and rhetorical assurances directed at the Muslim world, President Obama has embraced the Bush-Cheney national security agenda, from warrantless wiretapping to indefinite detention, and has extended the rationale for extra judicial killing on a global battlefield to include US citizens. By refusing to hold the Bush administration accountable for any of its transgressions of the law, the Democratic Party has kept the door open for future abuses of power. Meanwhile, the recent Supreme Court's *Citizens United* decision, freeing up limitless corporate spending on election campaign advertising, makes it increasingly unlikely that candidates with progressive agendas will be able to be prevail at either the state or federal level.

It appears that the national security surveillance apparatus described here will be harnessed by the 'Big Business-Big Government partnership' to manage the decline of the US from sole superpower status in the years ahead. But the outcome is by no means certain. Although constitutional rights and protections have been seriously eroded, they still do exist and can be used to bring challenges to government practices. And with the country on track to become a 'majority-minority' nation before the middle of the century, US history suggests that democratic participation can yet be re-vitalised.

Throughout that history, communities of colour have organised against the odds and overcome fear to demand significant change. The rising up of African Americans and their allies against the totalitarian rule of Jim Crow is but one example. We must begin now to prepare the way for what civil rights movement historian Vincent Harding has envisaged as the 're-emergence of our large-scale struggle for democracy . . . filled with participants of many colors, offering creative alternatives for the lives of us all'.[66]

NOTES

1. S. Saulny, 'Prayers and criticism in wake of Detroit imam's killing by FBI,' *New York Times* (30 October 2009).

2. FBI press release, 'Eleven members/associates of Ummah charged with federal violations: one subject fatally shot during arrest,' 28 October 2009. In fact, the former H. Rap Brown was convicted of murdering one officer and wounding another. The press and blogs have widely reproduced the error in the FBI's press release.

3. Microfilm edition, *FBI surveillance files: FBI files on black extremist organizations. Part 1: COIN-TELPRO files on black hate groups and the investigation of the Deacons for Defense and Justice*.

4. See 'Narrative timetable of H. Rap Brown,' <http://americanascherrypie.tripod.com/id3.html>.

5. E. M. Thelwell, 'H. Rap Brown/Jamil Al-Amin: a profoundly American story,' *Nation* (28 February 2002).

6. His conviction in 1990 on charges of conspiracy, the obstruction of justice, perjury and defrauding the government was overturned on a constitutional technicality the following year.

7. S. Harris, *The Watchers: the rise of America's surveillance state* (London, Penguin Books, 2010), p. 22.

8. See N. Blackstock, *COINTELPRO: the FBI's secret war on political freedom* (New York, Vintage Books, 1975) and *The Nelson Rockefeller Report to the President*, by the Commission on CIA Activities, June 1975 (New York, Manor Books, 1975).

9. The 1978 Foreign Intelligence Surveillance Act (FISA), which created a secret court to hear applications for the wiretapping of Americans, rarely turned down government requests. It was circumvented by the Bush administration when it instituted its post-9/11 warrantless wiretapping programme and has had its ability to serve as a break on government spying undermined by subsequent legislation.

10. T. Bunyan, 'Just over the horizon—the surveillance society and the state in the EU,' *Race & Class* (Vol. 51, no. 3, January–March 2010).

11. B. Gross, *Friendly Fascism: the new face of power in America* (Boston, South End Press, 1982), p. 271.

12. J. Markoff, 'Threats and responses: intelligence: Pentagon plans a computer system that would peek at personal data of Americans,' *New York Times* (9 November 2002).

13. G. Healy, 'Beware of Total Information Awareness,' Cato Institute (20 January 2003).

14. Shane Harris first revealed the NSA connection in 'TIA lives on,' *National Journal* (23 February 2006) and wrote about it at length in his 2010 book, *The Watchers*, op. cit.

15. P. Marks, 'Pentagon sets its sights on social networking websites,' *New Scientist* (9 June 2006).

16. S. Gorman, 'NSA's domestic spying grows as agency sweeps up data,' *Wall Street Journal* (10 March 2008).

17. R. Singel, 'Newly declassified files detail massive FBI data-mining project,' *Wired* (23 September 2008).

18. A. Ramasastry, 'The FBI STAR terrorist risk assessment program should raise renewed concerns about private sector data mining,' *Find Law* (24 July 2007).

19. Committee on Technical and Privacy Dimensions of Information for Terrorism Prevention and Other National Goals, *Protecting Individual Privacy in the Struggle Against Terrorists: a framework for program assessment* (National Research Council, October 2008).

20. Rep. Brad Miller, chairman of the Subcommittee on Investigations and Oversight of the Committee on Science and Technology, wrote to the Inspector General of the Office of the Director of National Intelligence criticising the performance of Boeing and other contractors and citing a government report that '413 government IT projects totaling more than $25 billion in FY 2008 alone were poorly planned, poorly performing or both' (21 August 2008). Congress exercises little oversight over the hidden, rapidly metastising homeland security industry which, according to a two-year investigation by the *Washington Post*, now involves an unknown amount of funding, at least 1,271 government organisations and 1,931 private companies, with 854,000 people—more than the population of Washington DC—holding top security clearance (see, <www.TopSecretAmerica.com>).

21. The American Civil Liberties Union (ACLU) has used both the federal Freedom of Information Act and state public records laws to seek information about fusion centres with mixed results. The ACLU of Massachusetts has produced a preliminary report based on the information it

has managed to obtain: 'When we are all suspects: a backgrounder on government surveillance in Massachusetts' (January 2010) which can be downloaded from <http://aclum.org/sos>.

22. 'Department of Justice evaluation and inspections report 1—2005–007' (June 2005).

23. M. German and J. Stanley, 'Fusion Center Update,' American Civil Liberties Union (July 2008).

24. *Mass Impact: the domestic war against terrorism in Massachusetts—are we on the right track?* (American Civil Liberties Union of Massachusetts, 2004), p. 19.

25. T. Cincotta, *Platform for Prejudice: how the nationwide suspicious activity reporting initiative invites racial profiling, erodes civil liberties and undermines security* (Political Research Associates, 2010).

26. Office of the Chief of Police, Los Angeles Police Department, Special order number 11, 'Reporting incidents potentially related to foreign or domestic terrorism' (5 March 2008).

27. *Information Sharing Environment (ISE), Functional Standard (FS), Suspicious Activity Reporting (SAR)*, Version 1.0, p.6.

28. <http://www.orbitrontech.com/coplink2.html>.

29. <http://66.181.249.50/pro8_co1030081.htm>.

30. K. Burke and J. Kayyem, 'The State of Homeland Security in the Commonwealth: Trends and Process' (October 2008).

31. 'When we are all suspects: a backgrounder on government surveillance in Massachusetts' (January 2010), p. 7.

32. <http://joerobertson.com/liberty/alex-jones-exposes-the-2009-virginia-terrorism-threat-assessment>.

33. S. Mufti, 'Islam in American prisons,' *IslamOnline.com* (31 August 2001).

34. *Out of the Shadows: getting ahead of prisoner radicalization*, a special report by the George Washington University Homeland Security Policy Institute and the University of Virginia Critical Incident Analysis Group (September 2006), executive summary, p. i.

[…]

55. As an example, Fawaz Damra, the imam of the Islamic Center of Cleveland, was stripped of his citizenship and deported to Israel for failing to reveal his ties to the Palestinian group Islamic Jihad when applying for US citizenship in 1993—which was four years before Islamic Jihad was put on the government's list of terrorist organisations.

56. S. Mufti, 'Islam in American prisons' *IslamOnline.com* (31 August 2001).

57. Office of the Inspector General, 'The Federal Bureau of Prisons monitoring of mail for high-risk inmates, Appendix VIII, the Federal Bureau of Investigation's response,' *Evaluation and Inspections Report I–2006–009* (September 2006).

58. 'Statement of John M. Vanyur before the Subcommittee on Intelligence, Information Sharing and Terrorism Risk Assessment Committee on Homeland Security, US House of Representatives, concerning Radicalization, Information Sharing and Community Outreach: Protecting the Homeland from Homegrown Terrorism' (5 April 2007).

59. Association of State Correctional Administrators, 'ASCA's reentry information sharing initiative,' Correctional intelligence, counterterrorism, gangs, and violent crime project, winter 2010.

60. S. Schwartz, 'Radical Muslims are taking over US prisons,' *Weekly Standard* (24 April 2006).

61. 'Judge refuses to dismiss Bronx synagogue bomb plot case,' *New York Times* (19 May 2010).

62. The case was still under investigation when five of the autopsy photos were posted online. <http://www.mlive.com/news/detroit/index.ssf/2010/04/civil_rights_group_releases_ph.html>.

63. D. Shanzer, C. Kurzman, E. Moosa, *Anti-terror Lessons of Muslim-Americans* (National Institute of Justice, 6 January 2010).

64. In his 8 April 2010 talk, Chomsky recalls how, in just a handful of years, anger with the 'incessant wrangling of Weimar politics' and its failure to deal with popular grievances was mobilised by 'forces dedicated to upholding the greatness of the nation and defending it against invented threats in a revitalized, armed and unified state, marching to a glorious future . . . The world is too complex for history to repeat, but there are nevertheless lessons to keep in mind.'

65. Gross, *Friendly Fascism*, op.cit., p. 162.

66. V. Harding, *Hope and History: why we must share the story of the movement* (Orbis Books, New York), p. 11.

*Nancy Murray is the director of education at the American Civil Liberties Union of Massachusetts, where she has researched and helped build campaigns against racism and government abuses of power.

Murray, Nancy. "Profiling in the Age of Total Information Awareness" *Race and Class* 52, vol. 2 (2010): 3–24. This text has been shortened. Passages left out are indicated by [. . .].

Used by permission.